Goin' back to
CALIFORN-I-A

Goin' back to
CALIFORN-I-A

CHRONICLE ONE—HELLS ANGELS

STEVE TODD

Steve
Todd

Dedication

To my beautiful children: Riley, and Isabelle.
Without your patience and love this
memoire would not have been possible.

How to Read this Memoire

This book was written over a two-year period, or 104 weeks. It is organized by the weekly calendar (Sunday – Saturday). As an example, the first two paragraphs below represent Saturday. The next two paragraphs represent Sunday.

Usually, but not always, the beginning of the week will start with Sunday or Monday and always end on a Friday or Saturday. *A line break with asterisks between Saturday and Sunday represents the beginning of a new week.*

On the bright side, we should have at least two investigators at church tomorrow. I hope everything goes well. I am happy to be a member of The Church of Jesus Christ of Latter-day Saints. I know the Lord will bless me if I am diligent and faithful in spreading the gospel of Jesus Christ.

I know the Lord watches over His missionaries. I have a fervent desire to meet, if not exceed our baptismal goals for this month. With the aid of my older brother, Jesus Christ, all things are possible.

***

Ryan came to church today, which was cool. Before Sacrament Meeting, Elder Hedelius and I rode to his house, packed our bicycles in the back of his pickup truck, and rode with him to church. Ryan seemed to enjoy the church service.

Elder Hedelius and I received a few referrals today. While we were greeting members, we bumped into a few people who were attending church for the first time, so I quickly wrote down their names and phone numbers.

Table of Contents

Preface

The purpose of this book is to share with my family and friends my experiences in serving a full-time, two-year church mission for The Church of Jesus Christ of Latter- day Saints (LDS or Mormon). I served in San Bernardino, California from July 1988–August 1990. I wrote in my missionary journal almost every day while serving in California. It was a marvelous experience. Recently, I decided to type and edit my journal/memoir and produce a book to give to posterity. Now I want to share it with you.

In summary, I experienced the emotional highs and lows of serving a mission for the church. There were many times when I had doors slammed in my face after prospecting all day. On other days, I experienced the exquisite joy of watching an investigator enter the waters of baptism. I'll also share how I became sidetracked from my original "mission plan" through correspondence with my long-distance girlfriend.

Most notably, I share my most beloved mission stories, including one where I was chased on my bicycle by ferocious Collies and Rottweilers.

Unlike much of the literature I have found online written by past-missionaries, this book is not anti-Mormon, nor does it bash the LDS Church in any way. I endured tremendous trials and tribulations during my mission that could have shaken my foundation and testimony in the restored gospel of Jesus Christ. However, I remained steadfast and endured to the end, not doubting for one second whether the LDS church was true or not.

In all honesty, this book isn't really a book at all. The following pages were taken directly from my very own personal missionary journal, word for word. I have only made minor edits, including grammatical and spelling corrections. Nothing else has been changed or altered. As a result, you—the reader—have the unique opportunity of experiencing exactly how my mission unfolded through the eyes of a very naïve and determined teenager. Although I consider many of my missionary experiences very personal and sacred, there's nothing "top-secret" within these pages either. This memoire is labor of love, and I want to share my love of the gospel of Jesus Christ with you.

In conclusion, my number-one goal is to share my memoire with family, friends—and you. My number-two goal is to share with you how important personal revelation is in your life. I can't over emphasize how important this is. It's one of the main catalysts for personal growth and happiness. Your personal relationship with God—the Father and his son, Jesus Christ—is paramount. During my darkest and saddest moments on my mission, the only things I had to rely on were my faith in Jesus Christ, my family's support, and hard work; that's it! In the end, nothing else matters. God, faith, and family is key. My personal testimony of the Savior is what carried me through from the depths of Hell to Heaven, and it is my desire that every person know and experience this miracle of our Savior's atonement and redeeming love for us.

Introduction

This missionary adventure begins in the luscious green hills of the great state of Georgia, travels to the rugged Rocky Mountains of Salt Lake City, Utah and focusses on its final decent to the very brown and smoggy landscape of Ontario, California.

Ever since I can remember, I wanted to serve a full-time, two-year mission for The Church of Jesus Christ of Latter-day Saints. Even as a small child, I sang the famous Primary song, "I Hope They Call Me on a Mission," with more gusto than any other.

As I grew older and more mature, so did my desire and passion to serve. By the time I turned nineteen-years old (the minimum age to serve a mission at the time), it was my destiny to serve an honorable mission. I was called by the living Prophet, Ezra Taft Benson, and inspired by God—Heavenly Father himself. How cool is that!? To a nineteen-year-old teenager who had once been held back in kindergarten due to ADHD, I was now ready to conquer the world!

My rich Mormon ancestry runs through four generations all the way back to the days of the Prophet, Joseph Smith.

My fourth great grandfather, Parley P. Pratt, was one of the original Twelve Apostles when the gospel of Jesus Christ was restored to the earth in 1830.

Both of my parents served missions and spent most of their successful careers working as entrepreneurs in the auto, property, and casualty insurance industries. My family originally moved from Huntington Beach, California to Atlanta, Georgia in August 1978, when my dad transferred with the Continental Can Company. Unbeknownst to me, just ten years later I would be moving BACK to California, only this time as an excited, focused, and inspired servant of the Lord.

I served my mission to San Bernardino, California. The original town was settled by five hundred Mormons sent by the Prophet Brigham Young in September of 1851. The one-hundred-and-fifty wagons traversed the Cajon Pass where the name of "Mormon Rocks" still pays tribute to their passage. Here the colonists purchased Rancho San Bernardino from the Lug Family and erected Fort San Bernardino, a five-acre village crowded within a 12-foot stockade.

The Native Americans first named this area the "Serrano Rocks," and it refers to the jutting sandstone formations that provided shelter for the Mormon colonists. These striking sandstone formations are riddled with small holes and caves: home to owls, lizards, and pack rats. Today, visitors love to mountain climb these beautiful rocks. This rich and beautiful Mormon history combined with my inspired calling from Heavenly Father is what gave me the passion and desire to baptize the entire San Bernardino Valley!

In conclusion, why did I title my memoir, *Goin' back to Californ-I-A*? Originally, I was inspired by a famous 1980's rap song entitled "Going back to Cali" by L.L. Cool J to write my own song about moving from Los Angeles to Atlanta in the 1970's. Then, 10-years later, I moved back to California, but this time on a mission from Heavenly Father. My song, "Goin' back to Californ-I-A" has a cool beat and laid-back melody, just like the great people of sunny Southern California.

I love y'all and hope you enjoy the read!

California San Bernardino Mission
1980 - 1990

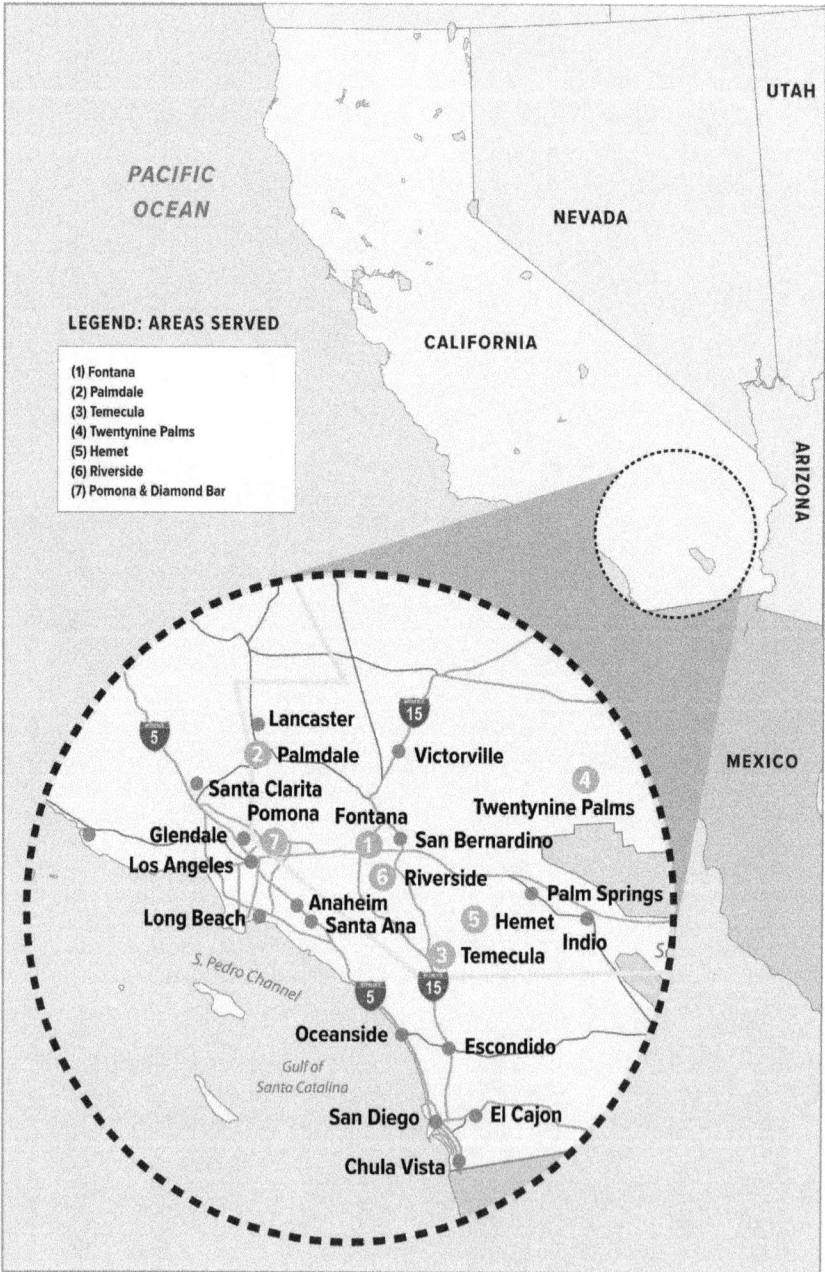

LEGEND: AREAS SERVED

(1) Fontana
(2) Palmdale
(3) Temecula
(4) Twentynine Palms
(5) Hemet
(6) Riverside
(7) Pomona & Diamond Bar

CHAPTER 1

The Great Wasatch Mountains

I'm going to start from the beginning because I have a ton of emotions going through my body. My mind is racing, and my heart is beating way too fast!

On May 21st, I met this beautiful girl, Kaesi McGurrin, at a church play. The gym was packed with over five hundred people, and I had to stand on a chair just to see what was going on stage. Upon reaching the summit, I looked towards the front of the hall and there she was—gracefully walking across the stage in full glory. It was love at first sight. We spent two wonderful months dating. Even though we argued whether we should go steady or not, our relationship worked out in the end.

Kaesi is a special girl, and she has a special family. I love her very much. During the past two-months, I not only met the woman of my dreams, but I graduated from North Springs High School in Atlanta, Georgia. And now, I am embarking on one of my biggest adventures, yet: serving a full-time, two-year church mission to San Bernardino, California. I am excited because I know I'm fulfilling my destiny to serve Jesus Christ and my fellow man!

My farewell talk went extremely well. It is customary (in The Church of Jesus Christ of Latter-day Saints) to deliver a talk during Sacrament Meeting[1] before heading to the Missionary Training Center (MTC) in Provo, Utah.

I was pleased with the speakers and musical number. I spoke for about twenty- minutes about my mission and the joy I feel in serving the Lord. The significance of what I am about to embark on over the next two-years has not fully hit me yet.

After church, my parents had an Open House for my friend (Melvin Windham) and I at our home in Dunwoody. Melvin is serving his church mission to South Korea. We both had family, friends, and neighbors stop by to bid us farewell. After one of my neighbors shook my hand, I looked down and noticed a $50 bill staring back at me.

In the weeks leading up to my departure, I accepted hugs from as many beautiful ladies as possible. One of the rules serving an LDS church mission is no dating or flirting with members of the opposite sex. In other words, I'm filling up my canteen before the well runs dry. In a nutshell, I enjoyed seeing everyone and had a wonderful time.

The night before I left Atlanta, the Stake President[2], President Tom Hammond, came over to the house and set me apart[3] as a full-time missionary. My entire family, the Whites, Scott Coleman, Dalen Youngblood, and Kaesi McGurrin were present.

When President Hammond laid his hands upon my head, he said, "It is important to remember your talents and your ability to meet and talk with people. You need to use the spirit in the mission field. The Lord is pleased with your decision to serve. The spirit and the Lord will help you learn the missionary discussions and other important principles of the gospel."

After the blessing, my dad handed me a document outlining the priesthood[4] line-of- authority for our family. I could see that my priesthood lineage runs all the way from my dad to President Thomas S. Monson[5] until it finally reaches the Savior, Jesus Christ. I have an awesome responsibility to serve an honorable mission.

Today is July 23rd, 1988. I left from Hartsfield-Jackson Airport at 8:20 a.m. and landed four hours later in Salt Lake City. During the flight, I read a book called Already to Harvest by Elder Hartman Rector, Jr.[6] I received the book from my Uncle Mike (on my mom's side of the family). Elder Rector suggests that every member need simply to "Open [Their] Mouth," and assures that The Spirit will guide us when we do.

During the plane ride, I chatted with a man next to me named Mr. Bob Allison, from Louisville, Kentucky. Bob was a scoutmaster with his local Boy Scout troop and was catching a connecting flight from Salt Lake to Montana to meet a few of his friends for a fishing trip.

After talking for a while, the whole time I was thinking, 'Should I introduce Bob to the *Book of Mormon*[7]?' I did not get a chance to offer him a copy of this holy scripture, but I did manage to get his mailing address. My plan, before I leave the Missionary Training Center (MTC), is to contact the mission president[8] in Kentucky and ask the elders to deliver a copy of the *Book of Mormon* to him. I am ready to serve!

As the plane began its descent out of the clouds, I turned my head to look out the window. Just then, the Great Salt Lake basin and the majestic Rocky Mountains with snowy caps came into full view. The mountains are so amazingly beautiful. The very first thing that came to my mind was...faith. It must have taken tremendous faith and endurance by the early Mormon pioneers[9] to travel cross-country, and eventually end their journey in the foreign land of Utah.

After de-boarding the plane, I met Aunt Elaine, Uncle Howard, and Uncle Ira with open arms at the airport. It was fun visiting with my relatives, including my step-grandmother, Gwen, who I hadn't seen since I was seven years old.

Today I spent time with my friend, Steve Prettyman, and his family in West Valley, Utah. Steve lived in Roswell, Georgia with his grandmother, who regularly volunteers to work at the Atlanta Temple[10]. In Roswell, "Steve and Steve" cruised in my parent's Chevy station wagon listening to Boston (my favorite rock'n roll band).

The city was celebrating the "Days of 47" with a large parade to commemorate the restored church's second prophet (Brigham Young), and the arrival of the Mormon pioneers to the Utah Valley on July 24th, 1847. It was cool watching the parade with my friend. I especially enjoyed seeing Prophet Ezra Taft Benson's float as it rolled down the street. I even saw the 1980's Dominos pizza float, Avoid the Noid character.

After the parade, we had lunch at Steve's house, who will be serving his church mission to Portland, Oregon soon. He is reporting to the MTC in a couple of weeks, so I will be able to see him again while I am there.

As I was standing on the front porch and preparing to leave, Steve's mother gave me a great big goodbye hug. Then she grew silent, and her eyes began to swell as tears rolled down her face. At first, I thought I must have said something wrong, but then she said, "You're the main reason why Steve's going on his mission." Her sincere comment made me feel special and important.

I grew up in a 1950's, "Leave it to Beaver"-style home. I was a well-behaved child until I became a teenager—when I pushed the limits with my parents. Despite this rebellious streak, I always knew right from wrong. I was also blessed with the ability to befriend people who were outcasts or "nerdy." My cousin, Steve, was a nerd, but we both had a good sense of humor, so we got along great. I still consider Steve to be one of my best friends.

I took Steve under my wing as a teen, and even got him a full-time job at McDonalds where I worked with a few of my church friends. I tried to be a good influence and we attended church every Sunday.

After leaving Steve's house, I enjoyed playing 18-holes of golf with my three Uncles: Burton, Ira, and Howard. I laughed to myself when Uncle Burton started giving Uncle Ira a tough time for shanking a few shots. In the end, we all played a nice round of golf, and it was fun hanging out with my uncles.

After having fun in the sun, we drove back to Uncle Howard and Aunt Elaine's house for lunch. My Aunts are awesome cooks, and so my belly was full of good food!

Aunt Elaine, worried that I had too much dirty laundry, offered to wash my clothes. However, Uncle Howard had a different idea, and said, "Elaine, quit treating him like a baby!" It was funny. I have always appreciated her kindness and for that she is one of my favorite aunts.

CHAPTER 2:

The School of the Prophets

The Missionary Training Center (MTC) in Provo is incredible! Joseph Smith and the early leaders used the term "school of the prophets" to describe a new school for the elders of the Church in Kirtland, Ohio. Today, the missionaries now refer to the MTC as the "school of the prophets." The spirit of the Lord, Jesus Christ, dwells here 24/7 days a week; 365 days a year. It's a marvelous experience to finally be of serving my Savior as a missionary. What a wonderful place to begin seriously learning of the scriptures.

The past two days have flown by because I have been so busy attending all of my classes and activities: Orientation, Missionary Discussion class, *Book of Mormon* class, and a couple of devotionals. My presiding district leader[11], Elder Crew, handed me a great big black notebook with my name engraved in gold that reads, Stephen M. Todd. Elder Crew is a super guy, and I can tell that he cares about us. I've been studying hard and reading all my class materials.. I have a strong desire to be the best missionary this world has ever seen! I know that, with the Lord's help, I can convert fifty of the Lord's children to His church so that they can live with Him again someday. I love the church and Jesus Christ. Missionary work is what I was born to do; I love it.

Our district name is the Barstow District—after Barstow, California—and we have an excellent group of missionaries. There are a total of nine missionaries in the Barstow District (eight elders and one sister): Donnae Tidwell, Jim Perkins, Vincent Thebault, Jared Heaton, Thomas Garner, Jason Lott, Conway Chidester, Jason Palmer, and...me.

There are four elders in my room: Elder Perkins, Elder Thebault, and Elder Heaton.

Elder Perkins, my companion, is from the state of Washington. Elder Thebault, from Canada, is 22-years-old; and Elder Heaton is from Washington, Utah. These guys are prepared and ready to serve a mission just like I am. We call our plain-and-dull-looking dorm rooms the "condominiums."

I really respect Elder Thebault's maturity, spirituality, and his dignity. The fact that Elder Thebault is 22-years old means he is three-years older than mostmissionaries who begin their service at 19-years old. I would like to emulate Elder Thebault's qualities.

The branch president will pick a permanent district leader this week. Elder Thebault does not think he will be called by the branch president to lead the district, but I know he will. I say in an obnoxious, but joking way, "Well, district leader, what shall I do next?" I love my family and this church, and I pray that I can become a great missionary; the type of missionary the Savior wants me to become one day. I am very blessed to be here on this earth to serve my fellow man.

Today I felt like all I did was eat and go to class. I seriously would not be surprised if I've gained five pounds. The good news is that "Exercise Hour" is part of our everyday agenda. This is the hour during our day when our district exercises. We have the option to play basketball, volleyball, or go for a long jog.

One of the best subjects we studied in class today was the 1st Discussion[12], "The Plan of Our Heavenly Father." Our instructor taught us that when The Spirit is present, Discussions can be incredible and extremely spiritual experiences. The main purpose of teaching the gospel is to help the investigator[13] receive an answer to their prayers from the Holy Spirit that the restored gospel is true.

After attending classes for twelve hours today, I am mentally and spiritually exhausted. It's an intense process to focus and have The Spirit with me all day, every day. However, I feel like I am engaged and asking God the right questions.

The elders in the Barstow District are great, and I love all of them. However, Elder Garner and Elder Thebault are my favorite companions. Elder Garner and I joke around quite a bit to break up the monotony; he is fun to be around. The MTC rocks the house! This is absolutely the best place to prepare for a church mission.

While moving from class to class today, I ran into a couple of my best friends from Georgia: Todd Dudley, and Scott Hammond. Elder Dudley will be serving in Mexico, and Elder Hammond will be going to Spain on his mission. Some things haven't changed since being in the mission field. I noticed that Todd is friendlier towards me, and that gives me confidence that we're still friends. On the other hand, Scott completely ignores me. I chuckle to myself, because everything with Scott was always about competition—apparently even on a church mission. I don't let his attitude bother me too much, but it would be nice if he would just say "hello" occasionally.

The MTC is a great place to learn and grow. The church is very well organized, and I feel The Spirit often. I'm having tons of fun and am growing spiritually. It's honestly like living in a different world. The temptations I had in Georgia with women and arguing with my parents are all gone. I feel protected by my Heavenly Father because I have a spiritual shield around me. I cannot wait until we touch down in California! I must always remember the Lord.

It's "Missionary Day" tomorrow. This is the scheduled day when Elder Perkins and I must role play a live Missionary Discussion. I am still learning the class material, but I'm confident we'll succeed our first day.

Well, I survived "Missionary Day." Elder Perkins and I taught the 1st Discussion twice. Each discussion lasts about an hour. The Spirit is the main tool for converting souls to the gospel of Jesus Christ. Without The Spirit of God, the investigator will not join the church for the right reasons. It is incredible how often I need to rely on The Spirit to guide and teach others. I'm a decent teacher, but I still need to develop better eye contact with the investigator. If I am sincere, care about my investigator's feelings, and they are open and humble themselves, then we will both will feel The Spirit of God and be edified together.

I believe the message of Jesus Christ and His gospel is the most important message of our day. I feel overwhelmed at times because there is so much to learn with scripture references and memorizing each principle of the discussions. I feel ill-equipped at times because of my own limiting beliefs. However, at the end of the day, I feel like I am making great progress. It is amazing to think that I am a missionary teaching about Jesus Christ! I know it's the right thing, and the best thing to do. I know that my Heavenly Father will bless me because He loves me. He loves all His children, proving it ultimately when He gave His only begotten son. "For God so loved the world, that he gave his only begotten Son, that whosoever believeth in him should not perish, but have everlasting life" John 3:16 (KJV).

Tomorrow is Sunday, and Elder Perkins and I have a Personal Priesthood Interview (PPI)[14] with the branch president[15], Elder Harvey. The first thing I noticed about Elder Harvey is that he has exceptionally large hands. Those hands also yield a tremendous handshake; when he squeezed my hands for the first time, I thought he may have broken them!! Every missionary in the district must have at least one interview before he or she leaves the MTC. Apparently, Elder Harvey just wants to talk and find out more about us.

This morning I jumped into the community shower with my roommates, and the first thing Elder Thebault said to me was, "Don't say a word!" I just looked at him and asked, "...Why?" He continued, "You talked in your sleep all last night. Something about your companion?? You talk all day, and then you talk all night... You don't know when to shut up!" I just smiled and laughed out loud.

I was curious, wondering what my friends back home are doing today; whether they're going out on dates or just messing around having a fun time. One would think that past friends and family would be on my mind constantly; but until now, thoughts of home honestly haven't crossed my mind. Since I'm committed to fulfilling my church mission, I often think about my family and friends on a spiritual level. I have not thought about the carnal or sensual world in a long time. A mission is a marvelous thing. The Lord is almighty!

Elder Garner and I have the best time here in the MTC. He is so cool because we are so much alike. We both like Chevy Chase and the movie "Fletch." Occasionally, Elder Garner requests, "Elder Todd, do an imitation of Fletch for us." Then I curl my lips, and with a southern "redneck" voice I say, "What are ya doing; some stunt flying or something?"

***

Today is Sunday and our district attended church all day. We had an hour of Sunday school in the morning with a three-hour break. Then we ate lunch and attended Sacrament Meeting. After church, we had three-hours of free time before our *Book of Mormon* class.

I felt pumped up after our *Book of Mormon* class with Elder Lind. He is a great instructor who teaches with passion and enthusiasm! I listened to every word and took meticulous notes. At the end of our meeting, we sang the song, "Behold a Royal Army," except we substituted the word "Victory" with "Baptize" and then sang "Baptize, Convert, and Families." It was fantastic because I felt motivated and inspired to spread God's word. I sang the new song all the way back to our condos. When we returned to our rooms, I posted my notes from class on my bedroom wall. Here is what I wrote down:

1. Get member referrals, work 70 + hours a week, 50% of my teaching pool will be baptized, work from 9:30 a.m.–9:30 p.m. every day.
2. Golden question and the approach, lacing and neighbors = referrals, seek less-active members, ask members for help, tract with The Spirit.
3. Working hard = Spirit = Conversion. This is the magic formula!
4. Expect success and "Light the Fire."
5. Teach the truthfulness of the *Book of Mormon*.
6. Think of all my blessings.

I mentioned earlier that Elder Thebault would probably be called of God to be a leader within our Branch, and I was right! Today he was called by Elder Harvey to be the assistant to the president. I knew Elder Thebault would rise quickly through the ranks! I, on the other hand, was called to be the "greeter" for our branch.

Tonight, I felt The Spirit, and it was incredible because when I align myself with God's commandments and have one goal to serve, The Spirit resides with me. We met for a Large Group Meeting (LGM) and listened to a presentation on the Prophet Joseph Smith and the restoration of the gospel. We watched several videos during the presentation and ended with a testimony meeting. I truly felt The Spirit of God burning within me, like a seed of the gospel—sprouting and growing in my soul (Alma 32).

I forget sometimes how beautiful and glorious the gospel of Jesus Christ is in my life. Jesus Christ and Heavenly Father absolutely love their children. The Holy Ghost can dwell within us if we live the teachings and commandments of the Lord.

Joseph Smith was an inspired man. He was a prophet of God who listened to his heart and prayed to his Father in Heaven to find out which church to join. The Spirit and the Holy Ghost can be so wonderful when God's children use inspiration to strengthen their own and others' lives.

A mission is such a great and marvelous work; it is the greatest event of my life thus far, and I love it! I was born to preach and teach the gospel. This is truly the greatest calling that can come to a young man. The Lord's children need to hear His message, the special message of Jesus Christ.

The next morning, we had a special guest speaker for our devotional: Elder Tom L. Perry, member of the Quorum of the Twelve Apostles[16]! Elder Perry was here to welcome our new mission president, Ed Pinegar, as President Durrant had recently completed his two-year church mission as president of the MTC. Apparently, this was President Pinegar's second mission call. (His first mission call was to southern England.) It's interesting to see the "changing of the guards", sort-of-speak, as I serve under two different mission presidents at the MTC. Here is what I wrote down from the speakers.

1. Edify—to improve morally and build personality.
2. Be wise, as found in Jacob 6:12.
3. Perfect the saints.
4. The six points of the "Foundation of Perfection."
    a. Revelation—from the ninth article of faith.
    b. Scriptures—Doctrine & Covenants 1: 37–38: "Search these commandments, for they are true and faithful, and the prophecies and promises which are in them shall all be fulfilled. What I the Lord have spoken, I have spoken, and I excuse not myself; and though the heavens and the earth pass away, my word shall not pass away, but shall all be fulfilled, whether by mine own voice or by the voice of my servants, it is the same."

    c. Holy Priesthood.

    d. Holy Ordinances.

    e. Development of personal talents and gifts.

    f. Keeping the commandments—Doctrine & Covenants 25: 15–16: " Keep my commandments continually, and a crown of righteousness thou shalt receive. And except thou do this, where I am you cannot come. And verily, verily, I say unto you, that this is my voice unto all. Amen."

5. Talents as found in Moroni 10:8: " And again, I exhort you, my brethren, that ye deny not the gifts of God, for they are many; and they come from the same God. And there are different ways that these gifts are administered; but it is the same God who worketh all in all; and they are given by the manifestations of The Spirit of God unto men, to profit them."

Later, around 3:30 p.m., I received my first haircut away from home. My mom always cut my hair over the years.... The barber said I needed a "California" haircut, and I obliged. Now I look sharp because my hair is "high and tight." After getting my haircut, Elder Perkins and I checked the mailbox. When I unlocked the mailbox door, it was empty. I long for letters around here; it's always an amazing feeling to rip open the envelope!

We finally get Preparation Day (P-day) tomorrow! P-day is our official day "off" from our regular proselyting efforts. It's the day we usually get to sleep in, do laundry, write letters, play basketball, or just relax and do nothing. However, this week, our district is getting up at 5:30 a.m. to do laundry and boy do I ever need clean clothes! By 7:00 a.m. we will be attending an endowment session at the Provo Temple. After the temple, we are thinking about going to the Utah Valley Mall and having the rest of the day to ourselves. I cannot wait!

***

I'll keep it short and simple tonight because it's past my bedtime. I had the unique opportunity of washing my own clothes for the first time today, and it was actually pretty fun. After doing laundry and cleaning up my bedroom, I went with the rest of the district to the Provo Temple, and it was fabulous. I love attending the temple because The Spirit is so peaceful and comforting to the soul. It is a sacred place where I will be married one day.

After our temple trip, we caught a bus going to the mall. While riding on the bus, I saw an old friend from Illinois and said, "Sister Sarah Smith! How's it going?" She almost didn't recognize me with my new haircut, white shirt, and name tag.

Later this evening I reflected deep within myself and realized that I need to improve in several areas like studying the discussions with more intent if I am going to become a great missionary. I know the Lord will bless me as I serve him well.

We had our first "Missionary Day" today, where we got to role play The Discussions[17] with other elders. Elder Perkins and I taught the 1st Discussion, "The Plan of Our Heavenly Father," to a pair of elders portraying investigators.

One of the investigators, Elder Bowman, played the role of an atheist and was giving us the most difficult time in the world. At one point, I became quite frustrated with Elder Bowman because he was asking the most absurd questions about the existence of God, our creator. I almost socked the guy right in the mouth! But I didn't let him get me down. I tried bearing my testimony[18] and everything—but nothing seemed to work. Finally, after a few agonizing minutes, he "let up" enough for us to move along with our discussion.

Today I just found out that my entire family is staying at my Aunt Florence's house, which is about a mile away from the MTC. My entire family is attending the Todd family reunion in town. I hope they don't stop by to visit me because I already said my "goodbyes." It's difficult not seeing my family, but I must learn to survive this experience on my own. Maybe what I'm really trying to say is...it's not difficult living on my own. I just hope my parents can accept it. It's difficult being the oldest of seven children and setting the example. I enjoy living on my own and any interference from my parents.

Here are a few random/cool things I've heard over the past few days:

1. "You remind me of someone, but I can't remember."
2. The MTC is the "School of the Prophets."
3. The last person to walk the halls at night is the Savior.
4. Bruce R. McConkie once said, "We do not Bible bash," as he crashed his fist to the pulpit. Again, "We do not Bible bash!" Finally, the third time, "We do not Bible bash! Then a word of silence, "But if we do...we win!"

I received absolutely no letters today. In fact, since beginning my training at the MTC, I haven't received a letter from anyone besides my parents. I really appreciate them taking the time to write, and I shouldn't complain. And yet every day after lunch, everyone from my district runs to the post office, and I'm usually met with disappointment when my eyes behold... nothing. I hate it when that happens.

Today we started learning the 2nd Discussion, "The Gospel of Jesus Christ." Tomorrow for Missionary Day will be applying our new teaching skills and putting them to the test. Elder Perkins and I will be role playing, both as an "investigator" and a "missionary." Memorizing the lessons is tough work, but I am learning a lot.

Elder Thebault and I are extremely competitive with one another. This past week, he and I have been competing to see who will be the best missionary in the district. During our competitive streak—and although we wouldn't admit it—we were getting on one another's nerves. We both have unique talents, one of which is pushing each other's hot buttons. As a result, we weren't on the best of terms. It even got to the point where we stopped speaking to one another. Every time he acted spiritual, I countered by acting crazy and wildly obnoxious. We went to the extremes on both ends of the spectrum, with Elder Thebault acting very mature and spiritual, and me acting immature.

The situation eventually came to a boiling point, and then we realized just how stupid we were acting towards one another. Elder Thebault finally asked, "Why do you disrespect me every time I give my opinion on my leadership position as an AP?" I could feel his sincerity for the very first time, and suddenly I felt bad for acting immature. "I apologize for being rude," I admitted. He likewise replied with an apology, and we had a nice talk as friends.

We both needed an attitude adjustment. I am committed to taking my role as a missionary more seriously, while Elder Thebault agreed to "lightened up" a little bit.

I learned a valuable lesson from this experience. By expressing my true feelings through transparency and honesty, I can resolve any issue. Additionally, I realized the importance of trust and respect in a companionship.

What a day! It is round three of Missionary Day. I have felt filled with The Spirit, and that is an incredibly peaceful feeling. Before tracting[19], I prepared myself by studying a painting of Jesus. After looking for only a few seconds, I was filled with The Spirit. I knew I had it, and my countenance showed it, because I could feel The Spirit of light gleaming all around me. It is my hope that I can consistently achieve this level of spiritual fortification while serving in the mission field. Missionaries can have The Spirit so strongly, and yet sometimes, I don't think we realize just how much we are protected.

As I was basking in The Spirit, Elder Perkins and I bumped into a couple of "mock" investigators, and The Spirit seemed to run right out the door. Missionary Day is beginning to get on my last nerves. I have been feeling pretty irritated, especially today. It's difficult to role play with my peers and practice feeling The

Spirit when they are constantly trying to stump and distract me with stupid questions about nit-picky principles of the gospel.

The elders in my district are great, and I am beginning to love them. I've been getting along better with everyone, including Elder Perkins and Elder Thebault. In fact, the entire district is getting along better.

The twelve-hour workdays at the MTC have begun wearing on Elder Garner and me, so we decided to have a wrestling match in his dorm room. He and I had a few built-up, frustrations, so instead of hurting each other with words, we killed each other physically...just kidding! However, we did have a wrestling match, and we were able to work out some of our frustrations. It was fun to just "let it all go" on the wrestling mat.

Today I received a message from the MTC Post Office that I have a package, but I can't pick it up until Monday. There's only one thing I want to say about that news: "It had better be a letter from Kaesi, or else!" I haven't received a blasted thing from her since I've been here, and I'm kinda ticked off about it, especially since I have written her four times. She has not written me once! I don't know what I'm going to do.... Maybe I'll write her a "Dear Jane letter...just kidding.

President Pinegar spoke at our devotional today and I enjoyed listening to his message, which he delivered with amazing power and authority. He talked about loving the people we teach. He stated, "It is important to work hard!" Then he talked about the *Book of Mormon* and how special this holy scripture is in our day.

Specifically, he stressed the need to feast upon the words of the *Book of Mormon* because it is a precious gift. The two main purposes of the *Book of Mormon* are (1) It shows the goodness of God to his children, and (2) Jesus is the Christ and the son of a living God. President Pinegar continued, "Teach from the *Book of Mormon* and follow Christ's example. It is important to have faith because faith leads to action and power." Listening to President Pinegar speak made me want to be the best missionary I can be, and his words resonated deep within my soul.

As I reflect on my relationship with my companions, I realize that things are getting better. Everything is just peachy. I love my family very much and hope the Lord will rain blessings upon them while I am serving in the mission field.

This morning during class, our instructor asked everyone to share their favorite *Book of Mormon* story. One of my favorite stories has always been the one about Helaman and the two-thousand stripling warriors. When I began to speak, I could tell I had everyone's attention. It is a powerful story!

The story begins in the *Book of Mormon* where 2,000 young men are led by an American Indian (General Helaman) to defend their people. The parents of these young men entered a covenant with God not to kill, even in defense against their enemies. Their sons, however, had not entered into this covenant. And so, despite their inexperience and youth, the stripling warriors fought because their mothers' promise that they would not be harmed during battle gave them courage to do so. Although many of these valiant men were wounded in battle, none of them were killed.

Today I received five letters and two care packages; one of which was from Kaesi. Finally, Kaesi sent me a care package! I was beginning to think she wasn't alive....

As I listened to her audio tape, she brought up a past incident that I care not to remember—because it hurt her feelings. It is something I shouldn't have done.

Although our relationship was great—most of the time—Kaesi and I argued sometimes. This is full disclosure, but the reason why we argued was because I went out on a date with a girl, Brandi Severson, about a month before I left Atlanta. When I brought Brandi home, I kissed her on the front porch. I told Kaesi about it afterwards and of course she got angry! Sister McGurrin called me a "turd," and it was a big ol' mess.

Why did I cheat on my girlfriend? Maybe it's because two-years is a long time to not date...and I didn't want to be tied down? Hindsight is 20/20. The reality is, and I should never gone steady with Kaesi...but it is what it is. Since the whole "Brandi incident," our relationship seems to have taken a turn for the worse. I take full responsibility for my actions and admit that I didn't want to reveal my mistake to Kaesi, but I did...there it is.

Long story short, the audio tape was bittersweet because Kaesi likes to make me feel guilty, and I don't know if she even realizes it...She also said some nice things, my favorite of which was, "I love you."

I really do not know how I feel about Kaesi. I mean. I'm spiritually and physically in a different world. I know that I care for her a great deal but loving her physically is not in the cards right now. Sometimes all I want to do is show her my love and affection, while at the same time, I want to help her gain a stronger testimony. Kaesi is great; I really couldn't ask for anyone better. I hope we can continue dating after my mission.

I have also learned to love my family more by serving a mission. I know my family loves me, and I know that they will be blessed while I am gone. They really do support my efforts, and that is especially important to me. All I can say is, 'Keep those letters coming in the mail!'

As I reflect on my spiritual experiences while at the MTC, I'm realizing that it's impossible to remember all the devotionals and classes I attend every day. I also love seeing missionaries from all diverse levels of society, many of whom have sacrificed their careers, education, and family just to be here. There are a few missionaries who had to repent and straighten out their lives to be worthy to serve the Lord. Some of the most common sins I've seen around here were partying too hard, drinking beer, and having sex. The miracle of forgiveness is a wonderful blessing.

We attended a devotional tonight about the Missionary Discussions and itemized the following goals:

1. Timeline: 3-week timeline to schedule the Discussions and have an investigator ready for baptism.
2. Action: Invite someone. Show them your love and continue to love them.

3. Spirit: "Live by The Spirit." Always be worthy to have The Spirit with you. Identify The Spirit with the investigators. Elders have the right to call upon The Spirit as found in John 14:26: "But the Comforter, which is the Holy Ghost, whom the Father will send in my name, he shall teach you all things, and bring all things to your remembrance, whatsoever I have said unto you."

4. Let the people open their scriptures and read John 14:26. Ask them questions to explain the Holy Ghost. "Can you see the wind? Can you feel the wind?" Explain to them what the Holy Ghost is.

One of the greatest highlights of my day occurred with my companion, Elder Perkins. We attended a Culture Meeting, and our teacher encouraged us to say a few positive words about our companions, and what we admired most about them.

Elder Perkins decided to go first. He said, "Elder Todd, you easily forget other people's mistakes. When other people say negative things about you, it does not seem to bother you." Elder Perkins continued, "You're tidy, and your side of the desk is cleaner than mine. [We both know that's not true!] You always smile." I replied, "Thank you, man; I appreciate it." Then our instructor concluded the meeting and said, "Before you retire for bed this evening, tell your companion that you love him."

After the meeting, we walked back to our condos and got dressed for bed. Elder Perkins was sitting on the top bunk reading his scriptures when I pulled out the piece of paper highlighting the things, I most admired about him. Then I read aloud, "You read the scriptures. You have a cooperative spirit. You follow the rules, especially the rule about being to class on time. And I have noticed that you have changed the most of anyone in the district. Your personal testimony is stronger." I looked up from my piece of paper and noticed that his countenance had changed; what I had said clearly touched his heart. Elder Perkins replied, "I'm not saying this just because the teacher said to, but I love you." It was awesome. I responded, "We will make it through the MTC and still be able to shake hands when this is all over!"

Everything is going great with my district. The missionaries are so awesome and so cool because we work as a team. Perhaps it feels so easy because we're keeping the commandments, following Jesus, and we have The Spirit with us.

Thank goodness tomorrow is P-day! We will finally get a chance to wash our clothes, write letters, and attend the temple. I cannot wait to go to the temple; it's the greatest place in the entire world. I cannot wait until I get to California. San Berdu, here I come!

***

All is quiet on the western front... I had a marvelous experience at the temple this morning. After our temple trip, we washed clothes and then decided to eat out for lunch. It was a fun afternoon.

When we returned from lunch, I wrote a few letters and made an audio tape for Kaesi. I hope she likes it because it came from my heart. I haven't received a letter from her in a few days. I did buy a *Book of Mormon* and had Bob Allison's name embossed on the front. (Bob was the gentleman I met on the airplane to Salt Lake City.) This afternoon, I mailed the package along with a letter to the mission office in Kentucky. I hope that he will accept my gift and allow the missionaries to teach him the gospel of Jesus Christ. I feel that serving a mission is such an honor.

The countdown begins: only five more days until we are in San Berdu! It is going to be an awesome experience. I want to be the best missionary I can be.

I received two letters from my sweetheart, Kaesi. In one of the letters, she shared her testimony about the love she has for her family. I am proud of her.

It's so weird how everything is going by so quickly, and there's not a thing in the world I can do about it. I live in a different world at the MTC—a better world. What I mean by a 'better world' is it's so calm and peaceful at the MTC. There are thousands of missionaries with one common goal. "This is my work and my glory to bring to pass the immortality and eternal life of man." Moses 1:39. I know that I will grow so much on my mission, and I cannot wait for the wonderful experience the Lord has in store for me in California.

During our Missionary Conference today, I had the privilege of listening to Elder Ballard of the Quorum of the Twelve Apostles and Elder Backman of the Seventy[20]. Elder Backman gave a great talk in which he encouraged us to concentrate on the "commitment pattern" for teaching the Discussions, including:

1. Build a plan with goals in mind.
2. Build trust. Show your love and care for the investigators. Show interest and ask appropriate questions that fit the needs of the investigator.
3. Prepare others to feel The Spirit.
4. Prepare to present the message. It is important to speak in a natural way. Use the scriptures and firsthand experiences.
5. Find out. Use questions that will help investigators express their own feelings.
6. Resolve concerns. Encourage the investigator to build their spiritual feelings. According to LeGrand Richards, "Don't take 'no' for an answer."
7. Make sure commitments are specific. Use the words, "will you," and positive motivation. Make sure the investigator understands their commitments.
8. Follow up and help investigators follow-through with their commitments. It is important to help investigators by being sincere and making daily contact to combat the opposition. Elder Richards

said he experienced faith-promoting experiences during his first mission.

Elder Ballard was more reserved but delivered a powerful message. He talked about proselyting and learning to speak with everyone we meet. Elder Ballard admonished us to live by Doctrine & Covenants 24:12 to spread the gospel: "And at all times, and it all places, he shall open his mouth and declare my gospel as with the voice of a trump, both day and night. And I will give unto him strength such as is not known among men."

In The Church of Jesus Christ of Latter-day Saints, we believe in four books of scripture including: the Holy Bible (we use the King James Version), the *Book of Mormon*, the Pearl of Great Price, and the Doctrine & Covenants. These are the "standard works," or the written canons formally accepted by our church. Being a complimentary set, we recognize that the books do not compete with one another. The Doctrine & Covenants is considered modern day revelation, written specifically for our day and time.

Elder Ballard continued by talking about his travels to Europe, during which he visited the country of Sweden. President Max Kimball served with him during his mission. (President Max Kimball was the former first counselor in the Sandy Springs Stake in Georgia.)

At any rate, Elder Ballard talked about "opening our mouths," and related this story: "One day we were riding on a bus when I asked President Kimball to speak with the person riding in the front seat. President Kimball replied with a puzzled look, 'Who are you referring to?' I pointed to the bus driver. So, President Kimball accepted the challenge. He got up from his seat and sat behind the bus driver." Elder Ballard continued, "When it was time to step off the bus, President Kimball wrote down the man's street address, phone number, and made an appointment to teach him the 1st Discussion. At that moment, our baptismal numbers were at an all-time high!

President Kimball said to me, 'It really works, doesn't it?'" Following this story, Elder Ballard concluded, "My sheep know my voice. Therefore, it is so important to speak with every living soul. Open your mouth."

Elder Garner and I ran all the way from our condos to the mailbox today. It was fantastic! I received seven letters and a care package, including one from my dad; I sure love him. He gave me the rundown on my finances and how he felt about me serving the Lord. On another note, I read that Brian Voyles was called of God to serve in Nova Scotia, Canada, and he reports to the MTC October 5th.

Three of the seven letters were from Kaesi, which was so awesome. I really cannot explain my feelings. She included a nice headshot photo and her Youth Conference pin. It felt just too good to be true; I absolutely loved it. I try not to think about her, but it is difficult sometimes because she is so awesome. While it's difficult to have the same feelings for her now that I am on mission, I know that I love her very much. The elders who live on my hall drooled all over her photo, but she's all mine.

Tomorrow is Missionary Day again, and Elder Perkins and I will be teaching the 3rd Discussion, "Restoration of the Gospel," and the 4th Discussion, "Eternal Progression." This is going to be fun because I feel more confident in my presentation abilities and the unity between Elder Perkins and I. We are getting along great, and he has definitely lightened up. Lately, he's learned to joke around with me, which is cool.

Elder Harvey asked me to speak on the Book of Mormon during Priesthood Meeting tomorrow, and I'm excited to share thoughts on Helaman's two-thousand stripling warriors. I know I've mentioned this before, but I love this story about faith, courage, obedience, and living the commandments of God.

I am tired of waiting and ready to go to California. I am prepared to do what I was born to do: preach the gospel to Heavenly Father's children, my brothers, and sisters. I cannot wait. I know that the work is difficult. In fact, I know it is extremely difficult, but I am going to work and endure to the end.

The Lord is pleased with me, because he knows the intentions of my heart. He knows how eager I am to live the commandments. The Lord loves me, and that is all that matters. I have a powerful desire to serve Jesus. Additionally, I need to have the self-assurance that my best is good enough for Him.

The spirit of the Lord, Jesus Christ, rings within my soul. I plan to live by Doctrine & Covenants 24:12, which says to "open my mouth" to those I come in contact within the San Bernardino Mission.

***

During church service today, Elder Garner was asked to share his testimony of the gospel. I was impressed with how humble he was in sharing his thoughts. The Spirit touched him in a way that he will never forget. My only goal in life right now is to baptize and help bring to pass the eternal life of man. I know that if I want to teach, I must teach with The Spirit. As all Sunday school teachers, local leaders, and all church members must understand: In order to share the gospel, one must obtain and teach by The Spirit.

Tomorrow is my last and final day here at the MTC. The church does a fantastic job teaching us the basic gospel principles so that we can take this unified message to the world. I am so glad I came here to learn more about the gospel. The Barstow District is excited about leaving for sunny California. I am a little scared, but that is surely par for the course.

We had a farewell party for one of our instructors, Sister Knott, tonight. She was one of my favorite teachers because she shares the gospel with a humble spirit. In addition, Brother Gibson is a stud, and I have learned a great deal from him.

I received three more letters and a care package from Kaesi today. She just doesn't quit writing, and I love reading her letters. I miss her so much, but I have learned to concentrate on my studies. This is the Lord's mission, and I am living on His time. Everything is going by so fast that I just can't believe it.

Yes! Today is our last day at the MTC! The Barstow District is "Goin' back Californ-I-A" tomorrow morning. I am so excited

I can hardly wait! The decisive moment has arrived; this is so awesome.

Since it is our P-day, we attended the temple; the best place on earth! I enjoy the temple because it is always calm and peaceful inside. It is a sacred and marvelous place to visit and perform temple ordinances.

I tried calling Kaesi's house to let her know about my travel plans and the layover in Phoenix, Arizona. However, she wasn't home, so I spoke with her mom instead. I like her family. After speaking with Sister McGurrin, I called my parents and we talked about my finances and travel plans. We had a nice talk about serving others. I love my family; they are seriously the best group of people a young man could possibly have.

It doesn't feel like I've been at the MTC for 3 weeks. Reality hit me a little bit today; the moment of truth is here. We are going to do the Lord's work. What a fantastic opportunity this will be; serving the Lord! My friendships have grown, and I feel close to the guys in my district. Each companionship has been strengthened in respect and love for one another. I am so thankful to my Heavenly Father for allowing me to go on a mission.

CHAPTER 3:

Welcome to San Bernardino

This is the biggest day of my life, and I'm speechless. I woke at 2:00 a.m., showered, and changed into my best suit. Then I carried my luggage to a chartered bus waiting outside the MTC. We had about 10-minutes before the bus departed to Salt Lake City, so I ran back inside and down the long hallway to say my final good- bye to my friend, Steve Prettyman. I crept into Steve's room so as not to awake his roommates and found him sleeping on the bottom bunk. I gently nudged him, and we gave one another a big hug. I whispered, "Steve, I am leaving, and I just wanted to tell you how much I appreciate your friendship. Let's write to one another every week, o.k.?" Steve replied, "O.K....I love you buddy." I said, "Love you, too, man" and crept back out the door.

At 4:30 a.m. the bus departed the MTC, and we arrived an hour later at the Salt Lake City International Airport. When I stepped off the bus, I was pleasantly surprised to see my aunts and uncles waiting for me at the gate. I enjoyed talking with them and appreciated all their support. I will always remember their kind words of encouragement. My extended family is incredibly special to me.

After we landed in Phoenix for an hour layover, I immediately telephoned Kaesi and talked to her for a few minutes. I love hearing her reassuring voice; totally made my day! After calling and speaking to my parents, we loaded our connecting flight to our final destination: the golden state of California.

The flight was generally uneventful until the airplane began its slow-and-steady decent from the hazy sky. As I peered out the window from the left-hand side of the plane, I noticed that there was low cloud cover. At first glance it appeared to be just clouds, but then a brown haze slowly appeared. That brown haze was the infamous SMOG that blankets the desert of California. I thought to myself, "San Bernardino is the Smog Capital of the World!"

Our airplane safely landed at the Ontario International Airport, and we taxied to the edge of the tarmac, close to the terminal. Once the ground support equipment arrived, we walked down the stairs, and I began to choke on the stale, dry, hot California air. The pungent stench left an awful sulfur "iron taste" in my mouth. The irony of the situation was that—at that moment—I knew that I was exactly where I needed to be, and it felt good to be home-away-from-home. Additionally—and unbeknownst to me at the time—I had another surprise waiting for me. As I was walking across the tarmac, I noticed this little red-headed lady waiving her hands frantically. I thought to myself, "These folks in California are nuts!" As we got closer to the terminal, I soon recognized my own grandparents, and gave them both a great big hug. When I glanced over at the assistants to the president, they laughed with joy and amusement.

After saying goodbye to Grandma and Grandpa, we gathered our luggage and loaded into the mission van. During the drive to the mission home, I could not help but notice all the smog again. It looked like a continuous filthy brown cloud that just kept rolling at the base of the mountains. We arrived at our new mission parent's home; the home of President and Sister Melvin Gourdin. After formally introducing ourselves, we took a driving test in one of the mission vehicles. Then each member of the Barstow District had a personal interview with President Gourdin.

The interview was a bit of a blur for me because I was thinking about my family, girlfriend, and all the comforts of home. As these things were going through my mind, reality began setting into place. I remember reading Doctrine & Covenants 88:119 with President Gourdin: "Organize yourselves; prepare every needful thing; and establish a house, even a house of prayer, a house of fasting, a house of faith, a house of learning, a house of glory, a house of order, a house of God."

Then he turned to 1 Corinthians 6:19–20: "What? Know ye not that your body is the temple of the Holy Ghost, which is in you, which ye have of God, and ye are not your own? For ye are bought with a price: therefore, glorify God in your body, and in your spirit, which are God's."

President Gourdin emphasized, "For ye are bought with a price by Jesus Christ." He admonished me to keep my mind and body clean, and to treat it as the temple of the Holy Ghost. I know that if I organize myself and prepare a house of order, The Spirit will reside with me.

After an exhausting day, I found myself deep in contemplation over the events from past few months: my mission call, high school graduation, dating Kaesi, my mission farewell, the MTC, and finally arriving in the mission field. The hardcore reality set in as I realized this would be my new home for the next two years. As that realization hit me like a ton of bricks, I could feel a knot form in the middle of my throat. For the first time in my life, I felt all alone. My first and immediate reaction was a desire to hop back on an airplane and fly back to the green, luscious hillsides in my beloved state of Georgia. However, I know deep down inside that this is where the Lord wants me.

Despite all my misgivings about this hot, dry, smoggy climate, I am glad to be here.

Companion
Jim Perkins
July-August 1988

CHAPTER 4:

Hells Angels

I am beginning to get used to California, and it is not particularly bad. I felt so discouraged and all alone again today. It is difficult trying to adjust to "The Smog Capital of the World." In all honesty, the smog is absolutely depressing. I think to myself, "How can anyone live here?" However, I am beginning to love the people.

Today I met my new trainer and companion, Elder Matthew Hedelius from Rigby, Idaho. Rigby is a small town in eastern Idaho near Rexburg—where BYU Idaho is located. Our newly assigned area is Fontana, and we leave tomorrow. Fontana is located about seven miles west of San Bernardino. I am excited to finally get to my assigned area! Elder Garner, Lott, Perkins, and I are spending the night at Brother and Sister George's house. Each member of my district has received their new assignment. It is sad to think that the Barstow District is no more. We are all splitting up, but I know we will stay connected through writing to one another.

The town of Fontana has long been known as a "rough and tough" location. Historically, it remained rural until WWII, when entrepreneur—Henry J. Kaiser—built Kaiser Steel. The steel company supplied steel plates for the pacific coast shipbuilding industry, and Mr. Kaiser's shipyards build hundreds of Liberty and Victory ships during the war.

However, war ships were not the only piece of hard metal to originate from the smoggy steel mills. A couple of years after the war ended the hot molten steel mills forged one of the most formidable and impenetrable gangs to ride a Harley Davidson motorcycle: the infamous Hells Angels. That is right! The Hell's Angels were born from the same steel mills that manufactured Liberty ships for the war effort. With that said, I find it ironic that "Hells Angels" quickly became associated with organized crime, drug dealing, trafficking of stolen goods, extortion, and even prostitution.

Another famous person with roots in South Fontana was Mr. Sammy Hagar from the awesome rock band, Van Halen! Thus, the rock 'n roll, blue-collar town of Fontana, California became the setting for my very first calling in the mission field.

Currently, I have mixed emotions about serving in California. This morning I asked myself, "Why am I on a mission...?" and have been searching for the answer ever since. Every time I think I have found the answer, I feel confused and torn between the world and my new spiritual life again. I suppose one reason I am feeling this way is because of the magnificent change that is taking place in my life, and within my own heart and soul.

Unfortunately, I cannot ignore my new and unfamiliar environment. I detest the smog, the tap water is disgusting, and I have a nasty chest cold. To be honest, I miss my home state of Georgia, my family, friends, and especially my sweet girlfriend. I miss all the wonderful comforts I possessed before my mission.

I also realize that I am being selfish, and that this mission is not for me...but for the Lord. He gave me all the good things in life; especially an awesome girlfriend. However, it's time I look deep within myself and begin acting like a man. It is possible to become selfless, but it's a big obstacle to overcome. It's proving extremely difficult for me to take that next leap of faith because I feel like I'm giving up so much of my own personal privileges and freedoms. However, I realize that I am gaining everything—including the blessings of being obedient to the Lord's commandments and taking steps to achieve my own salvation. Despite this knowledge, however, I still dearly miss my family, friends, and girlfriend.

In the grand scheme of things, the time spent on my mission is just a "blip" on the radar of eternity. At times I struggle, and doubt whether I will make it the full two-years of missionary service. However, when these doubts enter my mind, I say a silent prayer and immediately feel the companionship of the Holy Ghost. My mission is for the Lord, and that is a comforting thought.

Today we all attended a testimony meeting for the incoming and departing missionaries and I felt inspired to share my testimony before entering the spiritual field of battle. When I stepped foot in front of the podium to share my thoughts, I was so overcome with emotion and the Holy Ghost that I could not speak. I tried and tried to open my mouth, but the words would not come out. Feeling the power of The Spirit of God was one of the greatest moments in my life. A few seconds later, I regained my composure and shared my love of the Savior and passion serving a church mission.

I am finally in my new assigned area, and it's fantastic! Fontana is not a bad place; I actually like it. The first thing Elder Hedelius and I did on our first day together was ride our bicycles to the local grocery store, Albertson's. We bought our groceries for the week, then rode back to our humble apartment and spent the day putting away our food, unpacking our clothes, and tidying up the place.

Afterwards, Elder Hedelius made a few phone calls and introduced us to the local ward leadership. Then we reviewed our Area Proselyting Guide (APG)[21] to become familiar with any new investigators. The binder looked very thin to me. Sadly, it does not appear that anyone has written in it in a long time.

Tonight, we teamed-up with Brother Adams, one of the stake missionaries[22], who drove us to a member's home. There, we met Tammy Lewis, a sixteen-year-old mother of a precious little baby girl. Tammy has been living with her boyfriend, who is a less- active member of the church[23]. As part of our presentation, we watched the video[24] entitled, "Together Forever." Then we had a solid discussion about the *Book of Mormon*, and The Spirit was in their home. We had an enjoyable time.

I received a ton of letters today, including a couple from Kaesi. I miss her so much; I honestly think about Kaesi all the time. However, I know the Lord will bless Kaesi and her family while I am away serving the Lord.

I am still trying to get used to this nasty smog but suppose I can live with it. I just can't let it bother me so much. I know the Lord will watch over and protect me if I serve Him faithfully. This mission is great, and I love missionary work because I enjoy people!

Today we had a productive but exhausting afternoon, bicycling all over the City of Fontana. During our ten-mile trip, we visited five church members in the Fontana First and Fifth Wards[25]; it was fun! Elder Hedelius and I had the privilege of giving out four copies of *The Book of Mormon*. Out of these contacts, I feel that at least two of them will listen to the Missionary Discussions.

While riding my bike up and down a few hills, I really noticed the smog— specifically after mile five—when I began to breathe more deeply. The smog was so thick and nasty that it hurt to breathe, and my contact lenses felt like they had tiny granules of sand in them. My eyes watered as my lungs gasped for air. At times, my body couldn't bear the stinging sensation, and I felt absolutely awful. However, I knew the Lord was watching over me. I love my mission, and the Fontana Wards are full of amazing church members. I'm also grateful for Elder Hedelius because he is a cool companion and I'm learning a lot about how to become an effective missionary.

***

This morning we attended two church services with the Fontana First and Fifth Wards. In The Church of Jesus Christ of Latter-day Saints, the usual custom is to pray and fast for 24 hours, or two meals, on the first Sunday of each month. Even though it was not officially Fast Sunday, Elder Hedelius and I decided to pray and fast anyway. During our fast, we asked the Lord to soften the hearts of the people in Fontana who are ready to hear the gospel of Jesus Christ.

Currently, we do not have anyone in our finding or teaching pool, and our Area Proselyting Guide (APG) is empty. We have zero investigators to teach, and very few follow up visits. This is a stark reminder of how much work we need to do if we want to teach the gospel...

Apparently, the missionaries who served in Fontana before us were waiting on their visas to Brazil. We missionaries refer to them as "Visa Waiters" because they are typically only in an area for two to four weeks.

Today we fervently prayed to the Lord that He would "open up the windows of heaven," and bless this area with people to teach. Since we are responsible for missionary work in the Fontana First and Fifth Wards, we attended both Sacrament Meetings. A member of the bishopric[26] asked us to offer the opening and closing prayer in the Fontana First Ward, and we each spoke for a few minutes in the Fontana Fifth Ward.

The members of the church are great because they are very supportive of our efforts. Elder Hedelius and I handed out our dinner calendar to the Relief Society[27] and received five dinner signups for the month so far. I am looking forward to visiting with each member in their home in order to become acquainted, and to have a delicious home-cooked meal.

After church we decided to tract, and we handed out two more copies of the Book of Mormon. We concluded the afternoon by visiting a nursing home and met with a few less-active members. It is fulfilling to do the Lord's work on the Sabbath

Day. Our companionship is determined to teach and baptize. I know the Lord will bless us, and I love the work.

Preparation Day (P-day) was great. The first thing we decided to do was wash our dirty clothes at the local laundry mat. While waiting for the clothes to dry, we met Jim folding his clothes. He told us, "I stopped attending the LDS church as soon as I found out that you guys don't believe in the same Jesus as I do." Naturally, we responded, and talked for a few minutes about Jesus and what we believe in as a church.

Jim replied, "You guys don't know what you're talking about when it comes to the Savior," and then the conversation began to go sideways. I tried to diffuse the situation by asking him if it would be okay to schedule an appointment at his house to discuss the matter in more detail. Although he agreed, Elder Hedelius didn't like the whole thing at all. However, I think we can make a good impression on this guy.

I spent the rest of the day writing fifteen letters to my friends and family. After we mailed our letters at the post office, we did our grocery shopping for the week. I have great hopes that someone will write me a letter back!

I feel good about doing the Lord's work. Jesus watches over us because of His infinite love. God wants all His children to live with Him someday. Heavenly Father and Jesus Christ are wonderful, and I love them both. The Lord's work in Fontana will carry forth in all its glory, and Elder Hedelius and I will be successful as His servants.

It was cool attending my first Zone Conference[28] this morning. While there, I bumped into one of my old MTC roommates, Elder Heaton. He is a total stud because we were roommates in the MTC and we got to know one another.

After Zone Conference, we rode our bicycles to Tammy Lewis' house for our 2:00 p.m. appointment. When we arrived, however, we discovered she moved away. We decided to go to Plan B—and tracted. While tracting, Elder Hedelius and I were fortunate enough to deliver one copy of the *Book of Mormon* to a nice lady.

Next, we had a Family Presentation[29] appointment at 4:00 p.m. in North Fontana. Our appointment is near Foothill Boulevard, and it takes about 20 to 30 minutes to get there on a bicycle.

We presented the lesson, and it went o.k., I suppose. However, Elder Hedelius and I were expecting a more positive outcome than the one we received from the family.

We were not able to produce any new referrals. I don't blame the family because we were not as prepared as we could have been. That is our own fault.

After giving the Family Presentation, we decided to tract for at least one more hour. During that time, we delivered two more copies of the Book of Mormon, and one of the women stood out to both of us. At first, she refused to accept the Book of Mormon, but I was persistent and shared my testimony of its truthfulness and divinity. I felt the strong influence of The Spirit, and she accepted the gift. We will be following through with her soon, to see if she liked reading 3 Nephi Chapter 11[30] and Moroni's promise.

The next door we knocked on was a less-active member's home, the Whicstow family. Brother and Sister Whicstow were a jolly couple who invited us in for dinner. Sister Whicstow was kind enough cook us two delicious hamburger patties with pork and beans. During dinner, Brother and Sister Whicstow talked about their eighteen-year-old son who is serving in the U.S. Navy. Brother Whicstow, a church history buff and talked up a storm. Elder Hedelius and I enjoyed their hospitality.

At the end of each day, it is custom to check the mailbox before we retire for the evening. Tonight, I received four letters, and two were from Kaesi! I love it when I receive letters, especially from my sweetheart. I love my mission, and I know everything is going to work out, even if it is slow. I have faith in the Lord, Jesus Christ.

I just realized that I've been serving my church mission for almost one month, though I have been living in California for exactly one week. It honestly seems longer than that, but I know the time will go by quickly.

I had a few spiritual experiences today. This morning, Elder Hedelius and I followed through with a member referral. His name was George Gilbert, a ninety-one- year-old Catholic man. He lived alone in a small, cozy home. George is a cool dude because he is a kind and gentle man. He told us that, in his younger days, he was boxer. Apparently, he fought in fifty-nine matches and only lost four times. George sure liked to talk!

We tried to teach George the 1st Discussion, "The Plan of Our Heavenly Father," but he just kept talking—mostly about gospel principles. Elder Hedelius and I could not get a word in edgewise. It did not matter how hard we tried; nothing worked. At one point it became comical, and we accidentally forgot his last name, so we just called him Brother George. He did not seem to mind, and I don't even think he noticed.

Anyway, George was kind enough to give us both a compliment on our appearances. He said at least four times during our conversation, "You guys are wonderful and handsome." It made me feel good inside, knowing we are ambassadors of the Lord, and that we stand out from the crowd. People often notice our white shirts, dark pants, and nice haircuts.

We offered to give George a copy of the *Book of Mormon* and he accepted, even promising to read it. George said, "I am glad to see you guys on church missions doing the Lord's work. You're welcome to come back, anytime!"

The rest of the afternoon, we tracted in a local neighborhood and gave out five copies of the *Book of Mormon*. The Lord was with us. It was super-hot and humid because of the slight drizzle falling from the sky. Then my contact lenses started bothering me again, and I knew exactly what was causing the eye irritation—SMOG! (It does that to me occasionally.)

Tonight, we had a dinner appointment with the Cenatiempo's, a great family who prepared a delicious chicken dish for us. Brother Cenatiempo served his church mission in Atlanta about eight years ago. After his mission he became a schoolteacher. Brother and Sister Cenatiempo had three little daughters, all of whom are extremely cute. The youngest is only five weeks old and she is precious.

After dinner, we decided to show the video, "Together Forever," for the Family Presentation. I could feel the strong influence of The Spirit. After the video, I asked Brother and Sister Cenatiempo, "Do y'all know anyone who you could share the gospel with?" Brother Cenatiempo mentioned a couple of his friends who would be willing to hear the Missionary Discussions. While I was listening to him speak, I envisioned his friends entering the waters of baptism. It was as if the Holy Ghost had allowed me to see these individuals baptized in the waters of Mormon. It was one of the greatest feelings in the world because I felt peace in my heart.

I have a desire to work hard, be successful, and show love for the Savior. I will teach through The Spirit and baptize. I know I will baptize because the Lord has promised me blessings as I serve Him.

This morning I was ticked-off when I discovered my bicycle's tire was flatter than a doornail. Elder Hedelius and I spent a couple of hours walking to the bicycle shop and waiting for my tire to be repaired. Once my bicycle was roadworthy, we decided it was time to tract. It went well, and for the first time in my life, I met a Jehovah's Witness who didn't argue or yell at me. On the contrary, the lady was quite nice.

After tracting we decided to take a break and rode our bicycles to Kaiser Permanente Hospital to give a good sister a blessing. Her name was Sister Jannetta Sanford, and she had been suffering from blood clots in her legs. For this reason, she asked for a priesthood blessing[31]. She was thrilled to have us visit her in the hospital; it was so special. This was my first time anointing someone's head with consecrated oil. Then Elder Hedelius sealed the anointing and offered a blessing. I felt The Spirit as I lifted my hands from her head.

After visiting Sister Sanford, we headed to our very first confirmed teaching appointment at 5:00 p.m. with Kelly Kessel. We arrived on time, only to find a note on her front door saying she would be two hours late. When Kelly finally arrived, she was very apologetic.

We opened with a word of prayer and then decided to read from the book of Alma in the *Book of Mormon*, which was about faith. I shared one of my favorite stories about the two-thousand stripling warriors. The Spirit was present, and I felt like we formed a good bond with Kelly.

We had a productive day, which made me feel good. However, on our ride back home, I could sense something was wrong with Elder Hedelius. I asked him, "What's the matter?" The next thing I knew we were arguing back and forth and in the middle of our first verbal argument. I felt shocked and did not know what was going on.

However, we finally worked things out. The issue was simply stress. Elder Hedelius admitted that he tends to put a ton of pressure on himself to be an exemplary trainer and missionary. I think, like a pressure cooker, he needed to blow off a little steam. It is all good. Elder Hedelius is a super guy, and I love him most because he's one-hundred percent committed to serving his Heavenly Father.

When I finally laid down in my bed to relax and fall asleep, I closed my eyes and remembered talking with Sister Kessel's five-year old daughter. It brought back so many fond memories with my two baby sisters, Wendy, and Julie. I miss and love them and my other family so much.

Today, Elder Hedelius and I handed out eight more copies of the *Book of Mormon*. That is a total of thirty-one books for the week. We are tracting fools! If we continue at this pace, we are on track to deliver 124 copies of the *Book of Mormon* in a month. We have been working hard, and The Spirit has been making it possible.

While tracking we met a man named Jim, who invited us into his home. Jim said he was confused about some teachings and doctrines of the church, so he asked us questions about Joseph Smith and the *Book of Mormon*. Jim was very polite and seemed sincere when he welcomed us back to his home. I feel pretty good about teaching Jim the Missionary Discussions.

Tonight, Elder Hedelius and I had a dinner appointment with one of his friends, Reid Furniss, a twenty-nine-year-old single member who works as an accountant from Rigby, Idaho. Reid prepared a delicious Chinese meal; it was great! I especially enjoyed the old-fashioned homemade ice cream we had for dessert; it tasted so good! It is now 12:10 a.m. and I am exhausted.

This morning the Fontana District met together to review our week, since it is custom in the San Bernardino Mission to have a weekly District Meeting to review the week's activities. During the meeting, we also had a spiritual thought, and offered support to one another in the work. The elders in the Fontana District include Elder Waddoups, Elder Atwood, Elder Dredge, Elder Short, Elder Hedelius, and me. Elder Waddoups is our district leader.

After the meeting, Elder Hedelius and I went on splits[32] with other elders in our district. Elder Waddoups and I are also planning splits with members of the Fontana First Ward. It's a wonderful feeling to know that there are church members willing to volunteer and partner with the full-time missionaries as we seek to spread the gospel.

Elder Waddoups is super cool, and we get along great! He knows Dan Rogers, one of my friends back home in Georgia. In fact, Elder Waddoups and Dan were roommates at BYU-Provo. He has a ton of great ideas about tracting and door approaches.

While tracting we were invited into the home of Sister Garcia, a less-active member in the ward. When we arrived, however, Sister Garcia told us that she was completing the paperwork to have her name removed from the records of the church because she didn't agree with the law of tithing found in the Old Testament, Malachi 3:10, "Bring ye all the tithes into the storehouse, that there may be meat in mine house, and prove me now herewith, saith the Lord of hosts, if I will not open you the windows of heaven, and pour you out a blessing, that there shall not be room enough to receive it."

It was sad. Sister Garcia was a nice lady too. Her biggest issue was how the tithes (10% of earnings) were distributed among the church.

As I listened to Sister Garcia express such adamant resolve about removing her name from the membership records, my sadness slowly turned to anger. I just couldn't fathom why a child of God and a member of the church would ever want to leave for good! I became so emotional that Elder Waddoups had to lead the rest of the discussion. I was so disappointed to see this good sister make such a permanent decision to go astray and reject the gospel. I just hope Sister Garcia truly prays about it. On the positive side, we handed out eight copies of the *Book of Mormon* in under two-hours.

After tracting, Elder Hedelius and I headed back to our apartment to eat a late lunch. Then we followed through with a gentleman named Don Davis, who we gave a *Book of Mormon* to last week. Don is a nice guy and seems very sincere in his convictions. Though we were only able to speak with Don for a few minutes and weren't able to discuss the gospel during our visit, we will try again soon.

I am extremely disappointed in the results of my missionary efforts thus far. Even though we have scheduled some appointments, we have been unable to teach the Missionary Discussions. The few appointments we've had have either cancelled or, in Kelly's instance, showed up two-hours late. I want to teach the gospel of Jesus Christ so badly I can hardly stand it. I have one mission and one goal for serving in Fontana and that's teach and baptize!

After tracting this entire week, we hand-delivered thirty-one copies of the *Book of Mormon*, which is awesome! I feel pretty good about our accomplishment. There are many missionaries who don't have the opportunity to give out even ten copies of the *Book of Mormon* in a whole week.

Today I was feeling sorry for myself, so Elder Hedelius suggested we have companion study at the park, and we role-played the 2nd Discussion, "The Gospel of Jesus Christ." After our excursion and practice, I felt much better about myself. Then I thought, 'What better way to "drown my sorrows" than to tract?' And that is exactly what we did.

While tracting, we met two new people and spoke with them for 45-minutes, during which we had a polite discussion about the gospel. It was an interesting conversation, because we were able to talk about Heavenly Father's plan. I hope we can schedule an appointment to teach them in the future. Our newfound friends said they appreciated what we were doing to proselyte and spread the gospel. Although, overall, my mission has felt very "smoggy," I still love sunny Southern California.

***

This Sunday, Elder Hedelius and I woke up late for church. Aah! After Sacrament Meeting, we met with Brother Hadden, Mission Leader for the Fontana Fifth Ward. He is about 6'6, the size of an offensive tackle for the NFL, and his handshake is enough to break my hand, so I must be careful! When I fail to give him a firm handshake back, he makes me pay by crushing my hand; all the while with a pleasant smile on his face. He is actually a really super guy and has been giving us good information about the area.

After church, we had a dinner and teaching appointment with the Stallans family. Brother and Sister Stallan are less active and have two super cute children. We had a delicious dinner of ham, bacon, chicken, and vegetables. It sure beats the heck out of eating Honey Nut Cheerios! After dinner, we played with the children for a few minutes and then watched the video "Together Forever." We discussed the video and then taught them one of the Stake Missionary Discussions[33] for new members.

During the lesson, we demonstrated how to read and study the scriptures with Sister Stallan. It was neat to teach her how to study scriptures, because it is a powerful tool, she will use her entire life. Brother and Sister Stallan seemed very receptive to our message, and The Spirit was there.

I have faith that our teaching pool will begin to overflow next week. The Lord has promised us great blessings, and I know God will deliver. I also know the Lord keeps his promises when we keep ours. The Lord knows that we are working hard to teach people who are willing to learn about His gospel.

Today I purchased a pillowcase with a photograph of my face on it for Kaesi. I hope she enjoys my handsome face. In the accompanying letter, I asked her to give me a kiss every night before she goes to bed. Missionaries need love too! Kaesi mentioned in her last letter to expect a little surprise and told me that I would find out what it is this week. I cannot wait!

Tomorrow is P-day; what a relief. I'm looking forward to taking a break from all this tracting to watch a Disney movie. The mission rules state we can only watch "wholesome" Rated G or PG movies. Most importantly, I'm looking forward to sleeping in for a change.

Today, except for washing clothes and relaxing, we did absolutely nothing. We did meet the rest of the district at Elder Waddoups and Elder Atwood's apartment to watch videos and mess around.

I also received letters from Jeff Humphrey; Dad; and my sweetheart, Kaesi, who wrote me two beautiful letters. I really enjoyed reading them. Elder Hedelius has been encouraging me to focus on missionary work more and pay less attention to writing Kaesi letters. I believe he is right; he's a good guy and a great companion. This week should be great. I am looking forward to getting back to work.

Today I had the privilege of teaching my very first real-live discussion. Not only did I teach the 1st Discussion, but we also taught it twice in one day! Our first appointment was with Brother George Gilbert, the ninety-one-year-old ex-boxer who we met a couple of weeks ago. He shared with us how much he appreciates our visits and talking about the gospel.

George also confided in us that he has colon cancer. Despite this news, he is in good spirits and has a great attitude. He began talking about his dear mother and how much he loved her. Elder Hedelius and I were touched by George's words as he began to cry, with tears of joy running down his face. He said that when we visited, it felt like sun rays were shining through his home. What a marvelous experience to be in the same room with this wise and humble man.

Our second appointment was with Mr. Henry Smith, who has a strong conviction in the Holy Bible. Henry felt The Spirit and believes in the gospel message. I am striving to think positively and believe that things are beginning to look up. The Lord loves us and is willing to bless our area if we continue to work hard. My two-years are going to fly by, and I can't wait to baptize.

This morning we had a few humbling experiences. Our first appointment was with Brother George Albert. Through The Spirit, he shared with us his desire for baptism. However, he expressed one major issue. Most of his family are devout Catholics, and he is very dependent on his daughters for financial and emotional support. In other words, George must ask their permission to get baptized into The Church of Jesus Christ of Latter-Day Saints. We will continue to pray for George so that he can maintain his health and well-being and move forward with faith.

Our second appointment was with Margaret, who lives in the Mary Gold Apartments close to our home and is a single parent with a young toddler. During our initial visit, Margaret shared with us that her first born son was tragically hit by a bus and died. She was very receptive to the gospel message. Through The Spirit, she expressed a fervent desire to know more about the church.

I know the Lord will bless us if we keep his commandments, work hard, and have faith in Jesus Christ. This is His work, and we are simply His servants trying to teach our fellow man. I know that if I do my best and follow the promptings of The Spirit, the Lord will bless us. I feel close to the Lord. I know He loves me very much. I love my family, church, and my girlfriend. They all mean so much to me as I serve in this significant role of spreading the good news. I love the gospel with all my heart.

Today, Elder Hedelius and I had a couple of uplifting and humbling experiences. We prayed earnestly to the Lord, asking

Him to bless us while tracting in the area. The first few doors we knocked on left us very discouraged, as people repeatedly slammed doors in our faces. However, our faith prevailed, and we met a few genuinely nice people. Gratefully, we had the honor of handing out six copies of the *Book of Mormon*.

We were getting ready for our dinner appointment at Brother Todd Whicstow's house when we received a telephone call from a sister in the ward, who asked us to give her four-year old daughter, Chloe, a priesthood blessing.

When we arrived at their house, the mother began sharing with us what was happening to Chloe. She had been experiencing some terrible nightmares about life's battle between good versus evil.

Apparently, the dark side had been telling Chloe to do dreadful things. Her mother explained that the "bad people" were encouraging Chloe to hit her two-year-old little sister. According to Chloe, her Care Bears and stuffed animals traveled in the night, disguised as "bad characters" who tried to inflict harm on her as well. Furthermore, Chloe was told by the Care Bears that if she ever decided to tell her mother about the nightmares, they would inflict harm on the entire family.

However, the "good side" always prevails. Chloe also experiences good dreams, where she was counselled to listen to Jesus Christ and read the *Book of Mormon*.

These people were good and wholesome and approached Chloe as little children. Chloe's mother continued, "When I was pregnant with Chloe's little sister, she would calmly walk up to me and share wonderful things about specific blessings."

After Chloe's mom explained everything, Elder Hedelius and I laid our hands on little Chloe's head and gave her special blessing of comfort. It was one of the greatest experiences I have had on my mission thus far. We hold the Holy Priesthood of God to bless the lives of others. Chloe is a precious daughter of our Heavenly Father, and I know that, through the priesthood, her soul will be comforted. What a marvelous experience to exercise my priesthood to bless the lives of other people!

After our dinner appointment with the Whicstows, we visited a part-member family, the Lindseys. (Brother Lindsey is not a member.) We had a nice meeting with the family and will be teaching them the gospel in the next couple of weeks. I can't wait to continue teaching because it's my favorite part of serving a mission.

When we arrived home, I received a huge care package from the McGurrin family that included a new white shirt, a tie, cookies, M&M's, letters, and a couple of homemade audio tapes. The tapes were awesome. My mission is so wonderful, and I am incredibly happy to be here. I love my Heavenly Father and Jesus Christ, and I know that families can be together forever.

Last night I listened to Kaesi's audio tapes and was extremely impressed. There is no question in my mind that we love each other. However, I also realize that Kaesi is a great catch. She is an incredibly attractive 17-year-old and has a great personality. Additionally, she is a good Mormon girl! Kaesi will be graduating from high school and attending college soon. She has her whole life in front of her.

I began asking myself a few questions. "Will she find a new boyfriend at BYU? Or maybe find another guy to fall in love with?" Of course...who I am kidding? There is no doubt in my mind that she wants to experience life and find another boyfriend or two. She is young and in the prime of her life. I must prepare myself for the inevitable. Honestly, if Kaesi does find a boyfriend, I will be shaken for a while. However, I am well prepared to handle it.

When I was called by God and set a part as a full-time servant of Jesus Christ, I was given special gifts, talents, and abilities to teach with The Spirit of God. I am humbled that this is a part of my everyday life now and feel a gradual spiritual change taking place within my soul. I am developing into a true missionary of the Lord. I know I don't have all the answers to life's mysteries. However, with The Spirit's help in sharing my testimony of Jesus Christ, I can help others accept the gospel and join the true church.

My missionary service is tough at times. Sometimes it seems like my mission will last forever. However, when compared to eternity, serving two years is a just a "blip on the radar" of life. I feel the Lord's blessings upon me. I know deep down inside that He loves me, knows what is in my heart, and is fully aware of where I need to improve to become a better person and a better servant for Him.

This morning we attended our weekly District Meeting at the Randell building in Fontana. The bishop of the Fontana Fifth Ward asked us if we could give a member a priesthood blessing before she had surgery at Kaiser Permanente Hospital. Elder Hedelius and I raced towards the hospital on our bicycles and arrived at the hospital 35-minutes before the scheduled surgery.

As we walked through the clinic, Elder Hedelius and I reviewed the mechanics of the priesthood blessing to make sure I was prepared. I felt honored to have the opportunity to comfort this good sister in her moment of need. However, when we walked into the member's hospital room, it was empty. We were too late. I was terribly disappointed that we missed that opportunity to serve.

For the rest of the afternoon, we decided to follow-through with a few call-backs[34]. It was an exceptionally scorching summer day, but there was no smog!

Gratefully, my lungs are feeling great, as I'm breathing freshair again! It was so hot that some kind people felt sorry for us and invited us inside their home to feel the cool air-conditioning and have a drink of ice- cold water. After a long day of tracting and follow ups, we headed to Reid Furniss' house for our regular weekly dinner appointment. Reid is a great cook, and I really appreciate his hospitality.

***

Today, we rose early for our church meetings and went about our business of attending "all day" church. Later this evening, we have a dinner appointment with a less- active family, the Steileens, and I am sure the meal is going to taste great (since it's Fast Sunday). They have the cutest children ever! I always enjoy meeting with this nice family.

Since it is so blistering hot in sunny California, I decided to get a "flattop" haircut. I wonder what my family, friends, and Kaesi would say? It will be a pleasant change from all the heavy hair on my head. Our air-conditioning does not work in our apartment, so we decided to move our mattresses onto the roof and sleep outside tonight.

We have a few teaching appointments this week, and I am feeling better about our prospects. I hope and pray that we will get some baptismal commitments. I know the Lord will bless our efforts and that He loves us.

Today for our P-day activity, we played two-hand-touch football at Veteran Park. It was a bit of a drag because our district isn't particularly good at playing football.

At least I got to hang out with Elder Waddoups. He is so cool. The rest of the day I washed my dirty clothes, wrote letters, and made an audio tape for Kaesi. After some serious thought, I'm considering breaking up with her. And yet, I still can't help but think about our wonderful relationship. At this point, I've decided to write her only once a week. I am putting the Lord first in my life. For one, I am committed to reading the scriptures daily. It's critical to my spiritual growth and effectiveness as a minister of Jesus Christ to learn as much about the scriptures as I possibly can.

I have been missing my friends back in Georgia, and other friends on church missions. It is difficult not being able to see them—especially my best friend, Jeff Humphrey, who is serving in the Colorado Denver Mission. It will be another two-and- a-half years before I will be able to see him again. He is truly one of the best people I know. We've been friends for over seven years, and it is the type of friendship that will last at least another seventy!

Elder Hedelius and I have another solid week in front of us. I can't wait to baptize one of Heavenly Father's children.

It will be a great honor to bring one of them to the waters of baptism.

I finally did it. I got a flat top at the barber this morning. Most of my hair is gone now, which takes my "California haircut" to another level. I really like it because my head stays cool when the temperature reaches 112-degrees Fahrenheit.

This afternoon we tried to follow through with Mrs. Wright, a call-back from a *Book of Mormon* placement, but we talked to Mr. Jim Wright instead. He is a great guy. I know Jim felt The Spirit in his home. However, he is not currently searching for the truth. There was a point during our discussion when I identified The Spirit and shared my testimony, but to no avail. Jim said he could not accept any of it. Although we were disappointed in the outcome, we hope Jim realizes there is something missing in his life and will hear our message of peace and hope one day.

After a long sweltering day in the hot sun, it was time to head home and check the mailbox. To my shock and amazement, I received a disheartening letter from Kaesi; she practically read me the riot act!

In recent weeks, I have been struggling to end our boyfriend/girlfriend relationship for the last time. Elder Hedelius has chastised me about not focusing on the work and focusing on my girlfriend instead. In retrospect, I have been a little harsh in telling Kaesi to date other guys. She almost threatened to send me a "Dear John" letter. That made me mad!

I contemplated my next move, prayed about it, and telephoned her house. Kaesi's Mom answered the phone, but Kaisi was not home. I talked to Sister McGurrin for a few minutes and let her know why I was calling. We had a good talk, after which she told me that Kaesi was working and would not be home for at least a couple of hours.

When I called back a couple of hours later, Kaesi answered the telephone, and she honestly sounded like she was half asleep. We talked for a couple of hours and resolved our communication issues. It was cool speaking with her and trying to straighten things out. We both enjoyed the conversation. After I hung up the telephone, I promised myself not to ever call Kaesi again for the next two-years. Breaking the mission rules stresses me out.

Alternatively, I know the Lord will bless me if I keep His commandments. The zone leaders[35] asked me to speak in Multi-Zone Conference tomorrow about "How to Gain Member Referrals and Increase [Our] Teaching Pool." It should be interesting, since this will be my first official public-speaking opportunity in the mission field.

Today I spoke at Multi-Zone Conference. I feel it went well, and I even received some compliments on my talk. Participating in Zone Conference made me feel excited about this month. I know that if I obey my Heavenly Father and work hard, rich blessings are in store, and The Spirit will help Elder Hedelius and I reach our teaching and baptizing goals for September. Our goal is to teach five people a week and baptize two by the end of the month.

Later this evening, Elder Hedelius and I went on team-ups[36] with members from the Fontana First and Fifth Wards. I teamed-up with the elder's quorum president[37] of the Fontana First Ward, and Elder Hedelius teamed-up with a brother from the Fontana Fifth Ward.

First, the elder's quorum president and I followed through with a few call-backs. I loved discussing the Savior's visit to the American continent (34 A.D.), because the *Book of Mormon*'s greatest purpose is to testify of Jesus Christ.

After team-ups, I telephoned my parents to talk about my finances and my new bank account. I absolutely love my family, especially my parents. I'm realizing now that I couldn't appreciate their love until I moved 2,100 miles away. I have the greatest family in the world and am grateful to know that families can be together forever.

Today we decided to do a few additional hours of tracting, but the heat seemed to be getting to people's brains. We were working in the field and giving out copies of the *Book of Mormon* when Elder Hedelius and I met a man in his driveway.

He told us his name was Ryan, and that he was 41-years old. As we got closer, it became obvious that he had been drinking heavily, because we could smell alcohol all over him. However, he seemed interested in the church, so we gave him a copy of the *Book of Mormon*. Then he invited us into his house, and we watched the video "Together Forever."

I really wonder about Ryan...He seemed nice, but his behavior was not normal. He told us that the CIA was evil, and that the White House and U.S. Government are corrupt and "devilish." As we continued to watch the video, he wanted to re-play a few sections of the tape because "the CIA was nearby." Elder Hedelius and I told him that the CIA wasn't here, and yet Ryan insisted that the CIA—or any other government entity— was Satan. Nevertheless, we are going back tomorrow to teach him the 1st Discussion, and he said he wants to attend church this Sunday.

During our bike ride home, we met a man off the street. As he saw us bicycling, he yelled, "Hey you Mormons; come here!" Upon being summoned, we stopped near a school crossing and spoke with Jack, who said he was from Provo Utah. Jack also mentioned that he was a baptized member, and that he used to be a bishop. During our chat, school released, and children kept looking at Jack because he was in rags. When a large group of girls walked by, Jack—apparently growing tired of the children staring—said, "What are you looking at ugly!?" This guy was a trip!

I am happy to report that we ended the day on a positive note. We experienced one of our best teaching opportunities thus far and taught a part-member family[38] (the Lindseys) the 1st Discussion. Brother Lindsey is a cool guy and has been very receptive to the gospel. Elder Hedelius and I committed him to read and pray about the *Book of Mormon*.

After meeting with the Lindseys, we rode back to our apartment and made our usual stop at the mailbox, where I received letters from Jeff, Dad, and Kaesi. What can I say—I love them all! I especially like receiving letters from my girlfriend because she sprays the beautiful perfume, "Poison," all over the paper, and it smells awesome!

According to Kaesi, she has been going through significant trials and tribulations in her life, specifically though work, school, church, and even her parents. It made me think about how grateful I am to be serving a full-time mission, and not having to worry about life's usual everyday problems.

Right now, I have only one goal, which is articulated in the Pearl of Great Price, Moses 1:39: "For behold, this is my work and my glory—to bring to pass the immortality and eternal life of man." As I've mentioned this before, the Pearl of Great Price along with the Doctrine & Covenants is considered modern-day revelation, and one of the four canons of scripture in The Church of Jesus Christ of Latter-day Saints.

This morning we went on splits with the zone leaders, Elder Packard and Elder Rogers. Elder Rogers and I went to Ryan's house to teach the 1st Discussion. When we arrived, he was sober, and seemed to be in better spirits. I thought to myself, "Everything is cool." However, after we said the opening prayer, Ryan began talking about how evil the government was, and claimed he was working as a double-agent. Needless to say, we didn't get very far into the discussion. He did commit to driving us to church though, so this Sunday should be interesting.

After splits with the zone leaders, Elder Hedelius and I decided to tract. When we knocked on the first door, a nice gentleman named Tamer answered, and welcomed us into his home. He told us that he was from Egypt and was 22-years old. When we gave him a copy of the *Book of Mormon*, he committed to read it. We also taught Tamer the 1st Discussion. He is leaving to travel back to Egypt on Monday but seemed receptive and eager to learn more about the church. It was exciting because I feel Elder Hedelius and I have actually been meeting solid contacts in the field!

After a hot afternoon of tracting, we had an appointment at 4:00 p.m. with Brother and Sister Henry Smith. We taught

Henry the 2nd Discussion, "The Gospel of Jesus Christ." Brother Smith is 55-years old, is deeply religious, and likes to talk about deep doctrinal subjects. So far, he seems open to our teachings, and has agreed with everything we have discussed.

We then showed Henry and Sister Smith the video, "Together Forever." After watching the video, the Smiths shared a story about how they lost four family members in a horrible car accident. It was incredibly sad, but they felt The Spirit and we had a spiritual discussion.

While Brother Smith was looking for a scripture, I paused, looked Brother Smith in the eyes, and said, "Brother Smith...I know that this church is true, that Jesus Christ lives, and that the *Book of Mormon* is true. I am asking you to read, ponder, and pray about the *Book of Mormon*. The Spirit is with us today." Then I asked him, "How do you feel?" When Brother Smith responded that he "felt good," I replied, "That's the spirit letting you know that what we have discussed tonight is true. And now it's time for you to find out for yourself." I then offered him a challenge: "Will you read and pray about the *Book of Mormon*? Also, will you pray to find out if Joseph Smith was a prophet of God?"

Without hesitation, he said, "Yes." I'm not sure if he realized the magnitude of what he committed to? However, I do know that The Spirit touched his heart. And I know that Elder Hedelius and I will be baptizing souls; souls who will be coming to Jesus this month.

This afternoon, Elder Hedelius and I went on splits with the district. However, I found tracting with Elder Short frustrating because we only delivered two copies of the *Book of Mormon* the entire day. I know I shouldn't let it bother me, but I got feeling pretty depressed.

After a dismal day of tracting, Elder Hedelius and I reviewed our Area Proselyting Guide (APG). We have a few good investigators in our teaching pool, and I pray that the Lord will soften their hearts and open their minds to the truthfulness of the gospel. I want to bring souls unto Him through the waters of baptism.

On the bright side, we should have at least two investigators at church tomorrow. I hope everything goes well and that they keep their commitments. I am happy to be a member of The Church of Jesus Christ of Latter-day Saints because it feels good to keep the commandments. I know the Lord will bless me if I am diligent and faithful in spreading the gospel of Jesus Christ.

I know the Lord watches over His missionaries. I have a fervent desire to meet, if not exceed our baptismal goals for this month. With the aid of my older brother, Jesus Christ, all things are possible.

***

Ryan came to church today, which was cool. Before Sacrament Meeting, Elder Hedelius and I rode to his house, packed our bicycles in the back of his pickup truck, and rode with him to church. Ryan seemed to enjoy the church service.

Elder Hedelius and I received a few referrals today. While we were greeting members, we bumped into a few people who were attending church for the first time, so I quickly wrote down their names and phone numbers.

I know the Lord will bless us if we serve faithfully. I am excited about this month. I can envision the individuals entering the waters of baptism one by one. The Lord knows my thoughts, desires, and real feelings that are inside my heart. I love the California San Bernardino Mission—and I love my bike!

There is not that much to say tonight, so I will make this entry short. Today was P-day; yeah! It was interesting wearing normal clothes for a change, because people didn't look at us funny like they normally do. We washed our clothes at the laundromat, and I wrote my average of eleven letters to family members and friends. Then Elder Hedelius and I watched the basketball movie, Hoosiers, at the Bloomington building with the rest of the zone. I forgot how inspiring this movie was! Sometimes I feel like the Hoosiers because—in some ways— we're the underdogs.

The world and the adversary are like Goliath in the Holy Bible. It took courage for David to slay Goliath much like I must slay theoretical "giants" on my mission. I must have courage every day to stand up for what's right.

I know that the Lord will help us find, teach, and baptize people into His church. I have faith that if we work hard, the Lord will bless us. I love the gospel; it is so true. I am trying to keep a positive attitude!

This morning, Elder Waddoups and I taught Brother Henry Smith again. We had a good talk, but we didn't get into The Discussions because Brother Smith had not read nor prayed about the *Book of Mormon*, yet. He is a good man, and I know that if he prays earnestly about the scriptures, he will know the church is true.

The rest of the day was a flop! My bicycle tire was flat, so I had to pull out my repair kit and patch the tire. It took me a over an hour to repair it because I had to adjust the rear wheel exactly right with the bicycle chain.

After working on my bike, Elder Hedelius and I taught Brother Lindsey the 2nd Discussion, "The Gospel of Jesus Christ." It went very well. Brother Lindsey is very accepting of the gospel; he is a good guy and I enjoy his spirit.

Sometimes it seems like my mission will last forever. I think about home, my good friends, my car, and my sweet girlfriend. I long to be back with my friends. It's been so long since I've seen them.

However, I know beyond a shadow of a doubt that what I'm doing is the right thing. I really cannot look at the worldly things I once had with the same eyes, as I'm seeing more and more through spiritual eyes. One of my main goals as a missionary is to place my Heavenly Father and Jesus Christ first in my life. I'll tell you what; I'm not sure what the Lord has in store for me, but I know that great blessings will come to pass if I try and do better.

The gospel is so sweet and true; I have tasted it spiritually, and it is good. The stories and doctrines of *Book of Mormon* provide inspiration for my life. Jesus Christ really does live.

Today started out with a bang! My tire was flat—again. Apparently, the elders who borrowed this bicycle before me patched it one too many times. So Elder Hedelius and I had to take three bikes to "Rick's Bicycle City Shop" in Fontana: one for Elder Hedelius, one for me (so I could ride home), and then my green bike with the flat tire. Steering two bikes at once definitely made the trip awkward and interesting!

We finally arrived at "Rick's Bicycle City Shop" after walking the three bikes for two-and-a-half miles. I said to the manager, "I need a new inner tube for my rear tire." After I wheeled my bicycle forward and passed it off, I began my search for a new bike. I looked around the shop and eventually found a good mountain bike for $100.00. It was a sleek grey and silver color and was over 50% off because of its slightly-used condition. So, I said to myself, "Why not? I am opening my new checking account tomorrow, so I can get that bike." Ten minutes later, I left the shop a new bike owner, and left the old green bike once and for all.

The rest of the day, we followed through with call-backs from our *Book of Mormon* placements, which resulted in three good contacts. The Lord is blessing us, and I know we'll baptize.

We had an excellent appointment with the Mafis. Brother Mafi served his mission to New Mexico, and his wife is not a member. They are both super-cool people. Elder Hedelius and I planned to watch the church video, "Our Heavenly Father's Plan," with them. When we arrived, Sister Mafi offered us dinner, and there was no way we were going to refuse that offer! As we ate her delicious meal of chicken and rice, we had a nice dinner conversation. After the meal, we watched the video and talked for a few minutes.

During our discussion, we had a friendly conversation with Sister Mafi about her basic beliefs. She was very open and sincere about her feelings towards God, and I love that about her. The Spirit was there. When we talked about Jesus Christ, I noticed a twinkle in her eyes.

Sister Mafi said, "Before I approached you guys at the post office to ask you about the LDS church, my husband had been praying and fasting that I would soon hear the gospel. I felt The Spirit that day, and it told me to talk to you guys. It was so weird!" I thought to myself, "That's not weird. That's cool!"

Brother Mafi really wants her to join the church for all the right reasons. Sister Mafi is a deeply spiritual person, so I suspect she will read the *Book of Mormon* very thoroughly and sincerely. Sister Mafi cracks me up, because she is nice, but funny too! She also told us that she and Brother Mafi want to serve a mission someday when they retire. This morning I opened my new checking account, so now I can withdraw money.

Thank goodness...because I don't like living off traveler's checks. I love my new bicycle that's worth $250.00! Unlike my old one, it rides well, and everything works on it. To top it off, it only cost me $106.00 with sales tax.

Since it is transfer day, Elder Short's new companion is Elder Christensen, who is waiting for his visa to Brazil. That means Elder Davis is being transferred to another area. I'm not too bummed about that; he was a lazy missionary and got on my nerves. Elder Waddoups is staying at our apartment until his new companion, a greenie[39], arrives tomorrow.

Elder Waddoups and I received letters from Elder Dan Rogers, who expressed having a rough time in his area. He told us that The Spirit had left him; the whole nine yards....I am honestly worried about him. Dan has only completed one-year of college and so, it's important for him to complete a major goal in his life. Currently, he does not have a lot of options. Dan's a stud, and my good friend. I also know that the Lord can bless him, and I hope Dan relies on his relationship with the Savior to pull himself out of this funk.

Everything is looking cool in California, and I'm excited about my mission. However, I do need to develop the habit of getting to bed earlier, because 6:30 a.m. comes early, and the sleep deprivation is about killing me.

About a year ago, I remember getting so busy with school, my part-time job at McDonalds and early morning seminary that I lost a lot of sleep. About a week later, I got a bad cold.

Since then, I've decided that very little is worth it to not getting enough sleep, and I need at least 7–8 hours to function properly.

Today was an interesting day with Elder Waddoups and Elder Hedelius. However, "three's a crowd," because it was difficult to have any effective or meaningful conversations. Although we had one too many elders, we still had fun. We taught a Discussion this morning to a good guy; a black man named John. I felt like it was a success. We also visited a few of our investigators and followed through with three call-backs.

This afternoon we went on splits for an hour with the Spanish-American (Span-Am)⁴⁰ missionaries. I teamed-up with Elder Campbell, from Alabama. Elder Campbell is a big, clumsy guy with blond hair and a dimpled chin. When he speaks English or Spanish, it is easy to hear his Southern accent. He and I made a good team today. We gave out five copies of the *Book of Mormon*: two Spanish versions and three English versions. I love feeling like I'm doing my missionary duties when I am able to hand- deliver copies of this holy writ of scripture. Currently, we have two good call-backs to follow through with next week.

I didn't get a letter from Kaesi today. In fact, I haven't received a letter from her this entire week. I thought to myself, 'She must be super busy with school, work, church, and a social life.' This is the logical answer but, for real, I don't know what's going on with her. Do I sound a little worried? Well. maybe because I am! Things can change in any relationship over two-years. However, I do know this: if I put the Lord first in my life, everything else will fall into place.

I want to work harder, I want to be a better missionary, and I want to be a better representative of Jesus Christ. The Lord expects a lot out of me because I have the talent and ability to speak with people. I must strive to keep the commandments. In John 14:15 it says, "If ye love me, keep my commandments." I definitely love the Lord; therefore, I choose to keep his commandments. The gospel is true, and I know that if I am faithful, I will receive blessings.

Early this morning, I received a phone call from Elder Dan Rogers, from Arizona. Although his last letter said he had been struggling, he told me that he now had everything under control. It was neat speaking with an old buddy.

On the other hand, I've been thinking a lot about my other friend, Ben Dieterle. It's weird, but Ben has only written me once so far, and I don't know what's going on.

I mean, what can I do if he doesn't write me back? Our friendship doesn't seem the same; it's just strange. My only hope is that we can connect again and be close friends after my mission.

After reminiscing about a couple of old friends, I attended District Meeting with Elder Waddoups. I am excited for Elder Hedelius, because he is the new district leader! What a stud. He told us that we need to keep our minds on the work. We also have a new greenie in our district named Elder Stevenson, and he is from England. He is really skinny, and 6'5 tall! I don't know much about him, but he seems like a cool guy. Elder Waddoups has been assigned as his new trainer.

After District Meeting, we decided to kill two birds with one stone and watched BYU beat UTEP in football. While watching the game, we marked up[41] four copies of the *Book of Mormon*.

The football game was great. Towards the end of the fourth quarter, I was hollering and jumping up and down. I know that my dad was watching the football game at the Roswell Stake Center[42] in Georgia and doing the same thing. The final score was 31–27; yeah!

Later that night, we attended a baptism at the Arrow building for a young man named Mark. He had been reading and praying about The Church of Jesus Christ of Latter-day Saints for over eight-months, and finally received an answer from the Lord to be baptized into the church. Our zone leaders, Elder Packard, and Elder Rogers, were able to teach Mark. They are cool dudes, and I like them a lot.

The work here in Fontana will pick up. We have a couple of good investigators, and the Lord is blessing us. I must continue exercising my faith in the Lord that good things will happen in our area.

***

The next morning during Sunday school with the young-adult class, I gave a *Book of Mormon* presentation called "Lanny Owens." It is a highly effective way to present the *Book of Mormon* to others, and I feel like I did an excellent job. We want the church members to give the *Book of Mormon* to their friends. Of course, the goal is to increase our teaching pool.

After Sunday school and elder's quorum, we met with the Fontana Fifth Ward Correlation Meeting[43], and it was honestly very depressing. Brother Hadden was shocked by the lack of investigators we have in our teaching pool: only one with Brother Lindsey. Elder Hedelius likes to work at his own pace, whereas I'm the type of person who wants to 'find'em, teach'em, and then baptise'em.' Boom, boom, splash! Elder Hedelius and I had a good talk about working more effectively as a companionship.

After church, the rest of the afternoon went great. We had an early dinner at the Wickstrom's house, during which Brother Wickstrom introduced us to his cousin, Soni, who expressed an interest in taking The Discussions. I feel good about teaching her. After dinner, we went to the Kellans. They are a super family, and I know the Lord will give us the opportunity to baptize them into the gospel of Jesus Christ.

We spent the rest of the day in the Fifth Ward, visiting and talking to people. We met a super lady, Marva, who is anxious for us to follow up with her. I am excited because we may be able to add another person to our teaching pool. Then we tracted out Ms. Smith and gave her a *Book of Mormon*. I can see baptism in her eyes.

We wrapped up the evening by visiting with our faithful friends, the West family. They are from Texas, and Sister West's mom lives with them. They are less-active, but they love us to death. When we arrived, Brother West said, "Welcome Brethren," in his southern Texas voice. Then Grandma said, "I tell ya, buddy!" I loved their warm hospitality! After our visit, I was feeling pretty wiped-out; thank goodness we have P-day tomorrow.

This morning we telephoned Reid Furniss and asked if we could use his house to do laundry. He told us the key to his garage was located on the roof. After our conversation, Elder Hedelius and I gathered our dirty clothes and rode our bicycles to his house. However, when we arrived and searched for the hidden key, it was nowhere to be found. We looked all over the place, and still no key...so we decided to call Rick, one of Reid's friends. He said, "I put the key on the roof last night." We tried again to find the key, but our search was in vain. I grew frustrated and, to let off a little steam, I said (in a joking way), "Well maybe there's a bomb in the washing machine?" Of course, I knew full well there was no such device anywhere in the house.

After my comment, Elder Hedelius gave me a strange look and was not amused. Then he suggested that we kneel in the grass and pray. (Why hadn't I thought of that?) We knelt and prayed, asking our Heavenly Father to help us find the key to the garage door so we could wash our clothes. Then we rose to our feet and started looking again.

After we looked all over the roof and in the grass for the third time, we still couldn't find the key, and our patience was growing thin. As a last resort, we decided to check the sliding-glass door to the house. Lo-and-behold...it opened. Upon entering the house, we saw—laying the counter—the keys to the garage. Heavenly Father heard and answered our prayers.

After folding clothes, writing letters, and relaxing, we headed to our evening appointment with the Mafis. When we arrived, Brother Mafi was ill and asked if we could offer him a priesthood blessing. Elder Hedelius anointed his head, after which I sealed the anointing and offered a blessing. It was my first time ever giving a blessing and it was a fantastic opportunity to exercise my priesthood. It was an extremely spiritual experience because I was the mouthpiece for the Lord.

I feel Sister Mafi will soon be baptized. One day, she will pray to Heavenly Father and ask Him if the *Book of Mormon* is God's scripture. I know He answers prayers, just like He answered our prayers earlier today.

Today during our Zone Conference, we made two new goals for this month. (1) increase our teaching pool by 50%, and (2) baptize two new individuals per companionship. Elder Hedelius and I are shooting for four baptisms this month. I know we can achieve this goal if we are obedient to the mission rules. Elder Packard and Elder Rogers are studs; I love their spirituality.

After Zone Conference, we worked out in the field. Gratefully, Elder Hedelius and I are getting along better. I would say we have passed the honeymoon phase, and our companionship is beginning to grow and flourish as we have developed the spirit of cooperation.

It's a cold, cloudy, and wet day today; much different than the sunny, smoggy, 117-degree temperatures that we have become accustomed to this summer. Elder Hedelius is always cold, but I'm a macho guy, and can handle it. Things are going well for us; the Lord is pouring out his blessings and I am excited.

Elder Gene R. Cook, the Area President of Southern California, is coming to speak with us later this month. Additionally, another general authority will be visiting during the month of October. In preparation for the "top brass" coming to town, President Gourdin is conducting Personal Priesthood Interviews (PPIs) this Friday.

The purpose of the PPI is to have a personal, one-on-one meeting with the mission president. This is the usual custom for missionaries in the field, just as meeting with Elder Harvey was customary for my concluding week at the MTC. My conversation with President Gourdin will go something like this: "I confess I love my mission!" I want to be the best missionary I can be. I love the gospel with all my heart, might, mind, and soul.

Today we taught two 1st Discussions: what a day! However, our investigators have not been easy to teach. Brother Henry

Smith loved to go on tangents, but I used what I learned from the MTC and got us back to talking about the gospel of Jesus Christ.

It was interesting, because Brother Smith believes in everything we believe, but he still has a tough time accepting the *Book of Mormon*. As I listened to The Spirit, I felt impressed to turn to the "Articles of Faith."[44] As I read, Brother Smith did not say a word; he just listened. He can be a difficult dude to get through to sometimes, but he is eventually going to know that the *Book of Mormon* is the true word of God. I know if Elder Hedelius and I do our part, the Lord will do His.

Later this afternoon, we followed through with a few call-backs. We met Peter, who Elder Campbell and I gave a *Book of Mormon* to while tracting. He seemed really interested and asked us to come back tomorrow morning.

After visiting with our call-backs, Elder Hedelius and I went on team-ups with the ward missionaries. Elder Hedelius teamed-up with Brother Adams to visit Brother Lindsey, and Brother Fletcher and I teamed-up to visit the Mafis.

When we arrived at the Mafi home, we opened with a word of prayer and then I began teaching the 2nd Discussion, "The Gospel of Jesus Christ." Everything was going well until Sister Mafi started asking deep doctrinal questions about Adam and Eve. Once she got me on this tangent, I began digging my own grave. The next thing I knew, the spirit of contention was in the room. I quickly regained my composure and said a silent prayer that God's spirit would return. Miraculously, The Spirit did return, and we continued with a successful meeting.

After The Discussion, Sister Mafi cooked us a delicious meal and we had a nice dinner conversation. After Brother Fletcher and I left, we agreed that Sister Mafi really wants to know if the *Book of Mormon* is true. We reminded each other that the Lord answers prayers on His time; not our time. I will continue to work hard and leave the business of conversion up to the Lord.

Our daily routine typically consists of tracting, following up with call-backs, and teaching investigators. This morning, Elder

Hedelius and I met with one of our call-backs, Peter. He is an older, nice, retired gentleman who has been willing to listen to our gospel message. I know the Lord hears and answers my prayers, and that He softens the hearts of those who want to know the truth. Peter is a special child of our Heavenly Father, and I feel that Heavenly Father and Jesus Christ want Peter to be baptized.

After meeting with Peter, we had a lunch appointment with Sister Ward, who is a sweet widow and a member of the church. We ate a delicious beef stew and talked with her for a while.

After lunch we decided to go tracting and had the pleasant surprise of speaking with our lovely brothers and sisters; the open-minded and soft-hearted Jehovah's Witnesses (JW). Of course, I'm speaking sarcastically here...but they are some of the most interesting people I have ever met. I love them, and they love to put up a fight! I know the Holy Bible (KJV) well, but not as well as I should. A person needs a thorough understanding of the Bible to even strike up a conversation with the Jehovah's Witnesses.

I am trying to be honest when I say this, but I can see the devil's hand in some religions, and in their people. I'm not trying to speak ill or badly about other churches, but the Jehovah's Witnesses in Southern California are more aggressive verse the Jehovah's Witnesses I know in the deep south.

When we arrived home this evening, we discovered two new missionaries from the MTC who were moving into our apartment for the next couple of days. Elder Hedelius and I graciously gave them our extra bedding. I thought to myself, 'What would the church-lady say on Saturday Night Live? She would say, "Well, isn't that special!"'

I opened and read my mail before bed. Jeff Humphrey (I mean, Elder Humphrey) and I have been keeping in good contact. I miss him a lot, and it feels like forever before I'll be able to see him again. I have noticed that we have become a lot closer on our missions. In fact, we've probably become closer over the past seven-months than we have in the entire seven years we've known each other. He is so cool because he's dedicated to the gospel and one of the funniest people I know.

In addition to Jeff's letter, I received letters from my dad and from my little sister, Lynette. It is important to me that I keep in good contact with my family. On the other hand, I still haven't received a letter from Kaesi. I am mad and, to tell you the truth, I've stopped caring about it. It is just too hard carrying on a relationship 2,100 miles away. She is fantastic, but things do change—and sometimes not for the best.

Today we had Multi-Zone Conference with Zone 3 and had Personal Priesthood Interviews (PPIs) with President Gourdin. We enjoyed eight hours-worth of talks, singing, directing lessons, and an interview at the Rialto building. I am taking Elder Hedelius' advice and focusing on missionary work.

During my PPI with President Gourdin, he said, "You and your companion are going to do a lot of good things in Fontana." It sounds like my stay here will be at least a couple more months. Tomorrow, Elder Gene R. Cook is speaking with us; I'm looking forward to it!

After Multi-Zone Conference, we had to wait almost two hours for the bus to take us home. At first, we were at the wrong bus stop altogether, but we eventually got everything worked out.

After a long day of instruction, we finally arrived in Fontana. I was a little hyper after sitting all day, so Elder Stevenson (the tall greenie from London) and I went tracting together and gave away four copies of the *Book of Mormon*. Elder Stevenson is so cool; he taught me the English phrase, "You bloody fool!" Then we quoted some Monty Python and the Holy Grail on our walk back to my apartment.

Before arriving home, we stopped by the mailbox and picked up the mail. I finally received a letter from Kaesi, and I am not impressed with her at all. I know what she's doing, and her motives are piecing together like a puzzle. The bottom line is that Kaesi has not written me in two-and-a-half weeks. In the meantime, she wrote to my best friend, Jeff, and gave him a bunch of photos of herself. I did not get a single one. And then she has the nerve to write me this measly one-and-a-half-page letter that says absolutely nothing. I really hate sounding negative, but things just aren't working out.

Maybe I'm getting a little carried away. She has given me some wonderful things: a new white shirt, a tie, a Montblanc pen, and all sorts of cool stuff. I really shouldn't draw any conclusions, but it's difficult trying to figure things out on a mission. I have concluded that I shouldn't worry about it, so I'm just going to pretend like everything is fine and dandy.

While I was reading letters, Sister Mafi called us and said, "I'm getting too confused about some gospel topics, and I want to hold off on The Discussions for now." At first, Elder Hedelius and I were in shock, and we didn't know what to say. However, she continued, "You guys can still come over, talk, and have dinner with us."

I replied, "Okay; that sounds great." After I hung up the phone, Elder Hedelius and I decided to just fellowship the family. Sister Mafi will receive her own answer that the *Book of Mormon* is true when she is ready. I know that the Lord answers prayers.

This morning, my district and I caught the bus to Rialto. We were participating— along with other multiple zones—in Missionary Day at the Rialto Stake Center. The plan was to team-up with a fellow church member, and then tract for a couple of hours. Then we planned to reconvene at the stake center to hear Elder Gene R. Cook speak to us.

When we arrived, I teamed-up with Brother Malupo, a Samoan. He told me that he served his mission for two-and-a-half years! During our tracting efforts, Brother Malupo and I gave away four copies of the *Book of Mormon*. It was fun, and I really enjoyed spending time with him.

After tracting, we returned to the Rialto Stake Center to listen to Elder Cook. He offered some incredible spiritual guidance during his talk, which was titled, "The Lost Scriptures."

During his summary of this true story, Elder Cook told us that his property— including all his cash, luggage, and scriptures—were stolen from a mission van while visiting the Bolivia

Santa Cruz Mission. After searching up and down the streets with the mission office for hours, his scriptures were not found. Soon Elder and Sister Cook departed for their home in Quito, Ecuador. Over the next month, the missionaries in Bolivia kept searching for Elder Cook's lost scriptures. In the meantime, Elder Cook struggled spiritually because he failed to study the Word of God.

One night, however, he felt a spiritual impression: "Elder Cook, how long will you go on without reading and studying the scriptures?" Responding to this chastisement, he decided to borrow his wife's scriptures, and commenced reading from Genesis in the Old Testament.

Later that summer, a church employee from Bolivia brought a package from the mission president in La Paz to Ecuador and laid Elder Cook's scriptures on his desk. Elder Cook's scriptures had been miraculously found by a lady who was a member of the Pentecostal sect and had been returned to the La Paz Mission. From that day forward, Elder Cook promised the Lord that he would make better use of his time and spend more time reading his scriptures.

He told us that, "To this day, when I complete reading and marking my scriptures, I purchase a new set; always a "Quad" (Holy Bible, *Book of Mormon*, Pearl of Great Price, and Doctrine & Covenants). Elder Cook said, "The Spirit will continue to guide you, so don't get stuck on previous revelations you have received. Sometimes the Lord wants to give you more. The Lord wants to communicate and inspire His children. He does this through revelation, and often offers revelation through the scriptures."

He continued, admonishing us to use the aid of the scriptures and The Spirit when teaching. In his next short story, Elder Cook talked about an assistant to the president (AP) who wrote a beautiful talk and gave this same talk wherever he traveled across the mission field over the next six-months. While it was an amazing talk, it started missing something after a while: The Spirit. Elder Cook said, "It is important to allow the spirit to share with others your personal testimony. You shouldn't get caught up in the monologue of a beautiful talk."

Another true story that I've heard about Elder Cook was from the time he met the rock legend, Mick Jagger, on an airplane. This summary is from an excerpt from Elder Cook's talk, "The Eternal Nature of the Law of Chastity."

During a flight from Mexico to Dallas, Texas, Elder Cook was assigned a seat right next to Mick Jagger. Mick was traveling back to the U.S. after making one of his music videos. At first, Elder Cook didn't know who Mick Jagger was, until he pointed to his photo in a music magazine. At that point, the light bulb went off in his head, and he recognized the rocker.

After introducing himself, Elder Cook said, "What do you think the impact of your music is on young people?" Mick replied, "Our music is calculated to drive the kids to sex." Of course, Elder Cook was shocked at his response. The long story short is that Mick began to drink, and started yelling on the plane that the *Book of Mormon* was not true. This gave Elder Cook a real missionary opportunity, but to his knowledge, nothing came of it. (Gene. R. Cook, "Eternal Nature of the Law of Chastity, Ricks College, Idaho, 1989).

After Elder Cook concluded his talk, my district and I caught the next bus to Fontana. Upon arrival, we walked the rest of the way to our apartment. After grabbing a quick sandwich, Elder Hedelius and I followed through with a few call-backs and visited the Lindsey's home. Sister Lindsey was there, and she was kind enough to feed us and engage in some friendly conversation. I was grateful to Sister Lindsey for offering us a decent lunch, because I was starving from a long day in the field. I am happy to know her family.

After a nice late lunch break, we followed through with one of our call-backs, Mark. Although we visited with Mark and his wife and talked about religion, they were both extremely closed-minded and very one-sided. Mark kept saying, "I know the *Book of Mormon* is not of God and that your prophet is false." The situation was getting emotionally out of hand, so

Elder Hedelius and I decided to wrap up the meeting to avoid any further contention. After we rose from the living room couch, I walked over to Mark, placed my arm gently around his shoulder, and looked him in the eyes. Then I shared my personal testimony with him.

He could feel The Spirit. I know he did, though I know Mark wouldn't have admitted it even if I had asked him. However, I could see it in his eyes, and he was shaking.

I left him a challenge to continue reading and praying about the *Book of Mormon*. Mark invited Elder Hedelius and I to attend his church tomorrow. When we got home, we telephoned the assistants to the president (APs) to get permission to attend Mark's church service, but they said, "No."

After a day of prospecting, we rode our bicycles to our usual Saturday night dinner with Reid Furniss and Rick. We have great camaraderie with Rick, and the meals are always delicious. Before we left, Elder Hedelius and I committed Reid to attend General Conference[45] with us.

After visiting with Reid and Rick, we rode our bicycles back to our apartment, stepped through the front door, and lo-and-behold there were two visa-waiters sitting on our family room couch. After introducing ourselves, I learned that my new greenie was named Elder Dean Clark. His official mission call is to Brazil, but he's going to hang with me for a month-or-so until his visa arrives. Elder Clark seems like a stud and is from Provo Utah. I will fill in more details later ... I am dead tired, and ready for bed. It has been a long but productive day. I love the gospel of Jesus Christ.

***

This morning, Brother Mafi picked up Elder Clark and me before church. During the drive, he seemed upset that his wife didn't want to take The Discussions. I reassured him that Sister Mafi is a good person, and that if she really wants to know the truth, the Lord will answer her prayers. She is a child of God, and Heavenly Father loves all of His children.

Today, we had a solid Ward Correlation Meeting for the Fontana Fifth Ward, and I'm pumped up about finding some good investigators here. Brother Hadden's goal is to baptize three people a month; I know we can do it!

After church service, Elder Clark and I followed through with a few call-backs. One of our follow-up visits was with Mark Davio and his family. They seem nice and were willing to talk to us. I hope that, if we can just show them our love for the gospel, we can add them to our teaching pool.

After working in the field, we teamed-up with Brother Woods to teach the importance of the scriptures to Marva Lyken. The plan was to meet with Marva, and then return to the Woods' home to have dinner.

During our meeting with Marva and her family, we read some passages from the *Book of Mormon* that we had previously earmarked. Then I asked, "Have you prayed to know if the *Book of Mormon* is true?" She replied, "Yes, but I haven't received a clear answer, yet." We talked for a few more minutes about reading the scriptures every day before closing with a word of prayer, and then we left Marva's house.

After our visit with Marva, we enjoyed the best meal I've had since the start of my mission. Elder Clark and I loved it! It had been two months since he had enjoyed a home-cooked meal, so he was grinning from ear to ear. The Woods family treated us amazingly, as if we were one of their own children!

It was interesting to note the difference between a family who has the gospel, and The Spirit of the Lord in their home, verses a family who does not have the fullness of the restored gospel. The good news is so sweet and true. I love the gospel because it makes me happy as I walk in Jesus' footsteps. Since visiting with the Woods, I have been thinking about Kaesi a lot. I love her too.

Today was another P-day, so Elder Clark and I rode our bicycles to Reid's house to wash our dirty clothes. Reid showed us his British-made, MGB, two-door sports car in his garage. Before we left, we left a note on the windshield that read, "We took the MG for a spin, we hope you don't mind." We were only joking, of course.

We spent the rest of the afternoon completing our "to do" list of chores for a typical P-day: wrote letters, went grocery shopping, and cleaned the apartment. Then we had a dinner appointment with Todd Wickstrom and his family. Hopefully, Soni will commit to baptism this Friday. I know the Lord will bless us.

I am really looking forward to this week. Elder Clark and I are going to buckle-down and get things organized so that we don't miss any potential investigators. The work will carry forth!

I received a letter from Kaesi today, and I loved it. It was not a mushy letter but she said that she wanted to start over from the beginning. You know...hit the reset button and go from there. I love her because deep down I know she's a genuine, good person.

Today, September 27th, is the two-month mark since the beginning of my mission. The first thing Elder Clark said to me was, "Elder Todd, you were bearing your testimony in your sleep last night." That should tell anyone where my subconscious mind is at! Oh, I almost forgot—I have gained over 12 pounds since the start of my mission so I'm weighing in at a whopping 157 pounds.

This morning, Elder Clark and I had the opportunity of teaching Peter the 2nd Discussion, "The Gospel of Jesus Christ," and set up an appointment to teach the 3rd Discussion, "The Restoration." Peter is an older man, and a Catholic. He seems very humble and believes in the gospel principles we have taught him thus far. He talked about baptism, and how he feels this is the right thing to do. However, we taught him that the first step is to have faith, and then to pray. Peter understands that converting to another church often requires massive change. However, I know that Peter will be baptized if Elder Clark and I are faithful to our Heavenly Father.

After teaching Peter, we rode our bicycles all the way to the boonies of North Fontana and then up to Oleander Street. Elder Clark was about to die from exhaustion when he busted his bicycle and hurt his ankle. After that, we decided to head back to the apartment and eat lunch. We checked the mailbox, and I discovered a letter and a photo from Brandi Severson.

Brandi was a girl I asked out on a date and kissed before I left on my mission. She was also one of the reasons why Kaesi and I got into a fight earlier this summer. At any rate, Brandi wrote me a cool letter. She said, "I had a good time on our date, and you're a fun guy!" Her comment made me feel good inside because I like making other people happy. However, I am still in love with Kaesi because she is my baby!

After lunch, and after reading a couple of letters from home, we tried to repair Elder Clark's bicycle. First, we turned it upside down with the handlebars and seat on the floor. By the time we were finished, however, we had practically taken the entire bike apart—except for the chain because it wouldn't come off. I was so mad!

We finally came up with a game plan, hiked the four miles to Reid Furniss' house, and borrowed one of his bicycles. During the long "trek," I let Elder Clark ride my bicycle and I walked. I said to myself, 'This is not a fun activity.'

When we arrived at Reid's house, we found three bicycles: two modern looking bikes, and one that looked like it was built in the 1940's during WWII; an old timer bicycle. Elder Clark test-drove the two bicycles and didn't like either one of them, so I suggested, "Let's try the grandpa bike." And lo-and-behold, we had a winner!

After Elder Clark test-drove the "grandpa," bike, he loved it! "This is the one!" he shouted, as he threw his hands into the air and pedaled, hands-free. We are happy now, and he absolutely loves the bike. It is a smooth ride and, ironically, quite fast! I am humbled to admit that "grandpa bike" even beat me in a race.

The weather was smoggy and hot today. I can always tell when we have severe smog because my lungs and eyes bother me. I can't wait for winter, when the Santa Ana winds move the air pollution out towards the desert.

After tracting, we headed to the Mafi's for dinner. When we arrived, we sat down at the dining room table. Elder Clark was in an exceptionally good mood and kept laughing, which was hilarious! Brother and Sister Mafi are a funny couple. We enjoyed humorous conversation alongside our delicious meal.

This morning we taught Peter the 3rd Discussion, "The Restoration," and it went great, as usual. He is a good person, and he wants to choose what is right. The Lord wants Peter to join the church. However, it will be on the Lord's timetable and when he is ready for baptism.

After teaching Peter, we noticed that Elder Clark's rear bicycle tire was losing air. Upon further inspection, we found that he had picked up another nail. For some reason the roads are rough around here...so we headed back to our apartment to repair Elder Clark's flat tire, found the leak, and patched his inner tube. Then we prepared some lunch.

When we were ready to go out again, we noticed the sky had turned brown. I thought to myself, "Man; the smog must be getting really bad!" Earlier in the day, the sky had been bright blue, and I had been able to see the mountains perfectly!

Then we noticed that the brown mist was coming from the mountains, and that the brown color was slowly turning to black. There was a huge fire on the mountains! It looked like a volcano had erupted, and a huge cloud of smoke covered the sky. The wind was also blowing, and we could see that the fire was spreading rapidly. Elder Clark and I kept ourselves busy, taking photos from the roof of our apartment. The sun turned from yellow to a reddish orange, then to a dark-blood red, and finally, a deep purple. It was wild and caused me to reflect on the 'signs of the times' before the Second Coming of Jesus Christ. It was really something else! It seemed as if biblical prophecies were coming to pass, right before our very eyes.

In the book of Revelation, John saw plagues and wars being poured out after the seventh seal was opened. In Revelation 9:18 (KJV), it says, "By these three was the third part of men killed, by the fire, and by the smoke, and by the brimstone, which issued out of their mouths."

The news reported more than 1,100 firefighters have contained two San Bernardino County fires that charred 7,000 brushy hillside acres and caused the evacuation of 250 houses near Cajon Pass. The fire destroyed a ranch house and several buildings at a loss of $350,000. In addition, it caused about $85,000 damage to a mushroom farm north of Rancho Cucamonga.

Three people were injured. One resident suffered smoke inhalation. There appeared to be two different fires, and one was part of a controlled burn near Glen Helen Park. The other fire at Texas Mountain was highly suspicious and under investigation by the local authorities ("The State--News from October 4, 1988." L.A. Times Archives. https://www.latimes.com/archives/la-xpm-1988-10-04-mn-3337-story.html).

In an effort to distance ourselves from the fire and smoke, we decided to head south towards the Fontana Fifth Ward area, where we followed through with a couple of investigators and church members. Then we had about an hour left, so we tracted. It was difficult tracting, but I reminded myself that a mission is not supposed to be easy. However, following Jesus is worth it.

After tracting, we taught Brother Lindsey the 4th Discussion. This was my first time teaching the subject of "Eternal Progression" to an actual investigator, which was neat! Brother Lindsey asked some difficult, but sincere questions. I'm glad we teamed-up with Brother Adams, our stake mission leader, because he helped answer Brother Lindsey's questions. I feel good about Brother Lindsey being baptized in the gospel of Jesus Christ. I must continue to work, work, work, and work. I know beyond a shadow of a doubt that the Lord will bless me for my efforts. Even though the work in this area has not gone perfectly, I know people will join the church.

This morning we went on splits with the zone leaders to do a little tracting. Elder Packard and I teamed-up and decided to check out Veterans Park, where we met two men who admitted to not believing in Jesus. It was sad listening to them talk about their rough lives. They hadn't had any aspirations or goals when they were younger, and due to some poor decisions, they had accomplished very little in life. On the positive side, we had a friendly conversation with them about life in general.

We reconvened with the zone leaders for lunch at our apartment. After lunch, Elder Clark and I followed through with Henry Smith, a less-active member, and headed to his house to teach the 2nd Discussion.

I was feeling optimistic about presenting the "Gospel of Jesus Christ," but then Brother Smith's personality and beliefs dictated otherwise. He was extremely hardheaded and closed-minded to our beliefs. At one point, I grew so frustrated I could hardly stand it. We asked him to read, ponder, and pray about the *Book of Mormon*, but I honestly don't know if Henry's willing to take the next step in the conversion process. This was the third time we've challenged him to read the *Book of Mormon*. We closed with a word of prayer and left.

After our failed attempt to commit Henry to accept the remaining Missionary Discussions, Elder Clark and I got into a big argument. He really ticks me off sometimes. I am not saying that I don't tick him off, because I'm sure I do. I also think "ticking each other off" is part of missionary and companionship life. Sometimes we get along, and sometimes we don't. That is just the way it is.

Honestly, I believe we're actually just frustrated with Henry, and so we're taking our stress out on the companionship. Elder Clark and I need to take a deep breath and relax. Henry has his free agency to choose how he wants to live his life, and we need to respect him for his decision.

I received a very upbeat and positive letter from Dan Rogers today. He's a stud, and I hope we can remain good friends after our missions.

The work is slow, but things are picking up a little bit. However, we've still had no baptismal commitments, and that has been very frustrating. I told Dan in a letter that missionary work is one of the toughest jobs in the world. I am serious too. People cancel appointments, reject our message, and hand *Book of Mormons* back to us. Additionally, there are many "tough customers," like Henry Smith. It is totally brutal.

The trials must surely lighten up soon, and the work must move forward. I don't know what I must do to turn the work around in our favor. I mean, I'm doing my best! I am very frustrated. I don't doubt the Lord, but I do hope that the work picks up soon. I am anxious to fill our teaching pool and baptize. This is what I was called to do on a church mission for the Lord!

The next morning, Elder Clark and I went on splits with Elder Hedelius and his companion, Elder Carling. I teamed-up with Elder Carling, and Elder Clark teamed-up with Elder Hedelius. Elder Carling is quiet, but he has a cool demeanor. We decided to head to the park to prospect and met several people. In fact, three people accepted a copy of the *Book of Mormon*.

I know deep down that I sincerely like people. I like to show respect to others, and I feel good inside when people sense that I sincerely care about them. "People skills" is one of my best attributes, which is a very good thing when sharing the gospel.

The Lord will bless us only if we live by His commandments. The scriptures and the ancient prophets have taught us that rich blessings can only come through obedience to His laws. I know there are people out there who really want to know more about God's church and feel the need to be baptized. The Lord wants me to continue working hard, keep a prayer in my heart, and build my faith in Him.

Tonight, Elder Clark and I took a much-needed break from all of the tracting and decided to ride our bicycles to the stake center to watch BYU beat up Utah State. Astonishingly, the Cougars won 38–3; it was a good game. I loved it because the cougars stomped all over "Big Blue." I enjoyed getting pumped up and rooting for my football team.

I've been reflecting on my struggles lately, but things are generally peaceful. I couldn't ask for more, and I know that the Lord is watching over me. It is a great feeling to know that I'm living righteously and doing my part. The Spirit of God is a precious gift. I must continue working hard to improve my own life.

Today is the Saturday Session of the 158th General Conference. Elder Clark and I rode our bicycles to the stake center to watch the broadcast from Salt Lake City. President Ezra Taft Benson spoke during the first session, and said, "A few men have grasped the true vision of the *Book of Mormon.*" Here are a few bullet points from is talk:

1. We need to flood the earth with the *Book of Mormon.*
2. He encouraged family-to-family *Book of Mormon* placements.
3. We need to challenge investigators and families to read and pray about the *Book of Mormon.*
4. The *Book of Mormon* answers many of life's questions.

John K. Carmack talked about what a personal testimony means to him and explained that a testimony is a strong faith and conviction in Jesus Christ. There are three essential components to a testimony: a desire, to know that Jesus Christ lives, and a willingness to obey the commandments. He likened a testimony to a good seed, as described in Alma 32 from the *Book of Mormon.*

Elder Ballard talked about "Fellowshipping." He suggested the following when we fellowship: we must be warm and sensitive to The Spirit, show love and understanding, and demonstrate Christlike qualities. We must not only extend our love to relatives and friends, but to everyone.

Elder Wirthlin talked about "Temptations." He talked about how TV and media consistently produce shows that make alcohol and beer look appetizing, and how people believe that life was created to have a good time, all the time. In other words, "...eat and drink; for tomorrow we shall die," as found in Isaiah 22:13 (KJV). Elder Wirthlin stressed that this is a huge misconception and couldn't be farther from the truth. As I was listening to Elder Wirthlin's comments, The Spirit touched me, and I thought about the purpose of life...which is to gain a body, live worthily, and return to the presence of our Heavenly Father.

Elder Gene R. Cook, Area General Authority in Southern California, spoke about "Missionary Work." He said that it is a missionary's responsibility to call people to repentance and be baptized. He also stated that we need to encourage church members to pray and reflect on God. It is important to humble ourselves before Him. Then Elder Cook listed seven ways of inviting The Spirit of God into any discussion:

1. Pray.
2. Use the scriptures. Make sure to leave a special thought with each family we visit. Bring a paper copy of a verse to leave with the family.
3. Testify and bear our testimonies. The Spirit will bear witness of the gospel's truthfulness.
4. Use music. Alma 32.
5. Express our love and gratitude towards God and His children.
6. Share spiritual experiences.
7. Perform priesthood blessings and other ordinances.

After the Saturday Afternoon session, we headed home to eat dinner and get ready for the Priesthood Session. (The Priesthood Session is always my favorite because I enjoy feeling the camaraderie with other brethren.)

Afterward the Priesthood Session, we had a follow up visit with our friend, Henry Smith. This time we had a friendly conversation with him, and I felt much more at ease, as I was comforted by The Spirit. The Holy Ghost whispered to me, "You need to read Henry a story from 1 Nephi 8," which is about the *Book of Mormon* prophet, Lehi, and his vision of the tree of life.

During our visit, Elder Clark and I utilized all Seven Steps suggested by Elder Cook to call upon The Spirit—except for music. We decided not to sing a church hymn. After a brief discussion, I asked Henry, "Do you think the *Book of Mormon* is false?" He replied, "No, but I don't have a view. Either way, it's not false nor true."

I replied, "Fair enough, and I understand where you're coming from on that perspective." Then, I asked, "Do you mind if we offer a prayer and bless your home?" He replied, "Sure". So, we offered a blessing on his home and left as friends. Henry is a good guy. I hope somewhere down the road that Henry accepts the gospel during this earth life. If not here, I hope he will accept it in the spirit world. Despite not being able to convert Brother Henry Smith, I still feel the Lord blessing us, and I love the work.

***

This morning we rode our bicycles to the stake center to watch the final session of General Conference. I reflected on Elder Ballard's words about "Fellowshipping," and couldn't help but remember how the Lord blessed me as a priest in helping a few less-active young men back into activity. I think a couple of these young men returned to the church, and I continue to reach out and write letters to them because they are my friends. Elder L. Tom Perry spoke about love in the home. He said that, in order to nurture love in home, we need to have family prayer, read books of learning, love one another, and share our testimonies.

President Benson gave a very inspiring talk. He said, "America is a choice land, and the Constitution was inspired of God." He talked about Moroni's promise in Moroni 10: 3–5 and reiterated that the *Book of Mormon* is true. Today, the church and kingdom of God is growing. The church is better equipped to handle wickedness than ever before. Regardless, there will be battles fought between good and evil until the end of time. People will have the agency to choose between God's church and the devil's church. The righteous will be tested, and God's wrath will be upon the wicked. In the end, God's people will be saved. We can find true joy only in His church, The Church of Jesus Christ of Latter-day Saints.

I know the Lord is blessing me. I am beginning to become a better missionary and a better person. I must grow closer to the scriptures and, in turn, gain a better knowledge of myself.

This morning we played basketball as a zone, which was great, because I love exercise and being competitive! Elder Clark can play some serious basketball, and even played on his high school team.

After our P-day activities, we headed to our appointment with Soni, who is a cousin of Todd Wickstrom, and taught her the 2nd Discussion, "The Gospel of Jesus Christ." During our discussion, Soni asked us a good question about eternal progression and life after death. Of course, we answered her question, explaining that the purpose of this earth life was to prepare to meet God again. I have begun using The Spirit more to answer my investigator's questions about the gospel. It is The Spirit of understanding, as described in Doctrine & Covenants 50:22: "Wherefore, he that preacheth and he that receiveth, understand one another, and both are edified and rejoice together."

After teaching Soni, Elder Clark and I rode with the other Elders in the Fontana District to President and Sister Gourdin's house. That's right; Zone #4 was Zone of the Month! Each month, the zone with the most baptisms is rewarded at the President's house with a nice dinner and a movie. After dinner, we watched a John Wayne film, and followed the feature with a testimony meeting.

The entire evening felt amazing because we could celebrate a month's-worth of arduous work. Even though I have not baptized anyone yet, I can feel The Spirit and camaraderie within my zone. During President Gourdin's testimony, he gave us a few clever ideas on how we can help our investigators move along the path to conversion. On the way home, Elder Clark kept cracking me up. He even made the "strict" elder (Elder Hedelius) laugh. It was so funny!

This morning started out as a bummer day. After our fun-filled day yesterday, we had no choice but to complete our chores, so we washed our dirty clothes and wrote letters at Reid's house for around three-hours. Then we came back to our apartment and marked up eight copies of the *Book of Mormon* to hand out. After that task was complete, we went tracting on Hawthorne Street...which was interesting. We met some good people, and I know we will get some baptisms soon.

After tracting, we headed home and made our usual stop at the mailbox, but I didn't receive any letters for the second doggone day in a row! I'm not too depressed; it's just that I've written a lot of people! My attitude is, "If they write, they write. If they do not, well...they do not."

Anyway, I'm glad to be here in California. This mission is an answer to my prayers. I know that serving the Lord is pleasing to Him and I love it! This morning we followed through with Peter, who is going to the hospital tomorrow for a small procedure. We are keeping him in our prayers so that he has a speedy recovery. I also pray that he will accept the gospel.

After meeting with Peter, we headed to Bill's house. This was the first time I'd met Bill, because Elder Clark and Elder Rogers gave him a *Book of Mormon*. When they entered his house the first time, Bill was blaring "Highway to Hell" by AC/DC on his home stereo system. What an awesome song!

Bill is 29-years old, a recovering alcoholic, and recovering drug-user who recently turned his life around. We walked into his house as he was jamming to Led Zeppelin and "Black Dog" today. It would be incredible if Bill joined the church, and I feel confident that he will one day.

For the rest of the afternoon, Elder Clark, and I tracted but only gave away two copies of the *Book of Mormon*. We met Carmen, a 35-year-old woman who said she had a disability, but we did not know what she meant. She didn't have a physical handicap as far as we could tell, so maybe she has a mental disability? Carmen said, "I still get spanked!" We were definitely not expecting her to say those words. Hopefully, we can teach her in the right setting—emotionally and spiritually.

Our last afternoon appointment was with Bernie and Lauren McKenna. We did not get the full story, but apparently, they took all six Discussions a year ago. However, something happened with the previous elders, and they were not baptized. However, I have a peaceful feeling about this couple.

After visiting with the McKennas, Elder Clark and I went on team-ups with Brother Adams, one of the stake missionaries. We taught Brother Lindsey the 5th Discussion, "Living a Christlike Life." However, I was a little disappointed with him tonight because he didn't want to cooperate with us. I asked Brother Lindsey, "Can we pray now and ask the Lord if the Book of Mormon is the word of God?" to which he replied, "No." He then went on a tangent about the church that I really do not want to discuss. I pray that he makes the right decision because I know he has the truth. The bottom line is that Brother Lindsey doesn't want to make the commitments to learn more about the gospel. I pray the Lord will soften his heart.

To say the least, I am frustrated. It is extremely frustrating to work so hard and see so little results. On the other hand, no matter what, I am never giving up hope. Nope, not me! The Lord's work is too important. Elder Clark and I will win; we are on the Lord's team.

This morning started out slow for us. We only gave out one copy of the Book of Mormon in two-hours of tracting. Then we decided to switch gears, because sometimes anything is better than tracting. So, we followed through with the McKenna family. At first, they were adamant about not allowing us into their home, stating that they did not believe in our church. The bottom line was that they were not interested. However, I was filled with The Spirit, and I asked Mrs. McKenna, "If I can show you where the Book of Mormon is mentioned in the Bible, will you let us into your home?" She replied, "All right. Come on in," and waved us in.

Elder Clark and Bernie talked about hunting, fishing, guns, and the great outdoors. While Ms. McKenna and I had a nice little conversation about our church, the Holy Bible, and the Book of Mormon. Linda had a lot of good questions about The

Church of Jesus Christ of Latter-day Saints. I tried to answer them to the best of my ability, with the direction of The Spirit.

After spending two hours there tonight, we now have a follow-up visit next Thursday at 6:00 p.m. I pray The Spirit will be with us, and that it will continue touching their hearts. They need the gospel so badly in their lives.

The next day, Elder Clark and I met Bill again, and he told us a few wild stories about his issues with drugs and alcohol. He has been through a lot! We offered to give Bill a priesthood blessing to help him overcome the effects of his bad habits, and to help his leg heal. He said that he would like a blessing later, if his leg continued to bother him. I pray that he will be baptized.

After meeting with Bill, we taught Soni the 3rd Discussion on "The Restoration" and it went well. I'm not sure if she lacks the faith or what it is. but Soni said she is not ready for baptism. I haven't figured out a reason why she shouldn't' be baptized, because she has accepted all of the gospel principles, we have taught her so far.

After meeting with Soni we decided to go tracting and met a family with four little children. They asked us tto share an inspirational story with them and I thought to myself, 'The best story I can share with these children, is the story about Jesus...' So, we taught them the gospel of Jesus Christ and the 1st Discussion. I was surprised by how much they did not know about God and Jesus Christ. It made me feel very grateful to my parents, who taught me the gospel from a young age.

I received five letters today; a few good ones—and a couple not so good. I received a letter from Elder Garner, who said that my MTC companion, Elder Perkins, left the mission field a couple of weeks ago. What a bummer. I suppose Elder Perkins was not ready for his mission. I noticed how depressed he was at the MTC. Though I tried everything in my power to be his friend, Elder Perkins' heart and attitude was not in the work. I wish him all the best in his future endeavors.

The other letters were decent. I received a couple of letters from people I have not heard from in a long time, including a letter from my sweet girlfriend, Kaesi.

Surprisingly, the letter was very serious. She typed it up, and didn't even close it with "Your Friend," or "I Love You." She just signed her name.

I tell you what brother; she ripped me up one side and down the other for encouraging her to date other people and inviting her to read the *Book of Mormon*, then she shamed me for treating her like one of my investigators. I am on a church mission, for cryin' out loud! She really went overboard with this latest rant, but I could also see right through her and how immature she is. Her tantrum was almost funny.

When I let Elder Hedelius and Elder Waddoups read her so called "Dear John" letter, I do not think I'd ever seen either one of them laugh so hard. They said it was ridiculous. Elder Hedelius started mocking the letter from beginning to end. I laughed out loud too because I know she still loves me. However, I am going to play it cool and not write her for at least a month. She's gonna die, but hey; I'm not going to let anyone push me around. I am Elder Todd.

The work carries on. I pray every night for my family, friends, girlfriend, and the McGurrins. I pray for strength and testimony. I also pray for success and baptisms.

This morning we had our District Meeting. It usually only lasts an hour, but we had to review the Investigator Fireside[46] tomorrow, so that added another hour to the agenda.

Elder Clark and I break up the monotony of tracting by making sure we watch every BYU football home game broadcasted via satellite. We must support the Lord's team! BYU beat Colorado State 42–7 today; woohoo!

After the game, we rode our bicycles home to finish planning the fireside. Elder Clark and Elder Stevenson had a couple of appointments within the Fontana Sixth Ward, and Elder Waddoups and I reviewed our agenda and talks one last time. After we completed the fireside program, I talked to Elder Waddoups about Kaesi and the communication issues we have been having in our relationship. He said, "She's just immature." I replied and nodded my head, "You are right." I would say this 'boyfriend and girlfriend' relationship is cooling off fast. I still like her, but her letter was the "final straw that broke the camel's back."

***

This morning we attended church service and had a packed, fun-filled day. Elder Clark and I offered a presentation and performed a skit for the young adult class. I portrayed the prophet, Samuel the Lamanite, from the *Book of Mormon*, and Elder Clark portrayed Joseph Smith. It was a tender moment.

After Sunday school, we attended the elder's quorum in the Fontana Fifth Ward and had a very cool spiritual experience. A first-time visitor, Louis Martorella, attended church with his wife, Sunshine, who is a member of the church. When we spoke with Louis before the meeting, he said, "Guys, I've lived a very hard life. I spent some time in a juvenile detention center and got into a lot of trouble while growing up. I did not have the gospel in my life."

The subject in elder's quorum was on the priesthood and offering blessings to the sick and afflicted. These blessings are one reason why the priesthood is so important. Louis, who was sitting next to me during the meeting, quietly leaned over and said, "Hey, I can't help but ask questions. I feel something inside of me stirring. It's a good feeling." He continued and said, "What makes your church any different from another church? Where is the priesthood coming from? Who is Joseph Smith? He made your church in the 1800's, right?"

So, right in the middle of priesthood meeting, I quietly turned to him and taught the 3rd Discussion, "The Restoration." I said, "We believe in the great apostasy that the Apostle Paul talks about in 2 Thessalonians 2:3: "Let no man deceive you by any means: for that day shall not come, except there come a falling away first, and that man of sin be revealed, the son of perdition."

I continued, "We believe that Jesus' church was taken from the earth because of the people's wickedness." Then I talked about the need for a restoration, Joseph Smith, the *Book of Mormon*, and baptism. I reiterated how important it was for Jesus to be baptized by one who held the priesthood authority (John the Baptist).

After I taught Louis about the restored gospel, he turned to me and said, "Thanks. That really cleared up a lot of my questions. I understand now." It was so cool to hear him say that. The Spirit directed me in what to say, and I am grateful to the Lord for giving me this great experience.

After church, Elder Clark and I rode our bicycles home to eat and mark up a few copies of the *Book of Mormon*. After that, I started calling people on the telephone, and invited them to our Investigator Fireside.

About a week ago, Marva committed to join, so we stopped by her house unannounced and found her working in the backyard. Although she had committed to us earlier, she decided that she no longer wanted to go. However, after some gentle coaxing and encouragement, I was able to persuade her to join us. She freshened up, got dressed, and even brought a couple of her children along.

After re-committing Marva, we rode our bicycles to the church building. Since this was my first time participating in an Investigator Fireside, I was nervous before giving my talk. However, as I gave my presentation on the *Book of Mormon*, everything worked out well. Afterwards, Marva said, "I'm glad I came to the fireside." I wasn't sure at first, but I'm happy she felt The Spirit.

The neat thing about the whole experience was the events that led to Marva being there. She said, "I tried calling you guys earlier today to not bother coming over to the house, because I decided I wasn't going to the fireside." I looked at Marva with a confused look and said, "We wrote our phone number inside the front cover of the *Book of Mormon* a few days ago. You even called us, and we talked." Marva replied, "I know; and then I looked all through the book, but I couldn't find your phone number. It was nowhere to be found." At that point, she knew it was the hand of the Lord. Marva now desires to attend church and be baptized.

Today was P-day, but we didn't get our usual 7:00 a.m.–6:00 p.m. day off from normal duty. In the morning, Elder Stevenson and I washed our clothes, but that was it. After doing some minor chores, we had a Multi-Zone Conference with a general authority, Elder Ted E. Brewerton. He gave a spiritual talk, and it was a great conference.

After the meeting we returned to Fontana, but the rest of the evening was a bummer because we didn't get any real missionary work done. Elder Clark and I wrote letters, and then waited for Elder Waddxoups and Elder Stevenson to get back to the apartment.

When they returned, Elder Stevenson with a stern face said, "World War III has started. We just heard that Russia has just sunk all the American submarines. The U.S. aircraft carriers have been called to the Atlantic. President Ronald Reagan is going to create a peace treaty." Naturally, Elder Clark and I were in shock and did not know what to think. While it all turned out to be a big joke, we believed his story for a whole five minutes. Elder Stevenson is one of the funniest people I know; he is one silly elder. The British people have a great sense of humor, just like the movie Monty Python and the Holy Grail.

This morning started out interesting. Elder Stevenson and I teamed-up and rode our bicycles to the Bloomington building because I had to take another lousy "Master Teacher"[47] test. I was never good at taking tests in high school, and I am certainly no better now. I feel very comfortable teaching one-on-one, but for some reason, I have a difficult time memorizing all the Missionary Discussions.

After the test, we met with Peter and watched the new church video, "How Rare of a Possession, The Book of Mormon." Then we all knelt, and asked God if the Book of Mormon was true. I felt The Spirit, and Peter felt The Spirit, too. I know he will be baptized.

After teaching Peter about the Book of Mormon, we ran some major errands. We stopped by the bank, got cash, and went grocery shopping. Then we walked two miles back to my apartment fully loaded with food.

After putting our food away, we traveled to our 2:30 p.m. teaching appointment with Nancy, and the 1st Discussion went extremely well! Nancy is a very humble and sincere person, who we will surely baptize into the church.

After meeting with Nancy, we met Brother Broderick, Fontana First Ward's Mission Leader. For the rest of the evening, 'the three amigos' followed through with several investigators, including Soni. Then we decided to do some tracting, during which we hand-delivered a few copies of the *Book of Mormon* and had an enjoyable time.

I specifically pray for Soni that she will read and ask Heavenly Father if this holy writ of scripture is the word of God. I am an ambassador of the Lord, and I know that, if I exercise my faith, Heavenly Father will answer my prayers. My desire is to help my investigators repent and be baptized. I love my mission, and I love the church.

This morning we returned to our regular companionships.. Elder Clark and I decided to have companion study at the park, reviewed the 6th Discussion, "Membership in the Kingdom," and then planned our day.

Today we fasted for Ms. Reid, a lady who President Gourdin knows in his stake. Ms. Reid was involved in a horrible car accident and is currently in the intensive care unit at the hospital, so we have been fasting and praying for her, and for each of our investigators.

After companion study, we visited a family in the ward whose infant son has had a bad ear infection. This gave me the opportunity to exercise my priesthood, seal the anointing, and offer a blessing. It was so neat to be a mouthpiece for the Lord.

After working in the field, we checked our mailbox for letters, and I received a letter from my mom. She told me that the family has been blessed since I left on my mission, which was amazing news. I feel good that I made the right decision to serve the Lord.

I know that in due time—the Lord's time—He will give us the opportunity to baptize. I think to myself, 'When!?' I do not have an answer. However, I do know that if I am faithful and work hard, Elder Clark and I will baptize. I love this gospel. I love my mission call because it gives me strength, knowing that I received this special calling directly from God.

This morning Elder Clark and I went on splits with the zone leaders; Elder Clark teamed up with Elder Packard, and I teamed up with Elder Rogers. I supposed everything was cool—at least I thought that Elder Clark and I were cool.

Elder Rogers then took me out to get an ice-cream cone and have a "little talk." He said, "Elder Todd, things aren't going well between you and Elder Clark." Then Elder Rogers proceeded to dump all over me for being the missionary that I am. He said that I must change, stop being "so bold," and relax my missionary attitude. I think he handled the situation poorly, but I also took it well. I doubled down and said, "Elder Rogers, I appreciate you trying to help ease some of the contention between Elder Clark and me, but I'm going to work even harder at becoming the best missionary I can be. I don't think I need to let up on having an eye single to the glory of God."

After splits with the zone leaders, Elder Clark and I followed through with a few call-backs. Then we taught the 2nd Discussion, "The Gospel of Jesus Christ," to John, a black gentleman. It went well, and we picked up two new investigators from his family.

After teaching John, we headed back to the apartment and checked our mailbox, where I received my new mission portrait photos. (The photos turned out really well, and I look handsome! I really like them.) After admiring the photos, I forwarded thirteen of them to my family.

After lunch, we had an appointment with Soni to teach her the 4th Discussion, "Eternal Progression." When we arrived, however, she was not feeling well, and she asked for a priesthood blessing. It is always an honor to give people blessings of healing and comfort from their illnesses.

After the blessing, we decided to begin the Discussion. It

went well, and I asked Soni, "Would you like to kneel with us and pray about the *Book of Mormon?*" Soni agreed, prayed, and The Spirit was in her home. In fact, before Elder Clark and I had even left, she was feeling better from her cold.

After teaching Soni, we decided to return to our apartment for companion study. Albert, a 14-year-old boy, and his mother live in the apartment complex next to ours. When Albert noticed we were home, he came over to speak with us. He said, "Hey guys; I would like to become a missionary like you!" It would be amazing for Albert and his mom to join the church, because it would bring so much joy into their lives. (My pen just ran out of ink...)

Our appointment for the day is with the McKennas, a family who lives next door to the Millers. We had a polite discussion about the gospel, then watched the video, "Together Forever." After the video, we discussed a couple of differences between the teachings of The Church of Jesus Christ of Latter-day Saints and their church.

The conversation was simple at first, but then it became more involved. In fact, it was becoming a spiritual war. While we were not trying to harm anyone with scripture references, it felt like a spiritual battle. Elder Clark and I held our own viewpoints. Our spirits were stronger than theirs, and we held out stronger in the end because we had stronger convictions than they did. I felt pumped up, though I'm not sure they felt that way? Who's to say that they decide to get baptized one day. I said a prayer in my heart that The Spirit would prevail.

Near the end of our discussion, I concluded that it might be best to simply be the McKenna's friends, and not argue. After Elder Clark and I spent three-hours flipping through scriptures in the Holy Bible, I was exhausted.

After our gospel discussion with the McKennas tonight, we rode our bicycles home. When we arrived at our apartment, Elder Hedelius and I went on a long walk, and talked about the companionship between Elder Clark and me. We also talked about the "little talk" I'd had with Elder Rogers over ice-cream.

After venting for a bit, I feel better about my relationship with Elder Clark, and now I feel better about my relationship with Elder Hedelius too. Communication is the key.

As I reflect on the discussion, we had with the McKennas earlier today, I realize that I've never heard so much gripe over one man (Joseph Smith) and one holy book (the *Book of Mormon*) in all my life. The restored gospel is true, and I have a firm testimony that Jesus Christ does live.

Today, Elder Clark and I taught Peter the 4th Discussion. He is such a nice person, and he accepts all the gospel principles so well, but he has not changed his stance about reading the entire *Book of Mormon* yet.

For the rest of the afternoon, we did our usual follow-ups and call-backs, and then tracted for a couple of hours. Our biggest highlight of the day, however, was meeting with Marva in her home. We talked for about an hour and had an enjoyable conversation. I feel like she will be baptized, because she is so sincere about learning about the gospel.

After meeting with Marva, Elder Clark and I traveled to Louis Martorella's home. However, when we knocked on the front door he wasn't there, so we decided to stop by another part-member's home, the Street family. Brother Street's hobby is scuba diving. I learned to enjoy scuba diving after I attended a weekend trip to Gainesville, Florida, and went diving in Crystal River during my senior year of high school. It was a blast! Brother Street and I talked about several different things, and it was fun to share an interest in the same hobby.

After meeting with the Streets, we went back to speak with Louis, and he uttered the five words I've been waiting for over three-months to hear: "I want to be baptized." I am SO excited! Elder Clark and I have the Lord to thank for this miracle. It is His baptism, and I can't wait! Faith in Jesus + Working Hard = Baptism.

***

It has been a few days since I last wrote in my mission memoir. It's not that I don't have anything to write; it's because I'm lazy. Missionary work has been going well. The Lord has a lot in store for me on my mission, and I have a lot of work to do.

The work has been picking up speed. In other words, I am getting to the point where the mission is "it," I am finally settling in, and accepting fact that this is my life for the next two years. It is honestly great, because I feel committed, all the way!

Well...I received a letter and a care package from Kaesi this afternoon. The letter expressed how sorry she was for treating me so poorly. I looked inside the package and there was an inflated balloon that said, "I love you." I know Kaesi is sincere about her apology, and I forgive her, no problem. I just wish she would stick to dating member guys. I do not like her dating non-members because it makes me nervous. I guess I still care for her.

During our companion study, Elder Clark and I were discussing—of all things— missionary work. As we were talking, he said something to me that touched me, and made me feel important. Elder Clark said, "You will become an assistant to the president (AP) someday." I replied, "Why do you say that?" He said, "Because you are a 'go getter,' and I have never met anyone quite like you. You will be an AP someday." I said, "Wow; man. That means a lot. I really appreciate it."

That was one of the coolest things anyone has ever said to me. My secret formula is Faith in Jesus Christ + Working Hard = Success. If I can become the best missionary possible, the Lord will bless me and I will see great spiritual growth in my life. The church is true. I cannot deny it.

This morning we attended Zone Conference, which turned out to be an especially spiritually uplifting meeting. I really enjoyed it, especially when Elder Clark bore his testimony about how great of a trainer I have been for "teaching him the ropes" on the mission. He said some other nice things about me, in his own words. He really did give a good testimony.

After Zone Conference, I took the "Master Teacher" test again. This time, I know I passed it. It feels good knowing that I did well. It will be a proud moment when I receive my certificate with the words "Master Teacher" on it. I say this with tongue-in-cheek because I don't like taking tests now any more than I liked taking tests in high school.

Elder Clark and I had the opportunity of teaching two discussions today. We taught the 2nd Discussion, "The Gospel of Jesus Christ," to Nancy. I hope she accepts the principles and understands the importance of the gospel in her life. Elder Clark and I are ministers of Jesus Christ. Through our faith in Him, and if it is His will, Nancy will be baptized.

Then we met with Louis Martorella and taught him "The Plan of Our Heavenly Father." I know Louis will also be baptized, as we've already set a baptismal date for October 29th. It is so awesome to finally get a solid commitment for baptism!

I know I have grown spiritually and intellectually in the gospel, and that I have grown by leaps-and-bounds. However, I must still work on my obedience. I need to follow the Savior in all that I do so that The Spirit will be with me. This is key to my success. I also know that the Lord is watching over and protecting my immediate family while I'm gone.

I woke up this morning and completed my usual 30-minutes of scripture study. Then we had thirty-minutes of companion study. Missionary life continues. I am so excited about missionary work! My relationship with Elder Clark has improved because we can both see the light at the end of the tunnel. Through our faith and diligence, the Lord has blessed our companionship with the spirit of cooperation. The Lord continues to bless us, and I am thankful for that.

After breakfast, we tracted most of the day, met a few good people, and handed out copies of the *Book of Mormon*. Elder Clark and I pray for the opportunity to teach and baptize these individuals.

During our door knocking, we had some close encounters with a few angry dogs. Man; I hate California dogs! It seems like the dogs we encounter on the streets here are so aggressive! And yet, I know that, as servants of the Lord, we will be protected if we follow the rules.

During one of our visits, we came across a contact named Marcie who was a 'sight for sore eyes.' Her eyes could kill, and were a dark, penetrating brown. In other words, Marcie is good looking! I would definitely not mind if she joined the church.

My mind reflects on missionary work. We always have something to do because we are constantly trying to gather Israel. Naturally, there is a lot of work to be done, and this is one of the most important two-years of my entire life. I will serve the Lord until the end and will continue serving an honorable and faithful mission. The Lord expects a lot from me because I am a special witness of the Lord, Jesus Christ. Baptizing God's children is what I was called to do.

This morning while I was riding up Oleander Street, my bicycle's right pedal fell off the crank arm, but it wasn't too much of an issue because we were near a member's house. As a result, I was able to borrow a wrench and repaired the pedal. But then, only a mile down the road, my right pedal fell off the crank arm—again! I started thinking, 'Okay; something is seriously wrong with my pedal!'

After that, the rest of the day was a flop. We spent the afternoon finding parts for my bike and going to the post office for Elder Clark. After taking care of those errands, we went back into action.

We managed to visit with several part-member families late in the afternoon, then traveled to Soni's to watch "The First Vision" video. After the video, we talked about Heavenly Father and Jesus Christ appearing to Joseph Smith as resurrected, glorified beings. I said, "We know through Joseph Smith's first vision that Heavenly Father has a body of flesh and bones."

Soni replied, "I believe in the first vision, but I also believe that God is a spirit." The Spirit was there. I know I felt the presence of the Holy Ghost and I know that Soni believes the gospel is true, but she will not yet accept it. It is frustrating, but she has her own free agency. I feel deep down that Soni knows that if she sincerely prays about the Book of Mormon, she will get an answer from God, and I don't think she wants to get an answer.

After meeting with Soni we had an appointment with

Louis Martorella. However, when Louis answered the front door, he told us that he was not feeling well, and we had to reschedule. Our backup plan was to see Brother Street, our scuba diving friend.

After visiting with Brother Street, it was getting close to curfew, so we headed home and checked the mailbox where I received a sensational letter from Kaesi. The best part of the letter was the photo she included; it was out of this world. I mean— holy cow! It was one of the most incredible images I have ever seen in my entire life. It was a photo of Kaesi standing with just her towel on. That was it. There's no debate; she is mine; all mine.

I have been trying to focus on the work, and yet it still doesn't feel to me like I'm on a mission. The months have flown by in record time. Have I actually been on a mission for three months? Seriously, it seems like yesterday that I was sitting in a classroom learning about MacBeth in English class or dissecting a cat in Human Physiology. The events in my life are happening far too quickly, and my gut reaction is to try and hold the "pause button" on life.

Happy Birthday Kaesi. You are seventeen years old. I love the song, "Seventeen," by the band, Winger. "She was only seventeen!"

Today was another hard-earned missionary day, and we did not mess around. Our first morning appointment was with Peter, during which we watched two videos: "The First Vision" and "Restoration of the Priesthood." Peter loved both presentations and said, "Your gospel is beautiful. I thank you guys for coming out here on your missions." I pray for Peter to make the choice to be baptized.

After a wonderful meeting with Peter, we taught Sharon the 1st Discussion, and the conversation went well. Although Sharon needs to make a few changes in her life before she is ready for baptism, I know that if she makes the sacrifice and repents, she will be greatly blessed.

After teaching Sharon, we had a follow-up visit with Vicky. She is a call-back who we originally found through tracting, and it just so happens that Vicky's mother is a member of the church. Vicky was very sincere when she said, "I like attending church. Please don't give up on me." She continued, "The fact that you elders come by to see me tells me that you care." I thought to myself, 'We do care. We want to baptize you.' Before we left her house, Vicky gave Elder Clark and me both a Coca-Cola and some beef jerky. She was so nice.

After visiting with Vicky, we decided to tract the rest of the afternoon, and handed out four copies of the *Book of Mormon* in our assigned area. Then we decided to help Elder Waddoups and Elder Stevenson place books in their ward boundaries. By that time, however, we had worked up quite an appetite. Gratefully, we had a dinner appointment scheduled with the Steileens this evening, and it was a marvelous experience! We had delicious steak, potatoes, salad, and corn on the cobb. It tasted mouthwatering good.

After dinner, we returned home and retired to bed. As I was lying in bed thinking about our day, my thoughts drifted towards Kaesi. My feelings toward her are basically the same. I love her, and I will always care for her. She is a nice and beautiful girl. I hope we can invite the Lord into our relationship. If we can do that, then I believe we can continue to grow together.

Today turned out to be an absolutely fantastic day! In fact, it was a missionary's dream come true. The funniest thing about it was that the day began as a total disaster.

During District Meeting, many of the missionaries in my district—all with good intentions—were trying to lecture me on how I should be handling my investigator's concerns. I appreciated everyone's help, but elders can go overboard sometimes...and their hyper-focused attention to my flaws was driving me nuts!

After District Meeting, we headed to our apartment, but then I realized I'd forgotten the door key en-route. After that disgruntled realization, Elder Clark and I got into a stupid fight about trying to figure out a way to get into the apartment without the key. To be honest, he was very uncooperative. I was looking for solutions and all he wanted to do was play the 'blame game.' Weary of his onslaught, I took off on my bicycle to the manager's office in a huff and grabbed an extra key. My plan was to quickly return to my apartment.

A few minutes later, I returned to unlock the front door of the apartment, but Elder Clark was gone. One of the biggest mission rules is to be with your companion 24 hours a day, 7 days a week, 365 days a year...and yet here I was; all by myself.

Not knowing what else to do, I changed into my suit, made a sandwich, and rode my bike up to the Arrow building for a baptism. When I arrived, Elder Clark and the zone leaders were not there. Apparently, they were riding all over Fontana looking for me.

About ten to fifteen minutes later, Elder Clark and the zone leaders returned to the church building, and then we ran off to our appointment with John. Elder Clark and I had a great discussion with him, and I pray that John will be baptized. We invited him to read the *Book of Mormon*, and John said, that he would consider it, saying that he would give it some thought and prayer.

After following through with several of our investigators this afternoon, we decided to go home, eat, and then get ready for our appointment with Louis. When we arrived at the Martorella's home, Louis was excited to see us. The Lord prepared this man so that we could teach him the gospel, and tonight he said all the things a missionary wants to hear.

Louis said, "I couldn't remember what time we were meeting tonight; 6:00 p.m. or 7:00 p.m.... I forgot what time! But I knew you guys were coming over to the house."

He continued, "I was tired and ready to fall asleep when you guys knocked at the door. When I heard the knock, I got excited!" Louis explained that he had a tough childhood and ended up serving a couple of years in prison. He now has some health concerns and suffers from diabetes.

After speaking with Louis, the first time, I would never have guessed he would agree to listen to The Discussions. It made me realize that the Lord doesn't care about our outward appearances, nor what we've done in the past. We can always repent.

The Lord is only concerned with our heart and willingness to change. Louis is excited about joining the church and being baptized.

Currently, his only issue with the Word of Wisdom is smoking. And somehow, before we ever brought up the subject, he already knew that smoking was a no-go. He told us, "I want to quit for myself." He even talked about attending the temple and doing genealogy work for his family.

He told us a recent story about driving down the highway and seeing a good- looking lady. He said, "I started to have lustful thoughts for this woman, and I prayed, asking the Lord to get Satan out of my head." He continued, "I feel like the Lord is washing my insides out from all of the sin. I feel like I have been constipated for so long, and now .. I feel great!" Elder Clark and I laughed so hard we thought we were going to die. I appreciate Louis' honesty because I know I have had lustful thoughts too.

After asking Louis a few more questions, we discovered that he had already taken all the Missionary Discussions. While serving time in prison, a couple of elders taught him the gospel. Upon discovering this, we literally flipped through three discussions with him tonight. It was an incredible teaching opportunity.

After reviewing all major points from the first three Discussions, Brother Louis requested a priesthood blessing, stating that he had been suffering from a bad cold. In the blessing, we asked God to relieve his body of the infection. It was such a wonderful experience, and I felt so good inside.

As we walked to the door to leave, Louis said, "Elders, I was looking at my calendar and the 29th of October is coming up fast. You better make sure I get my discussions in before I get baptized." I replied, "Yes; we will make sure you're ready. And just to let you know, Elder Hedelius will interview you and ask this specific question: Why do you want to be baptized and join the church?" Louis replied, "You send Elder Hedelius over here and I'll tell him why!"

We spent two-and-a-half hours at Louis' house before it was time to leave, around 8:30 p.m. We then had an appointment to see Marva, and watched the video, "The First Vision." The entire family loved it! A couple of her children even showed an interest in attending church tomorrow; they are excited! Marva then promised me that she would join us at church in the morning.

When we got home from Marva's house, there was a letter from my dad laying on the kitchen table. In the letter, he offered some friendly advice about what to do about the Kaesi situation. He encouraged me to send her some beautiful flowers and included $15.00 check.

The gospel of Jesus Christ is so true. If men like Louis can change their lives, humble themselves, and be baptized, I have faith that other people can do the same. I love the gospel; it is so sweet and true!

***

I have been sick with a bad head and chest cold for the past couple of days, and my stomach hurt after our Sunday dinner appointment. I suppose I ate too much. As a result, I spent most of my P-day in bed. My head felt like it was swimming around. I feel much better today.

Louis Martorella is scheduled for baptism this Saturday, October 29th and I am so excited! However, our Ward Mission Leader, Brother Hadden, is giving us a tough time because he has "his way" of doing baptisms. The bottom line is that the Fontana Stake has a set baptismal date once a month that doesn't line up with Louis' date.

Additionally, Brother Hadden likes at least five to seven days' notice before any baptisms. He says he likes to prepare the program and make sure we have plenty of time for the baptismal interview.

In all honesty, I feel like he's trying to live the "letter of the law" when it's the "spirit of the law" that matters most. It's not reasonable to expect us to plan baptisms on one set date; that's not how the gospel works! When The Spirit converts and touches someone's heart, it's time to act. Oh, well...we will work something out.

I know the Lord is watching over us and that He is blessing us every step of the way. We must be obedient to the rules of the mission, have faith, and work hard in bringing to pass the eternal life of man. I love my mission; I was born to baptize and bring souls to Jesus.

This morning, Elder Clark and I taught Peter the 5th Discussion, "Living a Christlike Life." He is such a special person. However, Peter does not have any interest in joining us at church until after Thanksgiving. It would be nice to see him get baptized, but I don't know how long I will be serving in Fontana.

The rest of the afternoon, 'the three amigos'—consisting of Elder Hedelius, Elder Clark, and I—visited the Fontana Second Ward to follow through on an investigator appointment and some call-backs. When we arrived at our first appointment, Elder Hedelius' investigator was a no-show[48]. The rest of the afternoon was generally unproductive.

Even though most of the day was a bummer, I was still excited for our appointment with Louis. We were prepared for a fun-filled evening, complete with two discussions and a baptismal interview.

After teaching Louis, the 5th and 6th Discussions—which went well, just as expected—Elder Hedelius interviewed Louis for baptism. The only room where they could get some privacy was in Louis' garage, so off they went. Louis demonstrated a strong testimony of the gospel, and everything seemed to be going well until Elder Hedelius said, "I need to speak with President Gourdin before Louis can get baptized." Louis, Elder Clark, and I all looked at one another with a look of surprise.

During the formal baptismal interview, it is customary in The Church of Jesus Christ of Latter-day Saints for the interviewer to ask questions about serious sins. A serious sin encompasses abortion, murder, or committing a criminal act. For example, here are three questions that are asked.

1. Have you ever been involved in an abortion?
2. Have you ever been involved in a homosexual act?
3. Have you ever been arrested or have a criminal history?

If the investigator answers, "Yes," to any one of the questions above, then the matter must be brought to President Gourdin's attention. As of now, the mission president must interview Louis to determine if he is worthy for baptism into the Lord's church.

Elder Hedelius continued, "It could take anywhere from one to two weeks to schedule an interview with President Gourdin, so we may have to wait another week or so for his baptism." It's not that Louis doesn't have a testimony—because he definitely has one. It's just that certain items of business—that I am not fully aware of—must be discussed with President Gourdin.

You know...I do wonder sometimes about mission life. I've been through various trials over the past three months and am serious when I say that only the Lord knows the truth. In other words, only He knows what is in store for me in the future.

I mean...good gosh almighty! I have had trials with Elder Hedelius, Elder Clark, several investigators, a couple of missionaries, and the zone leaders. To make matters worse, we have a renegade ward mission leader—Brother Hadden—who's been trying to dictate when a person can get baptized. I have worked my absolute rear-end off since day one of my mission and am very frustrated. The Lord must have some type of purpose for me here in Fontana. I really shouldn't get depressed, and I have always worked hard in my church callings. But what do I have to show for it? Nothing. I have hardly seen any success in this area. Dang it! The Lord's ways are different than my ways; at least that is what I'm telling myself.

I must be positive and pump myself up somehow. I am never

giving up. My attitude is to baptize, baptize, and baptize. My formula is Faith + Working Hard = Baptism and Success. I believe that the Lord has specific missions for me to accomplish here, and things I need to do.

This morning I received a phone call from my good friend, Dan, my main man! He called to tell me that he had accidentally broken his foot. He was doing well and it sounds like he will fully recover. It's always neat to hear from one of my good friends, because we cheer one another up.

The rest of the day, the new 'three amigos'—consisting of Elder Hedelius, Elder Waddoups, and I—decided to work in the Fontana Second and Third Wards. It was fun working in Elder Hedelius' area again. We had lunch at a part-member's house, followed-through with a few call-backs, and then tracted.

I like working with Elder Hedelius and Elder Waddoups. They are good guys, and I have learned a lot from each of them. While tracting, I spoke with them about some of my frustrations with missionary work. After blowing off a little steam, I'm no longer feeling depressed or frustrated, and I'm finding it easier to have a positive attitude. Gratefully, I am still excited about missionary work.

After working in the field all day, I teamed-up with Elder Stevenson and Elder Waddoups for a dinner appointment in Southridge. The children loved us so much that they didn't want us to leave the house. What can I say; we are extremely popular people!

My basic philosophy is to just put my trust and faith in the Lord. I know He will make things right for me. Jesus will. I know He will.

Today is my three-month mark, and I'm excited because I feel like I've accomplished a lot in those three months. Apparently, this is the week of 'the three amigos,' because I teamed up with another threesome again. However, this time it was with Elder Waddoups and Elder Rogers.

This morning, we all walked together to Southridge and followed through with several call-backs and investigators. It felt like we walked two to three miles. The smog was especially bad today, and the pollution was bothering my eyes and contact lenses again.

After proselyting in the Southridge area, we decided to go back to the apartment for lunch, where we ate sandwiches and relaxed for a few minutes. Elder Clark and Elder Stevenson were laying down on the couch and recliner listening to a church tape when the telephone rang. I picked it up to find Elder Kipp, one of the assistants to the president, on the other line. He said, "Elder Todd; how is it going?" I replied, "Pretty good; and you?" Elder Kipp continued, "Great. Listen; you and Elder Hedelius are getting new companions today." I silently thought to myself, "Elder Clark just received his visa!" And sure enough, he did. He is now leaving us this Monday for Campinas, Brazil. I continued listening in silence as Elder Kipp gave me a few more details about the transfers.

When I hung up the telephone, I turned to Elder Hedelius and said, "You and I are getting new companions today." Then I turned and looked at Elder Clark and said, "You're leaving for Campinas, Brazil on Monday, dude!" You should have seen the look on his face when I told him the good news. Elder Clark was incredibly surprised; his expression was like a five-year-old child on Christmas day. He immediately jumped up from the couch and gave me the biggest hug I have ever had in my life. It was so cool because Elder Clark has worked his rear end off for this moment!

Later that afternoon, I met my new companion, Elder Evans, from St. Louis, Missouri. He is a visa waiter as well. Apparently, the country of Brazil has a tremendous backlog of visas. He seems like a real go-getter, so I decided to baptize Elder Evans with fire by taking him tracting.

While tracting, Elder Evans' bicycle pedal completely broke off the crank arm. It was kinda funny, because it reminded me of the time my pedal fell off only a week ago. Realizing I needed to ease up a bit, Elder Evans and I returned to the apartment and reviewed a few things about the California San Bernardino mission.

Elder Hedelius then told Elder Clark and me that Louis was scheduled for a baptismal interview by President Bringhurst—the Fontana Stake President—this Sunday at 8:00 a.m. Elder Clark really wants to see Louis get baptized before he leaves the U.S.A. for Brazil in a couple of days.

I love my mission, and how everyone works hard to accomplish the Lord's work. The neatest thing is that I know I have a family in Georgia who loves me no matter what. The knowledge that I can rely on my Heavenly Father and my earthly parents for love and support gives me great comfort, especially when I'm going through trials and tribulations.

This morning, 'the three amigos'—Elder Hedelius, Elder Waddoups, and I—all had companion study at the Fontana Library. We studied for two hours about the Fall of Adam, being saved by grace, works, and the wars between Gog and Magog.

In Revelation 20:12, St. John wrote, "And I saw the dead, small and great, stand before God; and the books were opened; and another book was opened, which is the book of life: and the dead were judged out of those things which were written in the books, according to their works."

After companion study, we traveled to Elder Hedelius' Ward and taught the 1st Discussion to two different investigators. After teaching, we went tracting and gave away four copies of the *Book of Mormon*.

Then Elder Clark and I became the "diamond duo" again. We had two dinner appointments scheduled for tonight. Our first dinner was with Brother Brill, and our second dinner appointment was with Brother and Sister Mafi.

Sister Mafi is always a great cook. We had an enjoyable time, and my tummy was filled. I also found it interesting that, while we were waiting for dinner to be served, the television was on. I really didn't realize how much filth is on the TV until I served a mission. It also dawned on me that I am on a totally different spiritual plateau than many members of the church.

After we rolled into our apartment, I talked with Elder Evans for a while. He has a lot of pizazz and is excited about missionary work. He wants to get out into the field to work and baptize.

I am not into life right now. It's weird, but...what I mean is...I haven't been in my assigned area of Fontana for the past couple of days. I enjoy spending time with the elders in my district, but I am also ready to focus and get to work. There are too many changes with all these visa waiters. I love them, and I know that President Gourdin loves them too. I'm hoping that, by next week, everything will turn back to normal. I praise and sing, Hallelujah!

Elder Clark is leaving the country on Monday. Man; I am going to miss him, even if we did have our moments. He is a cool guy, and I know he will do great on his mission in Brazil. I also know that the Lord is watching over me; I love the gospel.

Today started out slow but ended with a bang! We had our usual weekly District Meeting, after which the zone leaders joined us for an hour, and then we headed to lunch. Elder Waddoups refers to the zone leaders as "Zone Heads." It is a slang term, and I think it is funny.

After lunch, 'the three amigos'—consisting of Elder Waddoups, Elder Evans and I—traveled to the bicycle shop to get some parts for our bikes. Then we walked a block to the Fontana florist to wire a nice bouquet of beautiful flowers to Kaesi. It costs me nearly $25.00, but she's worth it.

After our short detour, we rode our bicycles back to the apartment to meet Elder Clark and Elder Stevenson. However, when we arrived, there was a note on the front door that read, "We're at the Fontana Stake Center watching the BYU vs. New Mexico game." At that, we rushed over to meet the elders, and watched the cougars give New Mexico a big fatgoose egg. The final score was 62-0. In fact, the game was going so well for the cougars that they put in their second-string quarterback, Ty Detmer. I bet my dad is so happy!

During the fourth quarter beat-down, Elder Evans felt like it was time to get to work again, so 'the three amigos' decided to leave the stake center with a few minutes left in regulation. Our plan was to follow-through with a few part-member families and call-backs. Elder Evans' new drive and enthusiasm for the work has been refreshing, and things are looking up for missionary work.

After working in the field for a few hours, we headed to Louis' home for our evening appointment. He is such a stud! This good man has a powerful desire to be baptized. We read 3 Nephi Chapter 11 with him, which talks about Jesus Christ visiting the people in North America after his resurrection. Louis really enjoyed our discussion. When it was time to say the closing prayer, I asked, "Louis, will you please offer the closing prayer for us tonight? I know God is looking forward to hearing from you." Louis reluctantly offered the prayer, and we thought he did a wonderful job. However, he did not agree, and his confidence was a little shaken. However, after we offered some additional encouraging words, Louis' spirit perked up again.

Louis is now scheduled to be baptized tomorrow, (Sunday) October 30th, at the Arrow building in Fontana, California. First, he must have an interview with the stake president at 8:00 a.m. This much I know: if the Lord wants him baptized, he will be baptized.

The last thing that we told Louis was to be positive and to keep his chin up. Elder Clark said, "You need to be careful with the adversary. He will try to tempt you and persuade you to do wrong. Please resist the temptation."

***

This morning began with a bang! Today was not only Louis' baptismal date, but it was also daylight savings time. Before we retired to bed last night, Elder Clark turned our clock back one hour (fall-back), and we were able to get an extra hour of sleep. However, Louis forgot it was day-light savings time....

The plan was to have Louis pick us up at our apartment at 7:45 a.m. and drive to his baptismal interview to meet with President Bringhurst. However, Louis came by at 6:45 a.m. (one-hour early) and knocked on our front door. He waited for a few minutes, and then remembered what we said about the adversary the night before. Louis thought that the devil was trying to steer him in the wrong direction because we did not answer the front door.

He has a fervent desire to meet President Bringhurst on-time, so he left without us. About an hour later, we finally figured out what happened. I immediately telephoned the stake president's office and I spoke with the stake clerk, who handed the receiver to President Bringhurst. He said, "Hi, Elder Todd; I need to speak with Elder Hedelius for a moment." Elder Hedelius then came to the phone, and they talked for about a minute.

After speaking with stake president, Elder Hedelius quietly hung up the telephone, turned to us, and said, "President Bringhurst has found Louis worthy to be baptized. The final decision is up to you guys and the Lord." Upon hearing the good news, all four of us (Elder Clark, Elder Evans, Elder Hedelius, and I) knelt and prayed. We felt the influence of The Spirit, and it felt amazing. I then telephoned Louis to tell him the good news and he was so happy!

After congratulating Louis on a job well done, Elder Clark telephoned his brother, Joe, who lives in San Diego, and invited him to attend Louis' baptism. The events leading up to his baptism were utterly amazing. We reviewed the program, and saw that Louis wanted me to perform his baptism and that Elder Clark would confirm him a member of The Church of Jesus Christ of Latter-day Saints.

At first, I was scared because of all the preparation we needed to accomplish in such a short time. During the past two days, however, we managed to get the baptism organized and ready with the Lord's help.

After making all the final preparations for the ordinance, we attended Louis Martorella's baptism at the church. Mark Adams gave a great talk. In fact, the music, conducting, and the opening and closing prayers were all fantastic. The Spirit was there in the Relief Society room, and it was a marvelous event.

It is customary in the church to have the baptismal service in the Relief Society room because that is where the font is located.

I am proud of myself. I am completely overcome with joy and happiness inside. We make a wonderful team—the Lord, Louis, Elder Clark, and me. Louis was so happy after his baptism. He said, "I feel like I woke up and just took a breath of fresh air. I feel super!" I could see the light in his eyes; it was so awesome.

Elder Clark did an excellent job with the confirmation, and the hand of the Lord was with us. He fulfilled one of his important mission duties here in California, and now God is calling him to another part of his vineyard in Brazil.

Jesus truly wanted Louis baptized tonight. Considering the way the events unfolded, I believe it was a small miracle for Louis to reach this point. The number of obstacles we all had to overcome was amazing, but with the Lord's help, all things became possible. In Matthew 19:26, it reads, "But Jesus beheld them, and said unto them, With men this is impossible; but with God all things are possible."

I feel that I am fulfilling my duties as a missionary. The Lord made this evening possible. I am so thankful for the opportunity to baptize Louis. I feel so good and proud of myself, and my confidence is rising. God is watching over me. "And, if it so be that you should labor all your days in crying repentance unto this people, and bring, save it one soul unto me, how great shall be your joy with him in the kingdom of my Father!" (Doctrine and Covenants 18:15)

Companions
Matthew Hedelius August – September 1988
Dean Clark September – October 1988

The McGurrin
family July 1988.
Kaesi is on the left.

The Todd family at
Hartsfield-Jackson
Airport July 1988

Golf outing with my
Uncle Howard, me,
Uncle Burton,
and Uncle Ira.

The Barstow District
in the MTC
July 1988.

The Louis
Martorella,
Jr. family in
Fontana
October 1988.

Elder Evans, Elder
Murdoch, and
Elder Hedelius
Christmas 1988.

Elder Hancock,
Rick Perales,
and me
Fontana
January 1989.

Brother Inman,
Marie, me, and
Marie's brother
in Fontana
January 1989

The Tomlinson
family and Rhonda
Youngbloom
Fontana
January 1989

CHAPTER 5:

The Infamous Santa Ana Winds (Devil Winds)

Today is Halloween. There is not that much to say other than, "Trick'o Treat!" It is also another fabulous P-day!

Elder Clark left for Brazil first thing this morning on a 17-hour flight from California to South America. That is some serious jet lag! He is a good guy, and even though we did have our moments, I really do love him. Godspeed; my brother!

Elder Evans and I spent the rest of the afternoon doing chores, and then the zone got together to play basketball. It was fun! On a personal note, Kaesi received her flowers today. I wish I could have been there to see her smiling face, and I hope she likes them. They cost me $25.00, so she'd better like them!

This morning, Elder Evans, and I tracted for a couple of hours. After celebrating Loui's baptism in the church for a day, we decided we needed to fill up our teaching pool again through tracting, and we met some good people. I have a new fervor for the work!

After lunch, we went out into the field again. However, within an hour, Elder Evans' bicycle (my old first bike), broke down three times. The first time, his chain broke in front of Fontana High School. Then the chain broke again while trying to visit some part-member families. After repairing the chain twice, Elder Evans got a flat tire. I acted like I was upset, but I really was not. After that, Elder Evans had to walk his bicycle all the way back to our apartment.

Upon our return, we checked the mailbox, and I received a new contact carrying case. In celebration, I immediately disposed of my old contact lenses and replaced them with the new ones. My new contacts work wonders; I can see again! I am sure they won't last long here due to the smog, which will do its fair share of damage.... Just kidding!

After repairing Elder Evans' bicycle, we traveled to the Wickstrom's home to watch a CBS TV show, "Go Towards the Light." The show was about a Mormon family and how they coped with the reality of their oldest son, Ben, dying from AIDS. It was so good, and very inspirational. I was so emotionally moved by the show that I felt like getting on my knees and thanking the Lord for my many blessings, including my good health.

The prophet Mormon was mentioned once or twice during the TV special. Ben's father talked about "The Plan of our Heavenly Father" and "Eternal Progression." He described the spirit as the hand, and our body as the glove, which is exactly how we teach the 4th Discussion. I was freaking out in a good way. My compliments to CBS for airing the show. It was produced first-class, and I give it four stars!

I can't imagine that anyone watching the show didn't feel The Spirit, and I believe that's a true statement. If someone didn't feel The Spirit, maybe they don't know what The Spirit is or what it's like feeling it for the first time. However, I felt The Spirit, and it made me feel good inside. The truth is so sweet and brings joy to my soul. The "Go Towards the Light" special is a "make you feel good" show. Of course, Ben's passing away was sad, but in the end, it made me happy to know that we will see our loved ones again in the eternities.

I often take having the Holy Ghost and a testimony of the true gospel for granted. While it is a sacrifice to live righteously, I think to myself, "Yes; it is...but so what.?" The gospel is true, and I accept it with all my heart. That is why I'm serving a church mission—to share with others the great joy that I have experienced through living the gospel of Jesus Christ.

I have a testimony of eternal progression, and so death doesn't seem so permanent or awful. Death is simply part of Heavenly Father's plan. While I have never lost a loved one—and I am sure that it's painful—I know that my loved ones who pass away will be happy living in the spirit world.

I love the gospel, and I know that Heavenly Father and Jesus Christ are watching over me. I am a servant and minister of my Lord and Savior, Jesus Christ. I depend on Him 24 hours a day, 7 days a week, 365 days a year. He is my friend, and I know that by following him, I am doing what is right. My family has been greatly blessed, which is one of the many reasons that serving is so great! In other words, my family benefits as well.

This morning I had to wash my clothes because I have been wearing the same underwear (garments) for the past two-and-a-half days. I have been so caught up in getting ready for Louis' baptism that I forgot to wash my clothes. Now I am clean, and I smell a lot better! The time I have spent serving the Lord has been flying by, and it's already November.

I received a few good letters today. Mama Todd outdid herself, writing the best letter by far. It was great! Mama wrote the most positive and uplifting letter that I've received from her in a while. She told me that I was a "good boy," and doing a fantastic job on my mission. It really inspired me; so much that I read her letter at least five times.

The rest of the afternoon, Elder Evans and I followed through with a few call-backs on our list. We have a couple of decent good contacts, and I'm looking forward to filling up the pipeline in our teaching pool. I want to be teaching on a regular basis. I've felt more at ease since the Lord blessed us with a baptism, and things are moving at a steady pace. I know my Heavenly Father has much in store for us.

This morning we met with Peter and read a few chapters from the *Book of Mormon*. Peter is holding steady to his commitment about joining us at church after Thanksgiving. I feel good about Peter. If it is the Lord's will, Peter will be baptized.

After meeting with Peter, we decided to follow through with some part-member families, after which we walked the streets for a couple of hours and did some good 'ol fashioned tracting. The bummer thing about it was that we only gave away one *Book of Mormon*. I felt depressed and could feel that the neighborhood we were tracting was not "the one."

After a dismal morning of tracting, we decided to regroup at home to eat lunch and adjust my bicycle. My crank arm and pedals have been constantly getting lose, so I flipped my bicycle onto its handlebars in the middle of the family room and proceeded to take the axle and crank from another beat-up, ten-speed bicycle, and replace it in on my bike. Elder Evans did most the work because he knows a lot about bikes. He also said I needed a new derailer, and that my existing derailer was shot. My hope is to travel down to Riverside on Monday to purchase a new derailer and rear bike rack. That way, I can carry my scriptures and extra copies of the *Book of Mormon*.

After adjusting my bike and having dinner, we traveled to Louis' house to say "hello" and to see how he was doing after his baptism. However, he wasn't home from work yet, so we decided to follow through with a few call-backs. It turned out that a little dog followed us all over the neighborhood. She was a small, rather ugly dog, and Elder Evans and I felt sorry for the poor thing. She followed us all the way home, so we named the dog "Alma," from the *Book of Mormon*. She will be staying with us for the night; hopefully we can find her a new home tomorrow.

Elder Packard just called our district to tell us the good news: our one baptism helped push Zone 4 over the top, and we are now "Zone of the Month!" That means the entire zone will be rewarded with a delicious meal and a movie again. We will have the privilege of meeting at the president's house on Monday.

This morning, Elder Evans and I went shopping for slacks at a few thrift stores in town. Since he's been wearing his suit pants while biking, he's been quickly wearing them out. After purchasing two pairs of slacks, we followed through with several part- member families, and it turned out to be a good afternoon.

After dinner, I read a couple of letters from home, specifi-cally a letter from Kaesi. To be honest, I was quite surprised I even received a letter from her, because she has been getting bad about returning letters lately. I feel like I'm getting the run-around, and that she is playing mind games with me. A couple of months ago, she sent me a "Dear John" letter. I waited three weeks to reply. After reading my letter, Kaesi came crawling back to me, apologizing for the way she treated me. I felt like she was being sincere, and we continued to exchange letters. I even sent her beautiful flowers.

Then I did not hear from her in a while. A couple of weeks later, I finally received a "thank you" letter for the flowers. Then in the same breath, she told me that she was not sorry for the "Dear John" letter. In other words, her apology didn't mean did-dly squat! Women! You cannot live with them, and you cannot live without them. I've tried to apologize for the whole Brandi situation. I take part-blame for creating havoc in our relation-ship, but good-grief-almighty; it's time to let things go and let bygones be bygones!

A part of me feels that I don't need this kind of treatment. I am on a church mission and trying to serve the Lord. When I kissed Brandi, I was young and being naive, and I didn't want to be tied down to one girl. I really do not need a girlfriend at all right now; it's too distracting....

But then, the other part of me is happy when I receive letters from her. Although the letters are far-and-few-between lately, I suppose not everyone can be as good as I am at writing letters. I really do not know what to think about Kaesi. I mean...I'm on a mission...so who needs women? I get the impression that she knows she has me in the palm of her hand for two years, while she can go out and date. It sounds lowdown, but that's the way it goes. I still love her. I also know she is great looking.

After stewing over my girlfriend situation, Elder Evans and I waited two-hours for Brother Broderick to bring us another case of *Book of Mormons*. The plan was to hand out twelve copies by the end of the evening. However, we only managed to give out five, which placed us at our goal of fourteen copies for the week. I was so tired when we went tracting, but we did it! The wonderful thing was that we gave out five *Book of Mormons* to some kindhearted people. We even met a lady named Pam, who had already had the Missionary Discussions, and even attended church once. She looks solid for baptism. Pam has not had The Discussions since last summer, so we can totally teach her again.

In addition to meeting our *Book of Mormon* placement goal, we met a part-member, Sister Sandgren, who has an 8-year-old son named C.J. She told us that she would like to see C.J. get baptized. This morning, we attended our regular weekly District Meeting; it was great!

Elder Ian Stevenson, the elder from London, was cracking me up. We talked about how irreverent the wards are here in Fontana. It has been getting so bad that our investigators are beginning to complain about the noise levels in Sacrament Meeting.

After District Meeting, Brother Broderick was nice enough to drive Elder Evans and me to Riverside to purchase a few bicycle parts. I bought a new rear derailer for $14.00 and a rear bike rack for $16.00, but I got a great deal.

After shopping for bicycle parts, Brother Broderick invited us to join his family for an all-you-can-eat afternoon at Sizzler. It cost $20.00 for both Elder Evans and I.

We had T-bone and ribs, and I was loving every minute of it. Elder Evans and I are thinking about helping Brother Broderick with some yard work. Aren't we nice elders?

After lunch, we went right back into the field. Of course, we went tracting and followed through with several members about *Book of Mormon* placements. While tracting, we met some goodhearted people, and it was clear that the Lord was really blessing us in this area of the vineyard.

After tracting for a few hours, we returned to the place where we left our bicycles except—they were both gone. We walked around and asked a few neighbors if they had seen anything unusual, or if someone had stolen our bicycles. However, everyone we asked said they hadn't seen our bikes. I could not believe it. I said to Elder Evans, "Do you think someone could have stolen our bicycles?" I mean...here we were doing the Lord's work, and now our bikes were gone? It was not possible. We decided to continue searching, and then about ten-minutes later, we discovered that one of the neighbors had moved our bicycles from the sidewalk into the backyard for safety reasons. Whew! Elder Evans and I had our bicycles back. It was time for a celebration, and we sang, "Hallelujah!"

I have not been thinking about Kaesi lately, even though my memoir suggests differently. It is just that I believe she did me wrong. She totally screwed up by treating our relationship like a yo-yo, and now it's my turn to return the favor. I know I have mentioned this before, but she keeps bringing up the past. My whole purpose in serving a mission is to help people repent and move on with their lives. This lady will not let me do it! She has the memory of an elephant. One little kiss, and the entire world has ended. Well...while I haven't decided what I am going to do yet, I'm sure I'll think of something.

The church is so true, and I love the gospel and Jesus Christ with all my heart. One of the main purposes of the Plan of Salvation is to be forgiven of our sins. Thank goodness for the Savior, who made it all possible. Jesus will always be paramount in my life, and my family comes in a close second. I know that what I am doing is right, and that it is what the Lord wants me to do. The gospel is true. It is as simple as that.

***

Today was Fast Sunday, so Elder Evans and I are fasting that our investigators and other individuals we meet will be baptized. This month is looking good, especially for the Fontana First Ward. I am excited and happy that the Lord has given us this opportunity to teach the gospel of Jesus Christ.

During Ward Correlation Meeting in the Fontana Fifth Ward, Brother Hadden was mellow. He did not mention anything about Louis except that he needed fellowshipping. The meeting moved forward without a hiccup, and everything appeared to be okay.

I know the Lord will bless Elder Evans and I if we follow the rules and obey the commandments of God. That is a BIG one. We are representatives of the Lord and Savior Jesus Christ, and as such, we have a huge responsibility to serve him while serving on a mission. This is the Lord's work. In other words, I am helping to bring souls to Jesus, and I am playing a huge role in Heavenly Father's plan. Why else would Satan be in the world, trying to stop and discourage us? Because we are going about our Father's business! The Plan of our Heavenly Father is a wonderful roadmap back to Him; it is serious and sacred, and Heavenly Father has made it possible for us to teach this special message to everyone. I love my family very much, and I love my mission.

After tracting for three months, I have developed an awareness of people in general. In other words, I have a theory on the average American person. My theory is that there are good and bad people in this world but, at the end of the day, I love people no matter where they fall on that spectrum.

Today was P-day, again! We woke around 9:00 a.m., ate breakfast, and showered. I love sleeping in on Mondays. Then we washed our dirty laundry. I tried to get a haircut, but all the stores were closed. I suppose they figure, 'its P-day for the missionaries,' and so the owners decide to close the barber shops and board up the bike stores....

Our zone is putting together a Christmas video called the "Mormon Rap." There are several missionaries in our zone who are singing the lyrics, and I am one of them! The gist of the song is to incorporate rap with humor, and we are filming it tomorrow at the stake center.

After completing our chores, we all met at President Gourdin's house for our "Zone of the Month" celebration. We ate lasagna and watched the movie, Lady Hawk. Then President Gourdin gave us some helpful hints regarding our investigators and teaching pool and admonished us to do the following: invite members to every discussion, ask for referrals from investigators, and contact investigators every day. I'm feeling excited about this month because the work is beginning to sizzle.

After our celebration at the mission president's house, we went home, and I decided to write Kaesi a letter. I told her that I am sick of her ignoring me, and that I was sick of all her garbage. She is finished. Just kidding. I wrote Kaesi the best letter I think I have ever written, and she will die when she receives it. She will love me to death. It is a good thing I am on a mission, because otherwise she would attack me. I love my mission, the Lord, my testimony, and my family and friends.

This morning, we taught Peter and read from the Book of Mormon. I pray that he will continue to read and pray about the scriptures.

After teaching Peter, we met at the stake center as a zone to film our Christmas video. It was great, and we had a lot of fun filming it. We all got in a semi-circle and did the "Mormon Rap." I rapped the words, "We've got the goals, we must achieve, and some of them you won't believe!" as I untied my tie and wrapped it around my head. I hope the video turns out good!

After producing our MTV-worthy music video, Elder Hedelius and I voted in the presidential election. George H. Bush will be the next president of the United States. I don't think California had a whole lot to do with it, but it was still fun voting. President Bush won 426 electoral votes and Michael

Dukakis had 111 electoral votes. I enjoy fulfilling my civic duties and responsibilities.

Tonight, Elder Evans and I had a dinner appointment at Reid Furniss' house. He is a generous guy; I like him. He offered to take us thrifting[49] in San Bernardino sometime. I definitely need some new slacks!

After dinner, Reid told me that he has been able to sleep better for the past month, after Elder Clark and I blessed his home. Reid also said that his friendship with Rick has improved. I love my mission because I love blessing other people's lives. Currently, this is exactly where I need to be in my life.

Today I feel an overwhelming pressure to do missionary work. I am hungry for baptisms this month, and I know we can do it with the special aid of our Heavenly Father. My whole mission in life is to find, teach, and baptize. I want to work hard, learn from my experiences, and follow the rules. I know the Lord is blessing me, and that He knows I will be an effective missionary. I must do my best. I love the scriptures, especially the *Book of Mormon*. It is the most inspirational canon of scripture I've ever read. Since the start of my mission, I've read at least thirty minutes to an hour from the *Book of Mormon* every morning for personal study.

We followed through and taught C.J. Sandgren the 1st Discussion. He is very shy, but a real nice kid who enjoys attending Cub Scouts and primary at church. He also has two cute sisters. I do not see a reason why he shouldn't get baptized.

This morning, I received a phone call from my grandparents, who live in Brea, California. They called to invite Elder Evans and me to dinner and to spend Thanksgiving with them and the Stirling family. There are rules against going to dinner with my grandparents outside the Fontana area. However, I must get permission from President Gourdin to leave the San Bernardino Mission because Brea is out of the mission area. However, anything is possible. If I do not ask, I will never know.

Later this afternoon, we picked up two new investigators: a person from tracting and a second person from a part-member family. The Lord is really blessing me when I do what I am supposed to do. I love my mission because it teaches me so many valuable things. The temporal world moves along at its own pace, but I am on a mission for the Lord and as such I'm on a higher "spiritual plane." I have grown so much; it's incredible. The Lord is really pouring down His blessings upon me.

In summary, today was an incredible one, and Elder Evans and I worked tirelessly all day long. We only took a thirty-minute break for lunch and then we were back out in the field. I like to keep busy, because I feel good knowing I have accomplished good things for the Lord.

The next morning, Elder Evans and I had a two-hour companion study on the Twelve Tribes of Israel. I learned a lot from studying Genesis in the Old Testament, and then we were trying to figure out what tribe Lehi came from. After some debate, we decided that he must have come from the tribe of Joseph. I learned a lot from our debate, and now have a better understanding of the Twelve Tribes of Israel.

After companion study, it was time to proselyte in the field. We met with five part- member families. However, no one accepted our invitation to come to church, nor to schedule any follow-up appointments to teach The Discussions. We did not find a whole lot of success, but I still felt good about the work we have been doing.

I do not regret my decision to go on a mission for one second. Serving the Lord is the greatest event of my life and is a wonderful blessing. Missionary work is tough, and it seems like it never gets any easier. We meet people every day—some good and some bad. And yet, the Lord knows the kind of effort I am putting forth. I really want to serve, and the Lord is going to bless me for doing so. I know He will.

Missionary work is tough, but I love it so much. Ever since I was a small boy in primary class at church, I have wanted to serve a mission and worship the Lord.

I was thinking today about all my old buddies on missions. I miss them so badly. The times we all shared on Boy Scout

super trips, summer camp, youth conferences, dances, etc....
These events and activities were the greatest...because I have
nothing but great memories of them.

I really cannot express in words how good it felt to be relaxed and comfortable hanging with my good, true-blue friends:
JR Howard, Ben Dieterle, and Jeff Humphrey were only a few.
Scott Hammond, Chris Autry, Brian Voyles, and Todd Dudley
were a few more. I miss these guys, and the good 'ol times we
shared together. I really do. I thank the Lord every day for allowing me to go on a mission.

This morning our zone had a "Missionary Tract Out," where
all the missionaries got together in one area went tracting.
During the event, Zone #4 placed over one hundred *Book of
Mormons*, and I teamed-up with a church member, Elder Creel,
and his daughter. We had remarkable success in placing five
Book of Mormons in one hour! The Lord truly answers prayers
and gives of His spirit, without which we could not teach.

After tracting, Elder Evans and I followed through with
five additional part-member families and three call-backs. We
also scheduled three teaching appointments. We were are on
a roll, and it was a productive day. I am getting really pumped
up about the work.

My confidence is growing as I continue to serve the Lord. I
contemplate the magnitude and responsibility I must help gather
the house of Israel in Southern California. I am on a mission serving my fellow man and my God. The change that has taken place
within my soul has been gradual. I have grown spiritually, ma-
tured emotionally, and of course—I am better looking than ever.
Just kidding! The Lord is watching over me though, and I know
additional blessings are in store if I continue to live righteously.

My thoughts drift to my personal life regarding Kaesi. I hav-
en't received a letter from her this week. It really does not bother
me. However, it makes me wonder. I don't know what to think
about our relationship as boyfriend and girlfriend anymore.

The other day, I was speaking with a return missionary
(RM), Steve Capps, in the Fontana Fifth Ward about Kaesi. He

said, "Things just change sometimes, between a man and a woman." He had a girlfriend during his mission. They wrote to one another for two-years. However, when he returned home, the relationship had changed. They grew apart because they were now two totally different people.

I am not thinking this is what is going to happen between Kaesi and Elder Todd, but I really don't know. Who is to say? Things have definitely changed a little, and to be honest, I have mixed feelings about her. I will keep trying to work on the relationship but, in the end, I must ask myself this question: "Will Kaesi help me become a better person, and vice versa?" I just hope she invests in her own self-development while I'm gone. As I strive to do the same, I know the Lord will bless me.

***

Today we had Ward Conference in the Fontana Fifth Ward, and President Bringhurst attended most of the meetings. During the "President's Meeting," he encouraged us to love our families, wives, and children. He said, "The love in a family unit is essential for a happy and lovely home. We can feel love from others when family practices love and unity. The family is the source of some of our greatest joys and happiness in life."

President Bringhurst's talk touched my heart and it made me realize an important principle: any "ah-ha" moment is a positive adjustment to my mission way of life and thinking, and I need to rely more heavily on the promptings of the Holy Ghost with the spirit of humility. Opposingly, I need to resist "Elder Todd's way of teaching." This is a faith promoting moment. I must humble myself if I am to develop spiritually. I know the Lord will bless me for my efforts. I love Jesus Christ and my mission call. President Bringhurst's inspired words also reminded me of the love I have for my remarkable family.

I slept in on P-day again, which is the most wonderful feeling in the world. When we finally got out of bed, we did our regular chores. Then we met with our zone to play a couple of hours of basketball this afternoon. I usually bring my pen and paper to finish writing my letters on the stage in-between games. It's also fun working up a sweat and being competitive with the guys.

After playing basketball and relaxing, we showered and changed into our batman suits (i.e., our regular mission attire). Then we had a second appointment with an investigator (Nancy), who we found through tracting. As she stood us up for the 1st Discussion a week ago, we decided to just break-the-ice and visit with her casually. She answered the front door and invited us to pick olives from her tree in the backyard. After picking a bowl full of olives, she invited us to dinner.

Our last appointment was with C.J. Sandgren. We taught him the 2nd Discussion, "The Gospel of Jesus Christ". He is such a good kid, and I like him a lot. We're excited that he committed to be baptized on the 26th of November. Elder Evans and I will have our second baptism! The Lord continues to bless us.

This morning we had Zone Conference. It was excellent and I received a lot of solid information. Elder Packard was transferred to another zone, and our new zone leader is now Elder Hancey. He is a sharp dude.

After losing one of our zone leaders, Elder Rogers and Elder Hancey were made the new "Zone Heads." Here is a list of things that Elder Hancey talked about:

1. Missionaries need to repent too.
2. Try to improve our attitude and follow The Spirit.
3. Fast and pray on a regular basis.
4. It is important to seek the Lord's guidance. When we do, we say what the Lord wants us to say.

Elder Hancey continued, listing a few ideas to help our investigators:

1. Allow investigators to feel The Spirit.
2. Investigators need to pray and ask God for themselves about the gospel.
3. Treat all investigators like members.
4. Picture investigators dressed in white and getting baptized.

The takeaway for me was that I need to be more obedient to the Lord while I am serving my mission. Also, I need to rely more on The Spirit when I teach. I know if I do these things, the Lord will greatly bless my companionship. He loves Elder Evans and I because He wants us to be happy and succeed.

After Zone Conference, we met with two investigators and read from the *Book of Mormon*. I feel the strong influence of The Spirit when I read God's word.

Later this evening, Elder Evans and I had a dinner appointment with the Goddard family and ate a delicious chili dish. Then we watched the video, "How Rare a Possession." It was such a great video! It was amazing to see how much faith Vincenzo Di Francesca, an Italian Pastor, had when he joined The Church of Jesus Christ of Latter-day Saints. The church is true no matter how you look at it.

Today we attended Multi Zone Conference. This was the second day in a row spent sitting down for eight long hours of instruction from The Spirit. I'm o.k. with one long day, but two in a row causes issue for me and the ADHD, which kicks in from time to time. As a result, I must do everything in my power to pay attention, and now I am absolutely exhausted.

The first speaker was Brother Warren, who developed a unique learning and memorization system using 3 x 5 index cards. Brother Warren utilized high school and college students to use his learning system, and those students made straight A's at BYU-Provo.

He then gave a three-hour presentation on how we can memorize our discussion scriptures quickly and easily. I really could have used Brother Warren's teaching method a few months ago when I was trying to obtain my "Master Teacher" certificate. His presentation was interesting. Brother Warren makes learning fun because we get to use our imagination when remembering individual names.

The last speaker was President Gourdin, who counseled us with ten things we could improve on individually while on our mission:

1. It's important to build a love for the people we labor with in California.
2. Increase the love we have for our parents.
3. Have an appreciation for working hard.
4. Understand the importance of teamwork.
5. Have a knowledge and love for the scriptures as the word of God.
6. Be available for inspiration in your life. Concerning the companionship of the Holy Ghost—live and work for it.
7. Have the humility to pray and seek to communicate directly with God.
8. Act in faith and be a doer of the word.
9. Guard the beauty and value of personal virtue.
10. Strengthen your testimony.

In addition to the ten values of love, President Gourdin encouraged us to visualize, in our minds, investigators dressed in white and standing in the water ready to be baptized. He also stressed the importance of a positive mental attitude.

After Multi-Zone Conference, Elder Evans and I taught Charlie Hammond the 1st Discussion. Charlie is 10-years old, and the son of a part-member family. I really like him a lot and know he will be baptized. The work is moving forward, and things are looking great. The Lord has blessed our companionship, and I know that He will continue to bless us as we live the commandments of God.

Before retiring to bed, Elder Evans and I had companion inventory[50]. I have had several companion inventory meetings with each of my companions. During this particular meeting, I read from Alma 7:23 in the *Book of Mormon*:

And now I would that ye should be humble, and be submissive and gentle; easy to be entreated; full of patience and long suffering; being temperate in all things; being diligent in keeping the commandments of God at all times; asking for whatsoever things ye stand in need, both spiritual and temporal; always returning thanks unto God for whatsoever things ye do receive.

In addition, we read Doctrine & Covenants 4:6. "Remember faith, virtue, knowledge, temperance, patience, brotherly kindness, godliness, charity, humility, diligence." Patience is a God-like quality. We need to obtain it in order to inherit the kingdom of God. I am going to try to develop this trait better. In conclusion, Elder Evans and I agreed that we need to develop more patience towards one another. We believe it is a goal we can achieve this month.

The next morning, Elder Evans and I went to the Fontana library to plan our day. We followed through with a couple part member families. After our visits, we decided to stop by Sister Causey's house. She could not talk long, but she scheduled a dinner appointment to have pizza at her place. Elder Evans and I really appreciated the kind gesture.

After working in the field all morning, we headed back to our apartment for lunch. While we were eating our sandwiches, the telephone rings. Elder Evans got up to answer it. And lo and behold it was President Gourdin and he asked to speak with me.

I know that the mission president only calls for two reasons: to make an emergency or midnight transfer or there is a specific issue. I quickly accessed that I was not being transferred from Fontana because regular transfers are not for at least two or three weeks.

I got up and Elder Evans handed me the phone. I grabbed the receiver and said, "Hello, President Gourdin." He asked, "Hi, Elder Todd. Do you know of anyone who you and Elder Evans encountered while tracting that may have gotten offended by something you guys said?" I thought for a second and said, "No."

President Gourdin asked, "Do you remember a Rachel Lee?" I replied, "Yes, that name rings a bell." He asked me, "Well, could you explain what happened?"

And I proceeded to tell him my side of the story. I said, "We introduced ourselves and got into somewhat of a heated discussion about the trinity. There was some contention between us. Elder Evans and I did not feel that we offended Rachel or her religion. In fact, we ended the conversation with a smile and shook hands."

After I spoke, President Gourdin told me her side of the story. President Gourdin said, "Rachel telephoned the mission office and was very upset. She said that if we ever stopped by her neighborhood again, she would call the police." I was surprised and I was not surprised. He continued, "Here is what I want you and Elder Evans to do. You are each going to write a letter apologizing for offending her. Then, drop your letters in Rachel's mailbox. I would not tract in her neighborhood for a least a month."

Naturally, President Gourdin gave me some counsel. He said, "Sometimes you need to teach with precaution when speaking with people and most importantly use the spirit." His last departing words, "Elder Todd, please be careful out there, o.k.?" I replied, "Yes, sir" and that was it. I hung up the phone and thought to myself, "This is total baloney." We will find out the outcome tomorrow.

I am not frustrated with President Gourdin, but I think the whole situation stinks. I smell a rat. The reason why I think the story is made up by Rachel is because there were two Jehovah Witnesses listening to our conversation next door. I believe it was the Jehovah Witnesses that called the mission office and not Rachel.

After dropping off our apology letters, we followed President Gourdin's counsel and tracted on the other side of Fontana First Ward. We were tracting on Owen Street and came upon a member's home, Sister Simmons. She lit up a cigarette and I assume she is less active. She invited us in her home, and we sat down.

Sister Simmons told us about her conversion story and how the missionaries and the church members play an active role in her life. She is a nice lady. She said, "I'm going through a lot right now. My husband and I are separated, and things aren't looking too good between us." Sister Simmons continued, and she had a pleasant grin on her face. "But, when things are going wrong in my life, somehow the Lord knows. He sends the missionaries or a ward member calls or checks up on me to see how I'm doing." She really wants us to come back to talk to her some more.

The rest of the day was uneventful, and we headed to our first of two dinner appointments this evening. One with the Wickstrom's and the other with the Causey family. I have a real good feeling about Sister Causey. I believe she will be baptized. We had a delicious pizza dinner and then watched the video, "The Plan of our Heavenly Father." It is an excellent video. After watching the video and feeling The Spirit, Sister Causey told us that she would read a couple chapters from the Book of Mormon.

After meeting with Sister Causey, we headed home. I reflected on the inspiring video and think about my own family back home in Georgia. I realize that my very own family is especially important to me. I love the gospel with all my heart. It fills my soul with joy and love. And I want to share it with everyone. I just pray the Lord will find me worthy enough to have His spirit to be with me always.

The next day brought the fury and the almighty winds from Santa Ana. All I can say is wind, wind, and more wind. The Santa Ana winds were whipping through Fontana like something fierce today. It was something else.

The name Santa Ana winds or "Santana Winds" is traced to Spanish California. According to historical records, the winds were called Caliente aliento de Satanas, or 'Hot breath of Satan,' due to their heat. They really do feel like Satan, breathing and spewing sand and dust everywhere.

We had a rough start to our morning and tracked for two and a half hours without placing one single copy of the Book of Mor-

mon. It was really depressing. We need to give away five copies of the *Book of Mormon* to reach our weekly goal of fourteen books. To add insult to injury, we had two appointments that were "no shows." We knocked on their doors and no one was home. We were exhausted and needed a much-deserved break from proselyting and the blasted wind, so we decided to head back to our apartment for lunch. This time, I did not receive a phone call from the President Gourdin for ticking off a non-member.

After recharging our physical batteries, we tracted some more, believing our fortune would change. However, we still had no luck placing copies of the *Book of Mormon*. At this point, I was getting frustrated.

We decided to switch things up and followed through with a call-back Elder Clark and Elder Stevenson had tracted out named Robyn. He is a cool guy, a young and handsome fellow. He said, "My wife just gave birth to our 9 lb. baby girl yesterday."

I replied, "Congratulations on the new bundle of joy." He continued, "I read 3 Nephi Chapter 11 and I really enjoyed the passage of scripture." We talked for a few minutes and scheduled a follow up visit. The good news brightened our spirits on an otherwise dismal day.

We felt encouraged, so we decided to do a couple more hours of tracting, and lo-and-behold we met a lady named Gail. She accepted a copy of the *Book of Mormon* and told us she was a Nazarene. Then Elder Evans heard a parrot talking inside the house and asked, "What kind of bird is that?" The next thing I know, I am standing in her backyard looking at several birds. (Elder Evans knows a few things about birds because he used to work at a pet store in Missouri before his mission.) Then Gail introduced us to her husband, Ralph. She said, "Ralph, I want you to stick your nose in this book." I chuckled to myself.

We talked about the birds for a few minutes and then Ralph and Gail invited us into their home. The next thing I knew, we are in their kitchen eating cake, cookies and drinking milk. It was delicious. We talked for about two hours. Ralph and Gail are some of the finest people I have met, super folks. We played with the birds and talked. Gail said, "I feel like I'm your mother telling you guys to wear your coats and eat more food." Then she looks at me and said, "Elder Todd, you're too skinny."

After meeting with this fine couple, the spirit of the Lord was upon us again. Elder Evans and I decided to ride through the neighborhood and follow the spirit as we delivered four copies of the *Book of Mormon* in just thirty minutes. We were doing well, with just one more delivery needed to reach our goal. However, Satan had other plans, and he really did not want us to place that last book. And, within a few minutes, the devil began working on our companionship and the people we met. One guy completely cussed us out—and we hadn't even said a word to him. We left in a huff, and naturally, Elder Evans and I grew frustrated with one another, and the frustration ended in an argument.

We decided to take another much-needed break after a long but productive day. After tracting, we headed to the Fontana First Ward Thanksgiving dinner at the church. When we arrived, we met a young lady who told us she wanted to hear the discussions and get baptized. I said, "Super, we have a gift to give you." The Lord loves to bless His faithful missionaries and, as a result, we delivered our fifth *Book of Mormon* for the day.

***

I have not written in my mission memoir for a couple of days because Elder Evans and I have been so busy. After the Ward Thanksgiving Party, we added another investigator at church on Sunday named Sally, whose boyfriend is a member. Elder Evans and I taught her the 1st Discussion during the investigator class. The Lord works in mysterious ways; it's fantastic.

After teaching Sally, we met Ivan. He seemed really interested and wanted to know more about the church. We have eight people in our teaching pool with a potential for five baptisms this month. I am excited. The Lord has truly blessed us. I pray that I can continue to be worthy of the many blessings that

He is giving me. There are certain things that I need to continue working on—like keeping my bedroom clean. I can hear my mother's voice in my head to "clean my room." Oh, no, the mother's curse is working.

The Thanksgiving Holiday is coming soon, and I cannot wait. It is going to be great. It's going to be weird spending the holidays without my family, but I suppose I can hack it.

The next day we were on fire with teaching appointments and taught three standard church Discussions. The Lord really is pouring out His spirit and blessings. I can see the hand of the Lord in all that we do. He has blessed us beyond measure. I'm thankful that my very own family in Georgia can share in the blessings that I am receiving here in California.

I believe one of our investigators, Nancy, who lives in the Fontana First Ward, will be baptized as soon as she attends church on Sunday. I feel good about Nancy, and I know that if she asks our Heavenly Father if The Church of Jesus Christ of Latter-day Saints is true, He will answer her prayer. She is a great lady. I pray that the Lord will help her understand the importance of the gospel and how it can affect her life in a positive and life-changing way.

After teaching Nancy, we met with C.J. Sandgren. He is progressing nicely, and I feel he will be baptized around the first week of December. Our third teaching appointment is with another golden investigator, Marie Inman. She is a foster child of Brother and Sister Inman; two wonderful people. This humble couple opens their home to foster and handicap children. Marie will be ready for baptism soon.

I thank the Lord for our many blessings. Currently, I know serving my mission in Fontana is where I need to be. I know that my older brother, Jesus Christ, lives. He has a tremendous love for each one of us; his brother and sisters. Missionary work is an incredible job. It is so important to share the gospel with others. I want to learn more about the gospel because I love it so much.

The next morning Elder Evans and I went on splits with the zone leaders. Elder Rogers and I went to the Fontana Fifth

Ward and met two families; it was great. We met the Tuomaia family. There are four potential baptisms in their home. The Lord loves blessing his missionaries.

After meeting with the families, Elder Rogers and I met the rest of the district at our apartment. Elder Hedelius, Elder Murdoch, and I visited one of their investigators in the Fontana Second Ward for lunch. Elder Murdoch is a brand-new missionary from the MTC. I was starving, so I ate a lot of turkey, potatoes, bread, and vegetables. I absolutely stuffed myself. The other elders biked home...but I just rolled.

After lunch, Elder Murdoch and I went tracting. Together with The Spirit, we really do make the best Tracting Team. Elder Murdoch is energetic and gung-ho like me, so we pack a one-two punch. We were fortunate enough to give away five copies of the *Book of Mormon* today. It was fun because we have a positive attitude.

Later in the evening, Elder Hedelius and Elder Evans were not feeling well, so they stayed at the apartment to rest while Elder Whyte, a Spanish Elder, and I went to a dinner appointment to teach Charlie Hammond the 2nd Discussion. The Lord continues to pour out His spirit, and Charlie is now scheduled for baptism on the 17th of December. I give credit to the Lord for everything I do because without the spirit, I am nothing. The Lord has tremendous and sacred power. I have grown tremendously since the beginning of my mission. I can feel my testimony grow, and I owe it all to the Lord.

Happy Turkey Day! We spent our Thanksgiving dinner with Reid Furniss and his family. The dinner was so delicious. We watched about twenty minutes-worth of football games and then two movie videos: "The Wizard of Oz" and "ET." I like "ET," especially when he says, "Phone home, phone home." It was a pleasant and relaxing afternoon.

After an exquisite meal, Elder Evans and I decided to get a couple of hours of missionary work in because we are missionaries. We traveled to Mae Williams' house to visit with her family.

We had an interesting conversation with Mae's father, Hugh Williams, and his friend, both of whom attend a local religious school. The conversation started out cordial and friendly. Then I turned to a scripture in the Holy Bible, and read it to the group. However, once I tried to comment or explain the verse in my own words, I could not get a word in edgewise because the gentlemen kept interrupting me every time I tried to speak. I started getting angry because they continued cutting me off, even mid-sentence. They absolutely would not allow me to explain myself. After some time, I realized that normal conversation with these two would be impossible, so I just let them talk and did not say much after that. I know that may be surprising to those who know me well, but it's the truth.

The Spirit did not return until Hugh and his friend left the house. At this point, Elder Evans and I were able to continue a friendly conversation with Mae. The Lord willing, I feel we can baptize her soon.

After a lively meeting with the Williams family, we returned to our apartment. I telephoned home just like ET (Elder Todd). It was great speaking with my parents and the rest of the family. I feel like I have the best family in the world, and I am thankful for each member of my family. I am so glad I have a loving, supportive, and caring support network back home. It brings me a lot of comfort during times of trouble and self-doubt. This is the Lord's work, and it will be carried forward. I love the gospel Jesus Christ with all my heart.

The next morning it was cold, wet, and extremely windy. Did I mention that the wind was blowing especially hard? It was the kind of weather that chills you to the bone! Despite the weather conditions, we decided to try some good 'ol fashion tracting. Elder Evans and I managed to deliver a grand total of fourteen copies of the *Book of Mormon* this week. The Lord has also blessed us with three solid call-backs.

We managed to dry off before our dinner appointment at the Causey's home. I'm not sure about Sister Causey, who seems to be hiding from The Spirit. Elder Evans and I will get on our knees and ask for guidance and wisdom from our Heavenly Father regarding her spiritual nature.

We received an update from the mission office regarding Rachel Lee's altercation a week ago. Rachel not only called President Gourdin, but she wrote him a personal letter. Wow! I completely missed the boat on this situation, thinking the Jehovah Witnesses were up to no good. On the contrary. In fact, I grossly underestimated Rachel's anger towards us. I cannot believe she went to all that trouble just to make Elder Evans and me look bad! The devil is out there, and he wants to try to stop us. However, I cannot deny the truth. The truth is of God, and I cannot deny God. I love being a missionary and I will persevere through trials and tribulations.

I am not sure if this is directly related to the Rachel dilemma or if we're pushing our companionship to the brink, but Elder Evans is the one person on this planet who's testing my patience to the max. Frustratingly, we got into another verbal fight tonight. Man, I only pray that he is willing to make an attitude adjustment and change his life to be in harmony with The Spirit.

The next morning, our district met at the Bloomington building for our weekly meeting. We all had to take the memorization test on the pathway to Master Teacher. It was fun, and I hope I did well.

After the meeting, we decided to go on splits. Elder Murdoch and I teamed up and Elder Hedelius and Elder Evans teamed up. Then Elder Murdoch and I followed through with a few people in his area; we had a fun time.

Later in the afternoon, we attended a Ward luncheon at the Bloomington building and had the opportunity of meeting several members and one new investigator. I noticed Elder Murdoch speaking with a handicap child. He really loves interacting with those who have special abilities. Elder Murdoch says he feels a tremendous amount of love radiating from their souls. He is a cool stud. I like him a lot because he is sincere about his convictions.

After the Ward function, Elder Evans and I went back to our apartment. Our companionship has experienced the ups and downs of missionary work, so we decided to blow off a little steam and clean our apartment—especially our bedroom. We just couldn't stand the clutter anymore and decided it was time to do some fall cleaning! We did "the works;" deep house-cleaning at its finest. First, we tackled our bedroom. We cleaned our closet and even under the bed. Then we vacuumed, took out the trash, and rearranged the furniture in our little 9 ft. x 9 ft. bedroom.

We were on such a roll, we decided not to stop there. Since dirt and debris tends to roll downhill, we vacuumed the stairs and downstairs living room. Then we swept and mopped the kitchen floor. We even repaired a broken door on the closet. Once we completed the bulk of our tasks, Elder Evans and I felt a lot better in our spik-and-span clean room. My mom would absolutely die with joy if she could see me now. Currently, we are living the good life; cleanliness is next to godliness.

***

The next day marks my fourth month serving my two-year church mission. When I look back, I am amazed that I've accomplished so much in so little time. Here are a few goals that I have achieved: (1) Successful mission farewell (2) Graduated from the MTC (3) I'm on my fourth companionship and trained two elders (4) Baptized Louis Martorella (5) Gave away numerous copies of the *Book of Mormon*.

After church service, our entire district ate lunch at an investigator's house in the Fontana Second Ward. It was a great meal and gave us the opportunity to fellowship with that beautiful family.

When we got home, Elder Evans and I saddled up our bicycles and rode towards a few investigators and part-member families in our ward. We made an appointment to teach The Discussions to Sister Ann Levinson and her son Sean. Sister

Levinson's mother is an active member, so Ann was exposed to the church growing up. The Levinson's are a nice family.

The next morning, our zone leaders drove our district to play basketball near South Ridge in the Fontana Sixth Ward. The games were held at a wealthy member's house, who just happens to own a full outdoor basketball court. The backboards were even made of glass. It was great and we had a blast.

After playing basketball, the zone met at the Rialto Stake Center to watch the video, "Princess Bride." That is a great movie. The first time I saw "Princess Bride" was about a year ago at our annual Young Men's scuba diving trip to Florida. The scuba diving trip was a lot of fun. "As you wish!"

The next day, all I can say is "wind, wind...and wind!" The Santa Ana winds blew hard all day long. I was exhausted by the time 12:00 noon came around. The wind fighting against my bicycle literally took all my energy. It was a tough day, to say the least.

Elder Evans and I tried hard to spread the gospel. However, despite our best efforts, we had several investigators cancel their appointments. We tried to make the best of it, so we tracted. However, it seemed like Murphy's Law was following us, and tracting turned out to be rather nonproductive. Our only teaching appointment with Marie Innam, turned out to be a bummer too.

We taught Marie the 2nd Discussion. I am not sure if it was the general feeling in the air, but she was very tired, and had a short attention span. The good news is that she agreed to be baptized the first week of January.

Although today was not one of my best days, I know the Lord is looking after me. The Lord is blessing me every minute of the day. My secret formula for success is Faith + Working Hard = The Spirit. The Spirit converts, and that leads to baptism. I love the gospel Jesus Christ with all my heart. My family is my pride and joy. I am thankful for each one of them.

The next morning during my personal scripture study, I'm in awe reading the *Book of Mormon*. I believe it is the most incredible book! We are so fortunate to have this book of sacred scripture in our midst today.

I am just beginning to scratch the service of the wonderful teachings that the *Book of Mormon* has to offer. If I obey the prophet's voice, the Lord has promised to bless me as a son of God. I absolutely love reading the word of God—the truth! Every time I read; I simply cannot put the book down. I get so engrossed in pondering the word.

I enjoy feasting upon the word of the ancient prophets who were inspired of God to testify of the Lord and Savior Jesus Christ.

Currently, I am reading Alma Chapter 18 about the Sons of Mosiah and Ammon. In this chapter, Alma talks about the great conversion among the Lamanites. It is an incredible and inspiring missionary story and is beautifully written. I love it!

After a day of proselyting, I had the unique opportunity of being in the "Eagle's Nest" at a Boy Scout Court of Honor held for Aaron Weitzel. It was fantastic! The Mayor of Fontana was there, and he personally congratulated Aaron.

It made me so proud, deep down inside my little scout soul, that I had become an Eagle. I was overcome with emotion and pride, remembering my own Eagle Scout of Honor. At the time, I was fourteen-years old and "graduated" together with Jeff Humphrey, Casey Barnes, and Mark Newton. So, of course, I welcomed Aaron Weitzel with open arms into the Eagle's Nest.

What a terrific honor! It was great getting my Eagle. I remember people clapping, cameras flashing, and the tremendous feeling of doing the right thing—success! It was a feeling that I will always cherish deep, deep inside my soul. I feel that the pathway to Eagle helped me make the decision to serve a mission. I overcame a lot of obstacles and completed two Eagle projects to achieve Scouting's highest rank.

The reason for two projects was due to me not getting permission from the Atlanta Area Council to do my first project. My dad invited me on a white-water canoe trip for Eagle Scouts in the Roswell, Georgia area. He allowed young men who completed their project before the river trip to attend. To meet the deadline, I rushed my Eagle Project without getting prior approval. Later the project was rejected because I didn't follow the rules. A powerful lesson for a 13-year-old....

After the river trip, I became so discouraged that I decided not to do another Eagle Project. However, shortly after my decision, Brother Paul Varney, (my Scoutmaster) stopped by my house to visit. We met and talked for a few minutes about how I was feeling. Then he left a small wooden plaque with the Eagle Badge and the words, "Do It Now," quoted by President Kimball inscribed on the bottom.

Brother Varney's small act of kindness inspired me to submit the paperwork for my second Eagle Project. Shortly after it was approved by the council, I completed my "successful run" in the Boy Scouts. Besides, building a wooden board game for children with learning disabilities was way more fun than my first project. Plus, I learned a powerful lesson: Persevere and never give up, even in the face of aversity!

I am proud to serve God. This is where I need to be. I am so thankful for the chance to go on a mission. I love the gospel with all my heart, and I have a strong testimony that serving as a missionary is a God-like quality.

The next morning, Elder Evans and I decided to ride to the park and hand out a few copies of the *Book of Mormon*. We did not hold back and looked for an opportunity to "open [our] mouth[s]," as Elder Rex Pinegar suggested in his book.

We met a guy named Jeff who is a Baptist. Jeff had an awful lot of questions for us. Man! It was tough, but The Spirit was with us, and it helped us testify to Jeff of the truthfulness of the gospel.

It felt like we were in a spiritual battle. Elder Evans and I were struggling with Jeff because of his doubts on Mormons and what we believe as a church. We were going back and forth, and I could not help but think about the story of Ammon when he converted all the stiff-necked people. Jeff claimed that he had read a couple of passages from the *Book of Mormon*. With the help of The Spirit, I was able to get Jeff committed to read a few more passages. So hopefully in the new future, Elder Evans and I will see him in the park again.

After speaking with Jeff, we rode back to our apartment to go on splits with Elder Hedelius and Elder Murdoch. The remainder of the day went great. Our district made up a song for Elder Murdoch. We took the idea from "Sufin Bird—Bird is the Word," by The Trashman. It goes something like this: "Murd, Murd, Murd...everyone knows about the Murd!"

So as Elder Hedelius, Elder Evans, and I were singing the song, Elder Murdoch came flying down the stairs, and about halfway through, began to "tuck and roll" into a ball, crashing into the wall at the bottom. Elder Hedelius then reached over to Elder Murdoch and started jokingly throwing him against the wall. Amid all playing and laughing, Elder Murdoch accidentally knocked a hole in the wall. It was so funny. You had to be there...but it was great!

I feel like I am growing leaps and bounds in my testimony of the gospel. The Lord has blessed me so much, and it is wonderful. The big San Bernardino "Christmas Conference" is tomorrow. It should be a lot of fun! I cannot wait to see all my old buddies from the MTC again. Yeah!

The day of "Christmas Conference," it was neat seeing all my MTC friends again. Everyone looked strong and healthy. I got a good feeling that everyone was enjoying their mission life.

The most important thing I learned today is the true meaning of Christmas: The birth of Jesus Christ, as found in Luke Chapter 2. The Christmas program was great, and it helped me understand why we celebrate this joyous occasion.

I grow stronger every day. My mission is so special because it helps me focus on what's truly important in this earth life. I think back to when I was just a small child in Primary being taught how important serving a mission is. It is especially important to spread the gospel and serve the Lord. This is what makes a mission so special and sacred. I love my mission.

Well, I decided to finally write Kaesi a letter, letting her know that I need to put all my time and energy into my mission and not into our dissolving relationship. I prayed about it, and I felt good about my decision to just be friends. I strongly feel that it is the best thing for both of us right now. I have no idea what she will say, but I know the Lord is supporting me one hundred percent of the way.

After District Meeting this morning, Elder Evans and I visited a couple of our investigators. And, as a result, we picked up one new investigator from a part-member family. We invited them to church tomorrow, and then we can hopefully find out when we can teach them.

After visiting a couple of investigators, we decided to visit a few call-backs. We had a spiritual experience with one lady. She believes strongly in Jesus Christ. She likes helping other people, and she really seemed sincere about it. She began to express her feelings for Jesus Christ when she started to cry. It was an incredible experience!

This dear Sister believes that it does not matter what church you go to; the important thing is to place Jesus Christ first in your life. We left a challenge with her to read and pray about the Book of Mormon. I just hope that she takes some time to read 3 Nephi Chapter 11 about Christ's visit to the Americas. I know she will enjoy reading it because it's all about Jesus Christ.

We met another call-back, and his name is Eddie. He is a religious man who believes strongly in Jesus Christ. Eddie is a large, intimidating black man with a deep, brash voice. However, he is really a cool dude. His brother is going through some tough times. We asked Eddie to join us in prayer to comfort his brother. Eddie's heart was touched. It was neat because this big burly man was humbled.

Well, I got the chance to meet Grandpa and Grandma tonight. They picked up Elder Evans and took us out to a nice Italian restaurant here in Fontana. It was neat talking to them and visiting with my awesome grandparents. They are super!

The church is true no matter which angle you look at it. It brings so much joy and happiness to those who accept and live by its teachings. Thank goodness for a loving Heavenly Father and our older brother Jesus Christ.

**

The next morning, we attended church service. It was great, as usual! I love going to church and meeting everyone. The Ward members love the missionaries.

We taught Marie Inman this afternoon. We reviewed the previous Discussions and read the introduction to the *Book of Mormon* in 3 Nephi Chapter 11. Marie has a learning disability and an extremely short attention span. However, through the Holy Ghost, we were able to teach and help her understand the real meaning of the gospel of Jesus Christ.

After our meeting with Marie, we had our first of two dinner appointments with the Mason Family. It was neat, and we had an enjoyable time with their family. Brother Mason and Elder Evans were trading corny jokes back and forth.

After eating with the Masons, we met with Brother Broderick, Ward Mission Leader in the Fontana First Ward, and had our second dinner appointment. Then we went on splits with Brother Broderick and his nephew, Carlin. He is eighteen-years old and is going on a mission soon.

Once we returned to our apartment, I let Carlin read my most recent letter to Kaesi. I wanted to get his feedback before sending the letter. He said, "This is one of the most incredible letters that I've ever read. This must have taken a lot of guts and maturity to write it. I felt The Spirit while reading it."

Before putting pen to paper, I prayed to Heavenly Father, asking for His help to say the things He wanted me to say. He really answered my prayers. I know the Lord answers prayers because he has answered mine. The gospel is true. And Heavenly father and Jesus Christ live. They love us all so much.

After doing our chores on P-day, we headed to Robyn's house to help him cut down a tree in his backyard. He is such a cool family man. We enjoyed helping Robyn in his yard. We have an appointment to show the church video, "The Plan of Our Heavenly Father," this week. We feel that Robyn's family will like it. He is a great guy! I pray that he will be receptive to The Spirit and accept baptism as a necessary step to his own salvation.

The next day it was hot. The weather warmed up and the wind died down. Elder Evans and I felt incredibly grateful to get a break from all the wind.

We decided to buy a live Christmas tree. Elder Evans and I picked it out. The Christmas tree lot was located on Juniper Street where we bought a Juniper tree. We gave the manager, Janet, a copy of the *Book of Mormon*. The Lord has blessed us so much! When we are obedient, he blesses us in return. The joy of missionary work can be incredibly great.

The next day was a regular workday in the field. Elder Evans and I had our first appointment with John, who we met through a Salt Lake City referral. John is a carpenter and a Born-Again Christian. My experience with the Born-Again is mixed. We discussed the gospel for almost two-hours, and it was interesting. After our meeting, John took us to his garage and showed us all his woodworking projects. He seemed interested in joining us at church, so I'm hopeful.

I received a letter from my friend Ben Dieterle. He told me that his older brother, John, died from a heart attack. Ben is heartbroken and does not know what to think. John had juvenile diabetes that created serious health issues for most of his life. I am worried about Ben because, from the tone of his letter, I can tell he has changed since serving his mission in Sweden. It is weird...but he is not the same person that I remember from the good 'ol days back in Georgia.

I reflect on my own immediate family, and they are the best. I love them all very much, and I need them a whole bunch. Family love is the greatest source of my joy and happiness. They are a great bunch of people. Elder Evans and I were asked to give a ten-minute presentation at the Investigator Fireside this Sunday. It should be neat because I enjoy speaking in front of people.

The next morning, the Santa Ana winds are back with a vengeance, and we biked through it all. It was a rather dreadful day today. It was incredible when the dust and sand flew up into our faces and felt like pins and needles in our skin. It hurt badly!

On the positive side, Elder Evans and I learned a powerful lesson today. It was cool, and I feel inspired me to write it here in my memoir.

We followed through with three part-member families. The Paulson family lived in an apartment complex, so we rode our bikes to their home through a parking lot. After knocking on the door a few times, we realized they were not home, so we left a note inviting them to attend the Investigator Fireside.

We began walking down the sidewalk towards our bicycles when we heard someone yelling at us, trying to get our attention. We immediately turned around and saw a lady, who we thought might be the manager. She asked, "Are you guys' Mormons?" We replied, "Yes," and I thought to myself, "Heck yeah!"

Her name is Ms. Holstrom. She said, "I really admired you guys for getting out here in this kind of weather. I want you guys to come in, but I'm busy right now. Can you come back another time because I want to hear what you have to say?" We both nodded our head and said, "Sure." She continued, "I've seen you guys before from my apartment window, but I couldn't get a hold of you." We gave her a copy of the *Book of Mormon*, jotted down her contact information, and departed.

It was so cool! Here we are, Ms. Holstrom basically ran after us, trying to get our attention, and she succeeded. I know it was by the grace of Heavenly Father that we were able to meet this nice lady. Elder Evans and I were just doing our job by working hard. By doing what the Lord asked us to do, we were seen out in public, and the Lord blessed us for our efforts. The gospel is so true. It is great because I enjoy receiving blessings.

Well, I'm really worn out tonight. Biking all day in this wind was incredible, but I love serving my Lord and Savior Jesus Christ. It is the greatest feeling in the world!

The next day, the infamous Santa Ana winds continued. The wind just howled through the town of Fontana, and it really wore us out! I think I must have burned fifty percentage of my energy by 12:00 noon. But the work must continue.

It is strange trying to explain my feelings right now about my mission and life- events that I have experienced up to this point. I know that I have only scratched the surface, and that there are many more spiritual experiences waiting for me in the future.

It is hard to imagine that I have only been on my mission for four short months. During this time, I have learned to dig deep down within myself and use Christlike qualities like compassion, being sensitive to the spirit, humor, seriousness, maturity, and humility. It is amazing to see how much I have progressed. I feel that I have grown more in the past four- months than I have the past year at home. The spirit of the Lord is so strong and peaceful. I know that Jesus Christ and our Heavenly Father live because I see miracles happen right before my very eyes every day.

Elder Evans and I had the wonderful opportunity of blessing Nora, a new member who just moved from Utah. Her Uncle, Elder Robert Lee, is a General Authority. Nora asked me to give her a priesthood blessing, and it was so neat. Through The Spirit, I said, "Your Heavenly Father loves you very much and he's concerned about your well-being." After the blessing, tears were rolling down her face. Nora told me that she is having some issues in her marriage. She felt great comfort in the blessing. I was so happy that I had this sacred opportunity to bless the lives of others in the gospel of Jesus Christ.

I was inspired this morning while taking a shower. I want to draft a paper on the importance of a mission called, "A Mission—A Blessing or a Sacrifice?" I am going to outline the highlights of my mission and the wonderful blessings that follow. It is a sacrifice that brings forth blessings.

We had a nice District Meeting this morning. Elder Evans and I were late, as usual. Afterward, most of the Zone 4 missionaries went to Rialto Stake Center to witness a baptism that the zone leaders were performing.

Tonight, at the "Know Your Religion" series, Brother Johnson talked about the importance of singing church hymns. It was excellent. The Spirit was there, and I realized the true importance of singing at church, home, and in our personal lives.

I reminisce the times growing up when we had "Family Home Evenings" in Georgia. It is the usual custom in the LDS church to meet with your family and have a spiritual thought or lesson every Monday night for Family Home Evening. We always began and ended the meeting with song and prayer. I was proud of my dad, who is a splendid example, and I look up to him a lot. I want to do the same in my own home when I get married and have a family. The gospel is true, and that is all there is to it.

***

Our Investigator Fireside in the Fontana First Ward went well last night. It was held at Bishop Freeman's house, and we had three non-members attend. Elder Evans spoke about Jesus Christ—His birth and resurrection. He did an excellent job! Then we watched the church video, "The First Vision." Afterwards, Elder Stephen Todd gave a presentation on "The Book of Mormon and It's Origin." Overall, the fireside went well.

It is so neat to be a part of Heavenly Father's team! I am a solider and representative of Jesus Christ. The Lord has blessed us with another investigator who is ready to enter the waters of baptism this Saturday. His name is Charlie Hammond. He is a neat kid who is excited about learning the gospel. I like him a lot. The Lord is blessing us beyond measure, and I thank Him for that.

The next morning, we had Zone Conference. It was awesome, and I got a lot out of it. Elder Rogers spoke about adversity in Deuteronomy 23:5, which states, "Nevertheless the Lord thy God would not hearken unto Balaam; but the Lord they God turned the curse into a blessing unto thee, because the Lord thy God loved thee." Elder Hancey talked about missionary work and finding people to teach. He also talked about how angels and the Holy Ghost are preparing the hearts of the children of men to hear the gospel message.

After Conference, we had an appointment with Sister Nancy Lee Evans, a lady who we have been teaching the gospel. We taught her the 4th Discussion, "Eternal Progression." The Spirit was there, and we were able to share our testimonies with Nancy many times. However, she has been a bit of a procrastinator. Nancy even confessed that "procrastination" is her middle name! So, I felt impressed to read a scripture about the subject. I just pray that she makes the right choice to read and pray about the gospel. I hope she does not wait until it is too late. It reminds me of the plaque I have hanging on my wall at home from my old Scoutmaster, Bro. Varney, with President Spencer W. Kimball's quote: "Do It Now."

After teaching Nancy, we had dinner at the Wickstrom's home tonight. It was cool speaking with them because they make sure we feel right at home. I really like them because they remind me of my own family. Brother Wickstrom and I had an enjoyable conversation. Sister Wickstrom's showed us a photo of her sister who is extremely good looking. Wow!

We picked up a few Christmas lights for our tree from the Bennett's (a less active family). The tree looks great! Elder Evans and I are currently teaching their daughter.

The Lord is really blessing us. It is wonderful to think that if we live and obey the commandments, the Lord will continue to pour out his blessings. After a long grueling day working out in the field I like to reflect and ask myself, "How did I do? Did I put forth my best effort?" Each day, it is a great feeling inside knowing my companion and I did a fantastic job with the aid of The Spirit! I feel good doing the Lord's work. This is the Lord's time; not mine. I am serving Him full-time for two years. I love my mission call because it came directly from Heavenly Father.

The next day, we met with Pam and her husband, who are foster parents. It is neat that they opened their home as a refuge for abused children. Pam said that 98% of the children were molested by a family member. It saddened my heart as we listened to the never-ending stories of children being physically and emotionally abused.

It made me think deeply about their situation. I know the gospel of Jesus Christ can help these children have a better tomorrow. There is just too much hate in this world. WAY too much! And I am so thankful for Jesus Christ, who can help us lead normal and healthy lives.

After meeting with Pam, we were introduced to a brand-new investigator, Rick Perales. We visited with him for a few minutes, and he seems like an outstanding person. I pray that we will be able to teach him the gospel of Jesus Christ. It is such an honor and privilege to share the gospel with others.

Elder Evans and I were privileged to give away eleven copies of the *Book of Mormon*. The Lord is blessing us. Missionary work is tough sledding! It is not easy, but it is such an important endeavor to help gather the house of Israel.

Charlie Hammond is ready for baptism this Saturday. Elder Hedelius is going to conduct the baptismal interview. Also, our district is scheduled to have Personal Priesthood Interviews (PPI) with President Gourdin. He sacrifices so much to be here serving the Lord.

The next day, I had a Personal Interview with President Gourdin. He is a great guy! I shared with him the issues that we are having with Brother Hadden and the Fontana Fifth Ward. We talked about two of the disagreements I have with Brother Hadden.

President Gourdin is aware that the Fontana Stake is scheduled Saturday, once a month, for baptisms. I said, "Baptisms should be open for when the investigator is ready. Why wait a couple of weeks?"

President Gourdin asked me to turn Alma 7:23 and to read it together with The Spirit. This is the same scripture that Elder Evans and I read during one of our companion inventory sessions.

And now I would that ye should be humble, and be submissive and gentle; easy to be entreated; full of patience and long suffering; being temperate in all things; being diligent in keeping the commandments of God at all times; asking for whatsoever things ye stand in need, both spiritual and temporal; always returning thanks unto God for whatsoever things ye do receive.

President Gourdin was truly kind, and he said that I need to be temperate in all things. More importantly, he admonished me to ACT and not RE-ACT to situations. He continued to counsel me, and said, "It really does not matter what someone says to you. We usually find a way to defend ourselves, but sometimes that just kindles the fire." I hope that the spirit and the Lord will help me improve as a person.

I believe Alma 7:23 is the most significant scripture that I have read so far on my mission. The second most significant scripture is Doctrine & Covenants 88: 119–121, which President Gourdin read during my initial interview in the mission field.

Organize yourselves; prepare every needful thing; and establish a house, even a house of prayer, a house of fasting, a house of learning, a house of glory, a house of order, a house of God; That your incomings may be in the name of the Lord; that your outgoings may be in the name of the Lord; that all your salutations may be in the name of the Lord, with uplifted hands unto the Most High.

Therefore, cease from all your light speeches, from all laughter, from all your lustful desires, from all your pride and light-mindedness, and from all your wicked doings.

After interviews with the President, Elder Hedelius and I rode our bicycles to Charlie Hammond's house to interview him for baptism. He passed with flying colors and his baptism is all set for this Saturday at 4:00 p.m. This is the Lord's baptism. I spoke with Louis Martorella, and he told me he is moving his family to Rialto. He is having financial difficulties and he's being forced to move there. I know that our kind and loving Heavenly Father is watching after him.

The next day was incredible weather-wise. It was dark, dreary, cold, and rainy all day long. However, the urge to serve and spread the gospel is strong within our companionship. Elder Evans and I carried forth the work and will of the Lord. I know we will be blessed for doing so. Even though the weather outside was nasty, we felt a ray of sunshine inside.

Charles Ray Hammond was baptized into the church. It was great! Brother Broderick's nephew, Carlen Johnson, baptized Charlie, and I confirmed him a member of the church. I always feel the strong influence of The Spirit at baptisms. My testimony grows stronger every time one of God's children enters the water of baptism.

I felt good confirming Charlie a member of The Church of Jesus Christ of Latter- day Saints. I have learned that the most important thing for a priesthood holder is to follow The Spirit. I say what The Spirit prompts me to say. I cannot go wrong because there is no way that The Spirit will guide me in the wrong direction.

We have a magnificent work, a marvelous work, and a wonder. I am just beginning to grasp the true importance of missionary work and I know that this church is true. The Lord has blessed our companionship greatly and I know that He will continue to bless us if we abide by His concepts and commandments.

***

The next morning it was dark and cold. We attended church service and to the rest of our Sunday commitments. The day can get exhausting after six-and-a-half hours of back-to- back meetings. However, I know deep down inside it is the right thing to do.

After church, we taught Marie Inman another Missionary Discussion this afternoon. During our meeting, Marie mentioned a couple of her concerns. Elder Evans and I are postponing her baptism a few weeks, or at least until January 7. Currently, we have Marie Inman, C.J. Sandgren, and Tammy Bennett scheduled for baptism next year.

After our meeting with Marie, Elder Evans and I headed to Rick Perales' home. He is a new investigator who is really interested in the church. We received a referral from Rick's girlfriend, Karen Tillett, who was a Sister missionary serving in the same Stake as Elder Evans in St. Louis, Missouri. That is dang cool!

Rick's a super guy and he wants to take the lessons. The Lord continues to place people in our path to teach and I am so blessed. The many trials and tribulations that I have gone through on my mission are turning out to be for my own good. Regardless of how you slice it or dice it though, the actual trial is still difficult.

After meeting with Rick, we visited Louis Martorella at his home this evening. His family is moving to Rialto tomorrow. They ran into some financial issues in their rental home. The district is volunteering to move their belongings to Rialto. Louis is a good guy, and I am proud of him. I cannot believe Christmas is one week away. The New Year is right around the corner.

The next morning, we moved the Martorella family to their new home. Louis' home is on a nice piece of property. Hopefully, things will work out with him and his family. Louis a great guy! He said, "Elder Todd, I want to still attend Fontana Fifth Ward. I like it there." I replied, "It would be great to have you!"

We headed back to Fontana. When we got back to our apartment, Elder Murdoch and I met with Brother Mecham at his house. We picked up a few personalized ornaments to send to our families back home. It is the thought that counts! It was great because we completed our Christmas shopping in less than two-hours.

The next morning, Elder Evans and I decided to get our hair cut. I like having my hair short because it is easier to manage. I am a clean-cut missionary now!

We visited several people on Arrow Street, including Ms. Holstrom (the lady who stopped us and asked questions about the Mormon Church). We met with her for about 20 minutes, and she talked about her daughter, who is a member of the church. Elder Evans and I will be teaching her soon.

According to Ms. Holstrom, her daughter is going through a rough divorce. It was sad to hear her story as tears were running down her face. She really loves her grandchildren. However, she may not be able to see them on Christmas because the ex-husband plans to take the children away.

After proselyting all day, we got home and found a great big package from UPS! I opened it up and it was from the McGurrin's. I quickly opened it up and inside the box there were five different packages all wrapped up. I was freaking out! My plan is not to go back to a "boyfriend and girlfriend"-type relationship with Kaesi, but I tell you what... she does not make it easy.

I may call Kaesi on Christmas day and ask her what the heck is going on. I am going to let her know that the best thing for our relationship is to remain "friends" through the rest of my mission. It is tough being out in the field, and it requires one hundred percent of my time and energy.

Elder Evans, and I have an appointment to meet at Rick's house, our golden investigator, tomorrow night. I am excited to teach him the lessons. I pray that The Spirit will be with us through the entire discussion.

The next day, Sister Stanley invited us over to her home and meet her foreign exchange students. We were introduced to eight beautiful young ladies from Japan. I have never met foreign exchange students from Japan before, so this was a new experience for me. The ladies were gorgeous, and they seem extraordinary. Maybe it's because I've been on my mission for five-months and even the telephone poles we pass every day are starting to look attractive. I do not know. Elder Evans and I had a friendly conversation with them.

After meeting with the ladies, Elder Evans and I have an appointment to teach the 1st Discussion to Christine Hilt, a nice black lady. We met Christine while helping replace her car headlights last Saturday afternoon. She is a super lady and I admire her sensitivity to care for her extremely ill mother. Christine is a splendid example of showing love and respect towards your parents. I pray that I will one day take care of my parents as well as she does.

After a nice Discussion with Christine, we met with Rick to teach "The Plan of Our Heavenly Father." Rick is a great person!

The Spirit was there. I am so happy, and my soul is filled with joy that Rick has made the decision on his own to hear and learn more about the gospel of Jesus Christ. He is one of the "elect" from the pre-existence.

One of the teachings in the church is the Plan of Salvation. We teach that each living soul on the earth was first born with a spiritual body as found in Jeremiah 1:5 (KJV). "Before I formed thee in the belly, I knew thee; and before thou camest forth out of the womb I sanctified thee, and I ordained the a prophet unto the nations."

After teaching the 1st Discussion, we talked about baptism and the possibility of setting a date next month. He is golden[51]!

After Rick's house, we raced home on our bicycles because my Grandpa and Grandma were coming over to our apartment. They came bearing gifts, including a big bag of fresh California oranges from my mom. She does not think I am eating enough fruits—and that is true. Moms always know what is best for their children! I had a good talk with my grandparents. Before leaving, Grandpa asked if I could offer a priesthood blessing of comfort with them. We knelt in the family room. I offered the blessing, and they really liked it. Christmas is near. This is a beautiful time of the year to celebrate Jesus' birth. The spirit of the Lord is so strong!

The next morning, we met with Ms. Holstrom. She liked our idea of dressing Elder Evans as Santa Claus and coming over on Christmas Eve for her two grandchildren. We are going to buy a couple of presents for each of them. It should be neat because we get to experience the true meaning of Christmas— serving others.

After discussing our Christmas Eve plans and following through with a few call-backs, we headed home for lunch. I received a telephone call from Elder Steve Prettyman this afternoon. It was cool to hear his voice again. He is really enjoying his mission. He is a stud. Elder Prettyman said "Steve, if it wasn't for you, I would have never wanted to go on a mission." It made me feel good inside knowing I helped a friend decide to go on a mission. I am not boasting in my ability, but it is cool knowing

I helped a friend decide to go on a mission. I am not boasting in my ability, but it is cool knowing I helped a friend make the right choice to serve the Lord.

Sister Platt, my old Sunday school teacher, wrote to me and said that Kip (Hardy) DeLay is scheduled for baptism soon. She writes, "Thanks to your good example." Boy, it must be 'Compliment Elder Todd Day' today.

I feel like I need all the compliments I can get, because I have received plenty of criticism, mockery, and abuse on my mission too. Believe or not, some of the criticism has come from within the church. In addition, I have had mission companions and a zone leader who have criticized my efforts. I try to remember that the scriptures say there is 'opposition in all things.'

It is incredible how many Born-Again Christians live here in California. While tracting, we met a guy named, Butch this evening. He is a pill. Butch is a good guy, but he is such a hypocrite. He often asks me not to do something, then promptly turns around and does the very thing he asked me not to do. Born-Agains are good people, but the ones I have met sure have a lot of nerve! It feels like a form of persecution, and it just strengthens my testimony even more. The Church of Jesus Christ of Latter- day Saints is the only true and living church upon the face of the whole earth. I know this beyond a shadow of a doubt. The Holy Ghost burns strong within me. Jesus Christ lives, and we are spirit children of our Heavenly Father.

Today was a productive day. With the great aid of The Spirit, Elder Evans and I were able to give away seven copies of the *Book of Mormon*. We met some good people who we pray will be able to receive the gospel.

Tomorrow is Christmas Eve; it is finally here! I am spending Christmas away from home for the first time and it is definitely different, but not bad either. Our district is having the best time serving others, helping them to feel the spirit of Christmas. Like a camera, we can help others bring the true picture of Christmas into focus.

This morning we met as a zone at the Rialto Building and watched the movie classic, "It's a Wonderful Life." It is an awesome movie and I love it! It has good 'ol fashion romance. The romance is cool and so is the message about Christmas. I really like it a lot because the movie has such a wholesome and warm message.

After our Zone Christmas party, Elder Evans and I taught Christine Hilt the 1st Discussion this afternoon. She accepted everything so well. She is a super investigator, and The Spirit was there while we talked with her. I am excited about having the golden opportunity to teach her. The Lord deserves all the credit and I thank him for that.

After teaching Christine, President Banks (First Counselor in the Fontana Stake) picked us up for Christmas Eve dinner with his family. The Banks have nine children. After dinner we read from Luke chapter 2 about the story of Jesus' birth. What a magnificent tradition reading this wonderful true story to the family. After the reading, each child received one gift to open. Elder Evans and I each received a present to open as well. We got shampoo, a pen, and a Nerf basketball shower basket. It was cool because I feel apart of the Banks' family now.

After a wonderful dinner and Christmas program, President Banks dropped us off at the Steileens home to eat some more food. Before we left, Sister Steileen walked over to me, gave me a hug, and kissed me on the cheek. I was not expecting that, and I blushed a little.

After our second dinner, we had to rush Elder Evans over to Ms. Holstrom's home so that we could dress him up as Santa Clause before the grandchildren went to bed. We borrowed the Santa outfit from Sister Goddard in the Ward. The boys, Daniel and Chris, loved the visit from Santa Claus. We all sat on Santa's lap, including Grandma. We all laughed and had a fun time with old Saint Nick.

After Santa's surprise visit, we returned to the North Pole (home) and changed into our pajamas. We were so excited about Christmas that we decided to have a wrestling match.

I always like to wrestle Elder Hedelius and put him in a headlock. He is so fun to wrestle and mess around with. We decided to move our mattresses downstairs and sleep next to the tree. Merry Christmas!

***

We arose at 7:00 a.m. to open our presents on Christmas day. I had a good Christmas with lots of presents. I received a sweater, T-shirt, tie, Ziggy doll, some candy, and a blue shirt from Kaesi. I received huge set of audio cassette tapes, "Lectures from the *Book of Mormon*," a journal, more candy, a tote bag to place my mission stuff in, and a couple Mormon Tabernacle Choir cassette tapes. It was great! After opening our gifts, Louis Martorella came over to pick us up for church. We had a special Sacrament Meeting combined with Fontana First and Fifth Wards from 9:00 a.m. – 10:00 a.m., and that was it. The rest of the day was "family day."

After church we stopped by the Killian family to get a puppy for Brother Louis' daughter, Rainbow. He was happy, and I know Rainbow will be thrilled, too. Louis dropped us off at our apartment and we wished one another a Merry Christmas. He's a great man and a good father.

The first telephone call I made this afternoon was with Kaesi and her family. It was neat to make an "approved" phone call for the first time in a couple of months. Kaesi and I talked for about 45-minutes, and I tried to convey to her my feelings to remain friends, but my efforts were in vain. I struggled to get my point across at all. It's interesting how differently we handle conflict-resolution. In the end, we left the conversation on a good note when Kaesi said, "I love you." Oh, well! We'll see how things go!

My second telephone call was to my family. I talked to Dad, Mom, and the whole bunch tonight. It was cool hearing everyone's voices. Dad and I had an enjoyable conversation about different religions, how the origin of the Christmas tree can be traced to the pagans, my relationship with Kaesi, and missionary life. It was super, and my family is the best!

My last phone call was to Elder Jeff, and we talked for about an hour. We had an awesome talk, too. He is so cool because I feel like I'm speaking with one of my brothers! I am glad we have become best friends. It was neat talking to Jeff, 'one Elder to another.' It is so cool to be on a mission. I feel great comfort knowing that I am doing the work of the Lord. The Church is true. The gospel of Jesus Christ is so sweet and simple.

It is P-day today and we decided to clean our apartment. We are trying to get it ready for apartment inspections. This is a yearly inspection by President & Sister Gourdin, where they personally visit each apartment in the mission—all two-hundred missionaries! This is a "white glove" inspection. I did my duty by cleaning both bathrooms: tub, floor, sink, and toilets. I put a lot of elbow grease into scrubbing the toilets. It looks great now. My mama would be proud!

After completing our regular chores, we decided to visit a couple of people and tract a neighborhood. We knocked on one door and a gentleman invited us into his home. We were excited until he mentioned that he's a member of a Western type "Buddhist" religion and played us one of his church audio tapes. Elder Evans and I sat there and listened to the strange chanting sounds coming from the boom box. It was totally weird and made me feel very uncomfortable. I knew right off the bat it was of the devil. We left immediately.

The twenty-seventh of every month marks another thirty-days in the mission field. So today I have been on my church mission for a total of five-months. I feel like I have grown a lot spiritually over a brief time.

I am experiencing another crisis in my missionary life again. I know the Lord is preparing me for something big in the future. I have had a tremendous number of trials and tribulations while serving my mission in Fontana and mostly from my peers in the church. I am referring to my companion, Elder Evans!

Wow, this guy is something else. I am trying to be his friend and help him serve in California while he waits for his Visa to Brazil. I have tried and tried, but I do not get any respect or even a simple thank you from him. He can be a difficult dude to get along with. I could name a half million things that are wrong with him, and another million things he needs to improve on to become a better person.

I know complaining does not do either one of us any good. All I can do is do my best, pray, and stay close to the Lord. The companionship issues with Elder Evans, along with normal pressures of being on a mission, has caused me to look deep within my own soul. A church hymn comes to mind: "I Need Thee Every Hour." I have concluded that enduring to the end is the best solution. The Lord wants me to grow even stronger. I want to serve Him.

While stewing in my frustration with Elder Evans, the zone leaders called and then came over to the apartment to meet with us individually. There is no mystery that the companionship has not been getting along lately. As usual, Elder Rogers took me out to get something to eat and talk. This is our third special interview together in the past couple of months. Elder Rogers said, "I have been hearing complaints about you from a couple of members in the Fontana Stake. It sounds like you are having issues with our companion again. What is going on?" The way he was talking, he made it sound like I was a dead-beat missionary not doing his job.

I explained that Brother Hadden couldn't get over the fact that Louis was baptized on a "non" Fontana Stake baptismal date. (Seriously; this guy really needs to take a chill pill and get over himself!)

After explaining my side of the story, we both started laughing our heads off. It felt good to finally get a few things off my shoulders and air some of my frustrations about companions, a ward mission leader, and a stake high council member. Elder Rogers and I continued to laugh for a couple of minutes and all the frustration just melted away. When I returned to the apartment, Elder Evans and I jumped back to the neutral zone. We were good!

The zone leaders suggested we go on splits with Elder Hedelius and Murdoch for the remainder of the day. So Elder Hedelius and I teamed up, and Elder Murdoch and Evans went together. We had a wonderful time. Elder Hedelius and I taught several discussions, and I learned a lot of good things, especially about bearing one's testimony of the restored gospel. It is so important because it invites The Spirit.

I must not forget that the Lord has blessed me. We are teaching some super people and have an abundance of baptisms coming up soon! I owe it all to the Lord.

The next morning, Elder Evans and I taught Rick the 2nd Discussion. It went fantastic! With the aid of The Spirit, Rick committed to baptism on January 17th, a day before mission transfers. He was excited, and I know he felt The Spirit. Rick said, "After you guys taught me the 1st Discussion, I felt great, and the rest of my day went very well." I am so thankful to the Lord for putting Rick in our path so that we could teach him.

After having a great discussion with Rick, we taught "The Gospel of Jesus Christ" to Christine Hilt. Christine's mother is extremely ill, and it is difficult for her to attend church. I think we will see if the Relief Society can help us take care of Christine's mother while she attends Sacrament Meeting. I feel at peace with Christine becoming a member.

The rest of the day we tracted. It was windy and cold. My hands were frozen. I did not realize that the weather in "sunny" Southern California could turn so cold. However, the Lord is blessing us for our efforts, and I know The Spirit is preparing the hearts of the people.

After a long, cold morning, it was time to return home and thaw out. I received a letter and a small package from Elder Jeff Humphrey. In his letter, Jeff mentioned how much he values our friendship and how he looks forward to getting back together after our missions. He is one heck of a fella. He is awesome! We are friends for life and forever! We both agree on one thing: Women are nothing but a temptation! Kaesi and Paula are just like the Born-Again Christians! Just kidding. On a side note, BYU beat Colorado 20–17 in the Freedom Bowl played in San Diego. Yeah!

The next morning, I received a telephone call from Rick's girlfriend, Karen. She wanted to know how things were progressing with Rick. She wanted to make sure he was accepting the gospel with The Spirit so he could build his own personal testimony. Karen is cool, and she is so excited that Rick made the decision to be baptized. Side note: We may have to move Rick's baptismal date up three days to January 14th because this is the date the Fontana Stake has set. Nonetheless, Karen is excited about being married in the Lord's temple. She is a neat gal and I know the Lord is blessing us both.

Elder Evans and I were fortunate enough to be able to give away twenty-two copies of the *Book of Mormon* this week. I am thankful for the Lord Jesus Christ, who made it possible for us to speak with all these people in Fontana. It is a unique opportunity to take the pulse of this town and see people respond to our message about the Savior.

I must admit, a lot of people call themselves "Christians," but then turn around and reject a short message and a sacred book about Jesus. It is disappointing to see so many people reject this glad message. They are the ones who are missing the chance to have the fullness of the gospel. I am not upset, but it is interesting to hear what people believe.

Things are going well. I want to continue working hard and do my best. It is important to begin losing myself in the work. I need to control my thoughts and only think about my missionary service now, rather than think about how much longer I must serve the Lord. I hope I can keep this in perspective throughout my mission. I must have laser-focus serving the Savior because giving of myself is the reason I decided to go on a full-time mission in the first place.

The next morning at District Meeting, we all took our "Memorization Test" at the Bloomington building. It is a test to make sure we have memorized all the scriptures in the

Missionary Discussions. This is a steppingstone to become a Master Teacher.

Elder Stevenson's companion, Elder Thompson, is another "Visa Waiter" to Brazil. He is serving his mission temporarily in California. He is from Indiana. Stevenson and Thompson are a cool companionship.

After the test, Elder Thompson shared some good news with the district. He said, "I finally received my Visa to Brazil. I am totally excited!" We all congratulated him, except Elder Evans. He had a look of shock and amazement on his face because he has been serving his mission a month longer than Elder Thompson. He could not believe his misfortune. There is no denying it now; Elder Evans is very trunky[52]! He cannot wait to go to Brazil.

I received a letter from Kip (Hardy) DeLay, a friend of Karl Bream and mine back home. I met Kip at Youth Conference right before I left on my mission. In his letter, he shared that he is getting baptized in January and that is so cool! Kip is in love with Jennifer Jewkes, and the situation is something else. He needs to take a long cold shower. If not, I am going to have to take a fire hose to cool this boy off. In Kip's defense, I must admit that I thought I was totally in love with a few girls growing up. If Kip's smart, he will just roll with the situation and let his crush subside. I, for one, have had to do that many times over crushes who did not feel the same way about me.

Elder Evans and I are speaking in Fontana Fifth Ward tomorrow on "How the Ensign Can Help Missionary Work." I am prepared, and all I'm asking the Lord for His spirit to be with me. If The Spirit is there, then that is all that matters.

It is weird knowing that today is New Year's Eve. Normally, I would be at a dance, having a fun time, going to parties, and staying out late back in my beloved state of Georgia! However, thinking about life before my mission really does not affect me.

And, just like the glorious holiday of Christmas, I am learning to live with it. As a representative of Jesus Christ, it is important to act accordingly. However, that does not mean we cannot have a little fun too!

A few elders from our zone came over to our apartment to celebrate New Year's Eve. We had a nice spread of Mexican food and watched the movie, "The Man from Snowy River." Elder Thompson and Elder Stevenson brought over confetti, horns, and hats. It was fun. We had our own little party!

It is January 1, 1989, and Fontana is going crazy! Fireworks, people screaming, and bottle rockets flying everywhere. It is complete pandemonium. Happy New Year! I hope the Lord will continue to bless me in my sacred calling to bring souls unto him in 1989. Let's Do It! Also, I hope that my family and friends will have a healthy and successful year.

***

My basic routine on a typical New Year's Day is to sleep in, wake up at 12:00 noon, and watch college football games for the rest of the day. Well...not this year. Elder Evans and I awoke at our usual time – 6:30 a.m. – and got ready for church. The New Year schedule is as follows: We have the Fontana Fifth Ward from 8:00 a.m. – 11:00 a.m. and then a "Ward Correlation Meeting" afterwards. After the meeting, we ride our bicycles home for lunch, and then meet back at church from 2:00 p.m. – 5:00 p.m. for the Fontana First Ward. Sunday means an entire day of church meetings and boy does it wear me out! We are talking about over 7-hours of straight church meetings. It is clear that I am not used to the new Ward schedules....

I was pleased with my talk today and The Spirit was present. I was prepared and therefore The Spirit directed me to say the things the Lord wanted me to say. My belief supports that "prayerful preparedness" is the key. I like giving talks in church because it is fun, and it gives me the opportunity to work on my communication skills.

As my confidence in utilizing The Spirit more effectively is growing, I have a better idea of how to control my emotions and use The Spirit to bear testimony. However, with more practice, I would like to work on my talk outline and organization so that my delivery is more direct. The most impressive talks I have listened to are those in which the speaker commands authority. I would like to practice more and be better prepared so that I can speak with that kind of power and authority also.

If Jesus Christ had a church upon the earth, it would be named after the Savior and his gospel, and not named after man. I know that The Church of Jesus Christ of Latter-day Saints is Christ's church, and it is the only true church. I love serving Him and spreading His gospel.

Well, as it says in the scriptures there must be an opposition in all things. Rick's girlfriend, Karen, telephoned our apartment to talk about a couple of Rick's concerns. He is confused about some of the principles of the church, specifically the priesthood.

While teaching Rick the 3rd Discussion, we noticed that he was a little jittery and uncomfortable about the subject. I know Rick should be baptized because The Spirit has born this witness to me. I also know that Rick has felt The Spirit and knows it is important to be baptized. However, the decision to be baptized is between the individual and the Lord. The Lord is in charge and will sometimes try our faith to test us. The Lord has the right to set obstacles in our path to help remind us of who we are serving. My success in the mission field is reliant on Him.

Things are going well, but missionary work is tough. Missionaries must get out in the field and work hard. If I do my best to spread the gospel, then the Lord is going to bless me for it. The Lord has prepared me for many wonderful things yet to come on my mission. What those experiences will be, I do not know. However, what I do know is that, so far, these experiences are strengthening my character and personal testimony. If I can always follow The Spirit in everything I do, the work of the Lord will continue to carry forth in its simplicity and purity.

Sometimes I cannot believe that I am on a full-time mission. A mission is so especially important. A scripture that comes to mind is found in the Pearl of Great Price. The Pearl of Great Price like the Doctrine & Covenants is considered modern- day revelation and is one of the four canons of scripture. "This is my work and my glory to bring to pass the immortality and eternal life of man" (Moses 1:39). I love feeling the joy and peace that comes from working for the Lord and my fellow man.

We spent most of the day cleaning our apartment for the Mission President's Inspection tomorrow morning at 10:00 a.m. I had the privilege of cleaning the downstairs bathroom and that was a lot of fun...NOT! It seemed like no matter how hard I scrubbed the toilet; I couldn't eliminate the ring nor a dark spot stained into the bottom of the bowl.

I am so excited about the baptisms we have scheduled for this Saturday. Elder Evans and I will have the opportunity to baptize and confirm them as members in the church. I just love baptisms because they are so wonderful!

We spoke with Rick this evening and he said, "I decided to push my baptismal date out a week or two. I feel we are moving too fast, and I ask you guys to slow down the pace of each Discussion." I replied, "That is not an issue to postpone your baptismal date." I know that Rick's baptism is on the Lord's timetable. Whenever the Lord feels that the time is right, that is when he will be baptized.

I love my Heavenly Father and my older brother, Jesus Christ. And I know that it is only through Jesus Christ that we can return and live with our Heavenly Father, as found in John 14:6 (KJV).

President and Sister Gourdin inspected our apartment this morning at 10:30 a.m. We passed with flying colors, and they told us it's a well-kept apartment. After the inspection, we all knelt in our family room while President Gourdin offered a prayer to bless our home and asked that The Spirit preside with us.

Later in the afternoon, Elder Hedelius and I went on splits to tract and visit with Marie Inman. While tracting, we encountered a house that had a large black collie laying underneath the porch. Elder Hedelius and I are not fond of mean California dogs. We've learned to be extremely careful because these dogs can be extremely aggressive. We approached the fence and shook the front gate to make sure the dog wasn't feeling tempted to leave his post. There was a slow drizzle, and the dog was seemingly trying to stay dry.

We debated whether we should risk life and limb to enter the premise. I asked Elder Hedelius, "How many missionaries have been bitten or seriously injured by dog bites?" He just smiled and said, "Elder Todd, we need to show more faith." At this point, we proceeded into the yard. I slowly opened the gate and walked in first, with Elder Hedelius walking directly behind me. I looked over my shoulder and asked him to leave the gate open in case of an emergency.

As we approached the large dog, he just looked at us in bewilderment and then a "not so friendly look" developed on his doggie face. I stopped in my tracks as Elder Hedelius slowly walked past me. I thought to myself, "Something just isn't right."

To get a holistic view of the situation, a person must know Elder Hedelius. In most situations—I'd say 99% of the time—he is a calm, cool, and level-headed guy.

However, the inevitable happened just as Elder Hedelius lowered his hand towards the dog. In a split second, I thought, "Something is going to happen!" Sure enough, the dog sensed Elder Hedelius's fear and jumped up on all four legs, showing the meanest pair of fangs I've ever seen!

Elder Hedelius was suddenly struck with complete and utter shock. He immediately froze and did the only thing he could do. He thrust his scriptures toward the angry dog, bent his knees and screamed as loud as he could, hoping to scare the dog into submission. I was already halfway across the front yard running towards the open gate when I heard Elder Hedelius and the dog in hot pursuit. We both flew past the gate and slammed it shut just as Cujo was about to make his escape. I have never laughed harder in my life. It was so funny. You had to be there. It was great! Elder Hedelius said that he lost about 5–10 lbs. from that experience.

After our close encounter with the four-legged monster, we visited Marie Inman. Elder Hedelius interviewed Marie for her baptism scheduled this Saturday, January 7th. When we arrived at our apartment later that evening, Elder Evans was in a cheerful mood, and I wondered why. He told us he was finally getting his Visa and going to Brazil! I'm now wondering who my new companion will be. Whoever it is, I hope he's not another Visa-mother (slang term for Visa-waiter).

I'm happy for Elder Evans because now I do not have to hear him complain all the time about how "California is not [his] mission." He is a good guy and wants to do well on his mission to Brazil. However, I had put up with a lot of grief from him. The bottom line is that we are just two very different people. Elder Evans leaves from LAX on Monday, January 9th, and of course I will be getting a new companion.

I get depressed sometimes when things don't go my way with missionary work, especially when we haven't scheduled any new appointments, and the work seems just plain slow. I feel like we are getting nothing accomplished. I feel that the best missionary work comes from my heart, is fueled with desire, and topped with a positive attitude.

Elder Evans and I visited a part-member family, the Kruegers. Brother Krueger is not a member and Sister Krueger is less active. We talked to her for a while about the gospel. When Sister Krueger was a teenager; she became rebellious and eventually fell away from the church. She did not understand the Plan of Salvation, especially the "Three degrees of glory," and she had a lot of misconceptions and questions about the subject, so Elder Evans and I explained the plan to her. Afterwards, she had a better understanding of the basic principles of the different kingdoms iof Heaven. We are hoping to schedule some additional appointments to teach her husband.

Tonight, we had a dinner appointment with Brother and Sister Christiansen. He is a neat guy and went to Montana on his mission. He told us a couple of spiritual experiences that he had while serving the Lord. Brother Christiansen is a very spiritual man. During the blessing on the food, he prayed and blessed Elder Evans that he would not get any worms while serving in Brazil...Ha! He also prayed that his body would be strong while serving the Lord. Brother Christiansen is very sincere about his convictions! I hope things go well with his new marriage.

Elder Evans and I are fasting and praying on Sunday for Mrs. Walker. Her daughter is Christine Hilt, who we are teaching. Mrs. Walker has Alzheimer's Disease, and we have been praying that she can be healed. We explained to Christine about priesthood blessings and how they are for the healing of the sick and afflicted.

Christine is a very spiritual person. I pray for faith and strength in Jesus Christ. Miracles will happen if we have faith, and if it is the will of our Heavenly Father. We are ministers and humble servants of Jesus Christ.

Tonight, was just delightsome! Marie Inmin, C.J. Sandgren, Tammy Bennett, and Miranda Lee were all baptized into the gospel of Jesus Christ. The Holy Ghost is such a wonderful feeling.

I had the unique opportunity of baptizing C.J. Sandgren. I love his believing spirit! I am so thankful to the Lord that he gave me this wonderful and most sacred opportunity. This is the Lord's work and His will. I am just one of His servants spreading forth the gospel of Jesus Christ.

After C.J.'s baptism, I had the opportunity to confirm C.J. a member of the church and confirm the gift of the Holy Ghost in the name of Jesus Christ. This was another very sacred and spiritual experience. I prayed for the sprit that I might say the things the Lord wanted me to say. I felt at peace with his blessing and knew I was directed by The Spirit. During C.J.'s confirmation, I said, "You will see great growth in your life if you stay close to Father in Heaven and follow his counsel. You will have an opportunity to serve a full-time mission someday."

Serving the Lord has brought many great blessings into my life. I feel so at peace with myself when someone makes the sacrifice to come unto Christ, repent, and be baptized. There is not a better feeling in the world! C.J. and Tammy are 8-years old, Miranda is 9-years old, and Marie is 14-years old. It was neat to see all the families there to support their children.

The Sandgrens are another part-member family. However, the entire family attended including C.J.'s dad, who is not a member. Also in attendance was the Richard Lee family. The Lord works in mighty ways, and it is so wonderful to think of the great love that he has for each of us. I want to continue diligently serving now and after my mission. In fact, I want to serve Jesus Christ my entire life.

I began to reminisce about my own baptism when I was 8-years old while living with my family in Crystal Lake, Illinois. My baptism was a spiritual and uplifting experience. I do not remember a lot due to the initial shock of entering the frigid waters in the baptismal font. Tragically, the water heater was broken and, as a result, there was no hot water. However, despite the frigid temperatures, the Holy Ghost warmed me up. When my dad raised me out of the water, I felt cleansed and refreshed. After my dad confirmed me a member of the church, I distinctly remember my mother putting her loving arms around me and asking, "How do you feel?" I replied, "I feel great!" Then, she continued, "I'm so proud of you." That was a marvelous time. I want to have a forever family.

Well...I completed reading and studying the *Book of Mormon: Another Testament of Jesus Christ* for the first time beginning my mission. I love this holy writ of scripture with all my heart because it is a book about Jesus Christ. It fills my soul and strengthens my testimony that He lives. The very first time I read the *Book of Mormon* was during high school, and it took me one-and-half years to read it from cover to cover. Now I will just start over, beginning with Chapter 1 of First Nephi, in addition to the Table of Contents, Introduction, and Testimonies of the Witnesses. I feel that it is important to read everything.

Our district is fasting and praying for Christine's mom, Mrs. Walker. We need to gather enough faith and strength so that we can give her a priesthood blessing that will allow her to improve her mental state despite suffering from the early stages of Alzheimer's. We need The Spirit to be with us. Faith is the key to blessings, and we hope that the will of the Father will be done.

In the *Book of Mormon*, Ether, Chapter 12 is an excellent reference on faith, especially Ether 12:6: "And now, I, Moroni, would speak somewhat concerning these things; I would show unto the world that faith is things which are hoped for and not seen; wherefore, dispute not because ye see not, for ye receive no witness until after the trial of your faith."

The principle of faith is found throughout the scriptures, and we need that faith to return and live with our Father in Heaven again. We can receive answers to difficult situations through fasting and prayer. Through our faith we can invite The Spirit to be with us.

I remember when I was a boy of 8-years old—the age of accountability in the LDS faith—trying to fast for exactly 24-hours. It was tough! I remember how sick I felt; the stomach pains were almost unbearable. However, I chose to endure to the end because of my faith; I knew it was the right thing to do. My dad always encouraged and praised me for my strength. My family's the greatest! I love them with every fiber of my being. I love the gospel of Jesus Christ and with His help, the work will move forward.

***

It was an incredible spiritual day at church. I was absolutely exhausted by the time we got home at 9:00 p.m. I refer to that kind of exhaustion as a "spiritual exhaustion" because of our new church schedule, meetings, and hours working in the field. On top of it all, we prayed and fasted for Mrs. Walker. I felt The Spirit extraordinarily strong.

During the Fontana First Ward, Brother Inmin confirmed Marie a member of The Church of Jesus Christ while Elder Evans, Brother William, and I all stood in the circle surrounding her. After Marie's confirmation, Elder Evans confirmed Miranda Lee a member of the church. It was such a neat experience. I felt the guiding light of The Spirit, and I know the Lord is pleased with our efforts.

An investigator, Tina; from Yucaipa, CA; visited our Sunday school class in the Fontana Fifth Ward. She said that she did not believe in attending church on a regular basis; however, she was a strong Christian. It was neat to see how much potential she had in the gospel due to her interest in the church. Tina had a lot of questions. Brother Hadden joined in the discussion and, with the aid of The Spirit of understanding, we were able to answer some of her questions. It reminded me of the scripture found in the Doctrine & Covenants (modern day scripture) 50:22 that reads: "Wherefore, he that preacheth and that receiveth, understand one another, and both are edified and rejoice together." I could see the potential that Tina has in becoming a member of The Lord's church.

Throughout the day I kept thinking about Mrs. Walker's blessing. I was reminded about faith in Ether 12, and the topic in elder's quorum was "humility." After church service, I felt humbled to have had the opportunity to stand in the circle to give Mrs. Walker a priesthood blessing. Elder Murdoch anointed her head with consecrated oil, and then Elder Evans sealed the anointing. It was so neat to be part of this special blessing.

Elder Evans gave an inspired prayer. It felt like the Holy Ghost was giving the blessing and the words coming from Elders Evans' mouth was coming straight from Heavenly Father. In the prayer, Mrs. Walker was blessed to stop being so aggressive towards Christine, requesting that the spirit of cooperation might prevail. She was also blessed to return to normal health if it was the will of the Father. It was a great testimony-builder and reminder to always rely on the Lord in all the things that I do.

Elder Evans and I broke our fast-during dinner at Ms. Holstrom's apartment. This would be Elder Evans' last American meal for the next two years. Mrs. Holmstrom expressed that she was going through a tough time with her family, specifically with Phoebe, her daughter. Phoebe's attitude and demeanor had changed-for-the-worse due to illegal drug use. Ms. Holstrom cried as she told us about all of her problems. It was so sad to witness, but there was not a lot we could do except promise to keep her in our prayers. And that is exactly what we did.

I know I am not a parent, and that one day I will find out how tough it is. But it is my feeling that if you teach your children correct principles from the beginning, they may not always choose the right, but eventually they'll come back to it. It is just too depressing to write about it. I can see how the gospel of Jesus Christ would make an enormous difference in their lives.

Well, I am rooming with Elder Hancey, a "zoney" (zone leader), until transfers, when my permanent companion will arrive. Zone Leaders have a bad reputation of focusing on stats and glory. However, Elder Hancey is a solid missionary, and it will be interesting to see how the next ten days unfold. I ask Heavenly Father to bless us with His Spirit, and that the work moves forward.

Elder Murdoch and I teamed up for the entire day. We had some interesting experiences and enjoyed one another's company. This morning we met with Peter Fedorka, an investigator who we have been teaching for the past four-and-a-half months. He is a good man, and we hope to see him at church.

After visiting with Peter, we biked to Rick's place, but he was not home. Karen, his girlfriend, called me this morning and told me that they had called off their engagement. Even though they are not dating anymore, we are still going to help Rick come unto Jesus—and Christ's church.

After following through with a few investigators, we met a family at the post office. They recognized our white shirts and introduced themselves. They were extremely poor and needed a place to stay. My heart went out to this family, and I wanted to help. However, I remembered that there is only so much the church can do. The family wanted to know if our church could help them out. It is sad to know that there are good people, leading good lives, and yet forced to live in the streets. It made me realize how blessed I am. I am beginning to understand the true scope of other people's problems; issues that many people face every day.

Elder Murdoch and I have a lunch appointment with Brother Reinfeldt to talk about a couple of his neighbors. I was not going to include this entry in my journal, but The Spirit has prompted me to write it down.

What impressed me the most about lunch was watching how relaxed and patient Brother Reinfeldt was with his children, especially his baby girl. They decided to prepare a couple of sandwiches, and Brother Reinfeldt's daughter picked up the butter knife and began spreading the mayonnaise on the bread. She was taking her time and fumbling the knife. Brother Reinfeldt could have easily taken the jar from her, but instead he helped her spread the mayonnaise on the bread by letting her do it herself. It was complete patience. That is how I want to be with my children, which is going to take self-control and patience.

Later in the evening, Elder Hancey and I visited the Tomlinson's, a part-member family in the Fontana Fifth Ward. The Spirit was present. While visiting with Sister Tomlinson and her sister, Rhonda Youngbloom, we noticed they both have an issue with smoking. We helped resolve their concerns by reading Doctrine & Covenants Section 89, which talks about the Word of Wisdom. Sister Tomlinson and her sister did not realize it was a commandment from God to only use tobacco for medicinal purposes. We also talked about the importance of church attendance and committed them to join us this Sunday. I pray that the Tomlinson sisters will feel of The Spirit, make new friends, and want to return to church each Sunday.

The infamous Santa Ana winds strike again! I have not felt this much wind in a long time. I tell you...the wind totally wears me out. I use every fiber of muscle and every ounce of energy just to cruise around town. I am beat!

Elder Hancey and I had a solid day. We managed to only give away one copy of the *Book of Mormon* but talked to several Born-Again Christians. It is neat teaching people the gospel. The Plan of Salvation teaches us that we lived in the pre-existence as spirits as found in Ecclesiastes 12:7 (KJV): "Then shall the dust return to the earth as it was: and the spirit shall return unto God who gave it." Even though we are in the flesh as human beings, I can clearly see the spiritual aspect of life. I not only view people as physical beings, but as my spiritual brothers and sisters. That is, in a sense, what it is like when I speak with people. I can also see clearly who the chosen spirits are and those who are not; those who like to argue and contend and those that do not.

Elder Hancey is an excellent missionary. He has been on his mission for eighteen months. He knows how to talk to people on their level and ask appropriate questions, and he shares his testimony often. He also quotes a lot of scriptures, a skill that I would like to personally develop.

I have been serving in Fontana for six months and transfers are weighing heavily on my mind. The next transfer date is on January the 18th, and I am not sure if I'm being re-assigned or not. It is all up to the Lord and His timetable. He is The Gardner, and I am just the servant. He knows who I need to become. I do not know about transfers, though. It sounds scary to tell you the truth! I mean...a new area, a new companion, new investigators, and new ward members. Wow! I pray for strength because I need it right now.

Yesterday was an interesting day with the winds clocking in at 80 mph. Despite the high winds, Elder Hancey and I managed to have a productive day. It was incredible though, because my legs feel like jelly after peddling all day!

I do not know exactly what is going on, but it seems like things just keep piling on my plate emotionally with a lot of contention and pressure from my last three companions. I feel like I have gone through the meat grinder, especially with Elder Evans and his whole attitude about not being in Brazil, combined with his lack- luster performance. I remember one time while repairing my bicycle, he said I was a perfectionist. It is funny that he said that, because I have never viewed or perceived myself that way.

Currently, I am having to deal with Elder Hancey. Our situation came to a head today because I've finally gotten sick and tired of being cut off right in the middle of Discussions and being treated like a fresh "green" missionary. I reminded Elder Hancey that I have trained two new companions in under six-months.

When we got home from our appointments, I immediately took my tie off, grabbed my coat, and took a long walk around our neighborhood to do some soul searching. Wow! I have had a lot of things on my mind and a ton of stress since I have left Georgia. The Lord has taught me to have patience and temperance in all things, especially here in California. I feel like the Lord is really preparing me for something big on the horizon. For what, you ask? Honestly, I do not know yet.

When I walked through the apartment door, I saw Elder Hedelius, and we talked for a while. He sympathized and said that people have been keeping things against me that they should have forgiven a long time ago. I one hundred percent agreed with him. I am really ticked off at Elder Hancey for the junk I must put up with, including no respect! The dude makes me feel totally useless at teaching appointments because he constantly cuts me off even when it's my turn to speak.

After speaking with Elder Hedelius, I brushed my teeth, cleaned my contact lenses, and went straight to bed. Even when Elder Hancey asked me a question, I did not say a word, but went right to sleep.

The next morning, I decided that no matter how angry I felt at Elder Hancey, I would try to do something Christlike. In other words, I would try and think of something that the Savior would do in a comparable situation, perhaps a small act of thoughtful service. So, when Elder Hancey jumped into the shower, I immediately straightened up his side of the room and made his bed. I felt at peace with myself despite all the persecution.

On the other side, I have learned a tremendous amount from Elder Hancey. He uses The Spirit, and that is a huge plus. He collaborates well with members, and he knows his Discussions like the back of his hand. He is smooth with his delivery and communication. Elder Hancey also does an excellent job when speaking with investigators and he tries to find out their specific needs and wants. Overall, I enjoy collaborating with him, and have decided that he is not a bad guy.

My saving grace was that I received a letter from Mom. I tell you...through the thick and thin of things, my family is always there for me. That is right! They are my very own family, and you just can't beat 'em!

My little sister, Julie, had to have her arm re-broken by the doctor because her bone was not healing properly. Julie said to the doctor, "I'm the youngest of seven and this is the first time I've been first in anything!" Mom says that she has a good sense of humor and a really good attitude about the whole situation. Julie is a super little girl.

The most important thing in my life right now is Jesus Christ. The Savior is my personal friend no matter what. He is The Gardner, and he knows what he wants me to become.

It was a mad dash to District Meeting this morning. Elder Hancey and I were late as usual. My new companion is Elder Rogers' little brother, who is eighteen-years old and from Arizona. Elder Rogers, Jr. is on a two-week church mission visiting his older brother. He is a cool guy, and we seem to get along just great! Elder Hancey will be back in the early part of next week.

My new companion and I visited several members in the Ward and delivered several copies of the *Book of Mormon*. It took much longer than I expected to deliver the books. We stopped by the Wood family's home in Fontana Fifth Ward and delivered five *Book of Mormons*. Sister Wood decided to give away several copies as late Christmas gifts to her friends.

She suggested we give a copy of the *Book of Mormon* to her next-door neighbor. Junior and I visited the neighbor's house and introduced ourselves. When we walked up the driveway, we noticed the husband and wife standing by their vehicle. At first the family was cordial and friendly as the father was re-organizing his trunk. We said, "Hello!" and immediately one of the women—assuming it was his wife—ran inside the house.

We continued our conversation with the husband, but noticed he was clearly uncomfortable with the situation. I immediately got right to the point and began my introduction into the *Book of Mormon*. The Spirit was present, and this good brother felt it and responded in a positive way. The gentleman was not jumping up and down for joy by the time we left, but it was still cool to see that when we put our faith and trust in the Lord, remarkable things happen. It was a wonderful experience. The Spirit is the key to conversion. I have also decided that I need to develop better eye contact when sharing my testimony with others.

This weekend in Fontana is Stake Conference. President and Sister Gourdin were sitting on the stand when we arrived. Sister Gourdin gave a great talk on Isaiah 61:1-3 (KJV). Verse 1 reads, "The Spirit of the Lord God is upon me; because the Lord hath anointed me to preach good tidings unto the meek; he hath sent me to bind up the brokenhearted, to proclaim liberty to the captives, and the opening of the prison to them that are bound."

It was neat shaking their hands after the meeting. The Gourdins are great people, and they really do a lot for us. I found out that Elder Hedelius was called to be a new zone leader. He is getting transferred and I'm so happy for him. I know Elder Hedelius will do great things in his new-assigned area.

***

Today was a momentous day packed full of all sorts of spiritual experiences, beautiful women, talks, blessing the sick, lessons to be learned, and investigators at Stake Conference. We arose early and attended the Young Adult session at 8:00 a.m. with Elder Pinnock, a member of the Quorum of the Seventy.

He gave an incredibly good talk on morality, the Word of Wisdom, and goal setting. Elder Pinnock read a great scripture on morality found in 1 Corinthians 6:14-20 and Doctrine & Covenants 88:119–121. In 1 Corinthians 6:15 (KJV) it says, "Know ye not that your bodies are the members of Christ? Shall I then take the members of Christ and make them the members of a harlot. God forbid." President Pinnock continued reading in Chapters 18–20:

Flee fornication. Every sin that a man doeth is without the body; but he that committeth fornication sinneth against his own body. What? Know ye not that your body is the temple of the Holy Ghost, which is in you, which ye have of God, and ye are not your own? For ye are bought with a price; therefore, glorify God in your body, and in your spirit, which are God's.

Regarding the Word of Wisdom (health code), he talked about the two serious issues teenagers face, including alcohol and illegal drugs. He concluded, emphasizing that we should set lofty goals and then give our every effort to achieve those goals.

During church service, Junior was freaking out and drooling over the Stake President's daughter, who—if I do say so myself—is exceptionally good looking. I laughed to myself at how ridiculous Junior was acting. In the mission field, we like to say that—with regards to attractive women—you can only look once, and if you don't, you are not a man. However, if you look twice, you are not a missionary.

At the 10:00 a.m. session, President Banks from the Fontana First Ward spoke with us about spirituality in the home. He stressed that if we invite The Spirit to reside within our four walls, we will have greater success in the home.

Sister Capps gave an excellent talk about her re-activation to church. She named several people who helped her return to activity, but she said that the "one" person who helped her the most was her best friend, Jesus Christ.

The regional representative spoke about the mission of Jesus Christ and the purpose of the atonement. What a marvelous gift the resurrection is to humankind and what a tremendous blessing it is to have in our lives.

After the intermediate hymn, President Gourdin gave a wonderful talk on missionary work. He quoted a scripture from Alma 31:5.

And now, as the preaching of the word had a great tendency to lead the people to do that which was just—yea, it had more powerful effect upon the minds of the people than the sword, or anything else, which had happened unto them—therefore Alma thought it was expedient that they should try the virtue of the word of God.

President Gourdin concluded, "We not only want The Spirit to help change people's lives, but we also want Jesus Christ to change their hearts as well." He strongly encouraged us to love one another.

To summarize his talk, President Bringhurst bore his testimony of patriarchal blessings. He instructed us that we must seek the Lord in all that we do and stressed that thoughts ultimately direct our lives. As members of the church, we must be the first to forgive others and share our testimonies with our friends.

The concluding speaker was Elder Pinnock who talked about meeting together often. In Proverbs 23:7 (KJV) it says, "For as he thinketh in his heart, so is he: Eat and drink, saith he to thee; but his heart is not with thee."

In addition to enjoying an amazing Stake Conference, the Tomlinson family and Rick came to church today. It was a great blessing to sit with them. Sister Gourdin came up to me after Stake Conference and said, "Elder Todd, was that an investigator family I saw you sitting with?" I replied, "Yes ma'am. We have several investigators at church today."

After church service, we switched companionships and Elder Hancey came back for at least a few more days until transfers. I am grateful the Lord decided to give me a break from Elder Hancey for a while. Elder Hedelius and Elder Murdoch invited us to a dinner appointment. After a delicious meal, we attended a Spanish baptism.

When we got home from the baptism, the telephone was ringing. I picked up the phone and it was Little-star Martorella. She was calling to let us know that her mother, Sunshine Sitka, had fallen and broke her hip. Sunshine was rushed to the San Bernardino Community Hospital not far away. Little-star asked if Elder Hancey and I could administer to her mother and of course, we jumped at the chance to assist the Martorella Family. About 30-minutes later, Brother Martorella picked us up and we traveled to the San Bernardino Community Hospital.

When we arrived at the hospital, we quickly walked to Sunshine's room. Elder Hancey anointed Sunshine's head with consecrated oil and I had the privilege of sealing the anointing and giving her a blessing. It was a marvelous spiritual experience. I patiently waited for The Spirit. It was there and I recognized His presence. I closed the blessing in the name of Jesus Christ. I am learning to better recognize The Spirit when it enters the room. I used to think that the Holy Ghost manifested itself as an overwhelming feeling of joy, but that is simply not always the case. Most of the time for me, The Spirit is incredibly quiet; a still small voice working in the hearts of the children of men. It is always a great feeling.

***

After a long and productive day of worship, Elder Hancey and I had a nice long talk. Most of the conversation was about the incident surrounding Brother Hadden and Louis Martorella's baptism. Apparently, Brother Hadden was still harboring ill feelings towards me for not following his protocol for Stake baptisms. I recall reading a letter from my dad stating that Brother Hadden had called and spoken to him about it. This made me think, 'This dude is a control freak!' Why in the world would it make a difference when an investigator is baptized? If the person accepts Jesus Christ, repents, and tries to keep the commandments, why would they not be baptized on a day of their choosing?

At any rate, Elder Hancey and I discussed how things could run more smoothly in the mission. He reiterated what President Gourdin told me last year in our Personal Priesthood Interview. I need to work on being more humble, patient, and temperate. In other words, I can let Brother Hadden run the missionary efforts for the Fontana Fifth Ward and try follow his rules.

I am tired, and it's time for bed. I can't believe how much I've learned on my mission in the short five-and-a-half months I've been here. I think the first six months of my mission will be the toughest. The Lord has put me through many trials and tribulations, but they have all been for my good and benefit. The Lord knows what He wants me to become.

We are number one in the California San Bernardino Mission! Zone Four has the highest number of baptisms for the month of December. We are "Zone of the Month" again.

After P-day, we traveled to the mission home to have a delicious meal and watch a G rated movie. After dinner, President Gourdin encouraged the zone and said the following.

Please continue working hard towards your goals. Keep doing what you are doing and get back to Book of Mormon placements. Place the books with love and care. You need to repent, have faith, and thank the Lord for allowing individuals to come unto Christ. It is important to continue doing good works and pray often. If we do these things, Heavenly Father will reveal the answers to us in our prayers, and we will have more opportunities to teach others.

Then Sister Gourdin said that if we achieve two-hundred baptisms in a single month, the entire mission can attend the temple. That would be so awesome. It is the usual custom that missionaries do not attend the temple while serving in the field. Our goal is to teach the gospel to the living.

The next day, Elder Murdoch and I taught Rick the 3rd Discussion, "The Restoration," which is all about the priesthood. The Spirit was there, and Rick told us that he felt he must know everything about the gospel before he is baptized. He said, "Elder Todd, I want you to baptize me." I replied, "I will be honored and thrilled to baptize you, Rick!" It is so exciting to see people join the true church of Jesus Christ. I pray for the continued support of the Holy Ghost so that I can be an effective advocate in building forth the kingdom of our Heavenly Father. The Lord answers prayers.

After our meeting with Rick, we were riding our bicycles to one of Elder Murdoch's appointments and met a couple people on the street. We talked to them for a few minutes, but we were running late, so we scheduled a meeting with them on Friday evening.

I received a letter from Kaesi this afternoon and it sounded like she'd been through a lot in just a week. Kaesi said that she was "held-up" at gun point during work by some dude. He demanded all the money, grabbed it, and took off. To make matters worse, a couple of days later, her living room caught on fire and Kaesi was almost burned. Kaesi's mom was away but felt inspired to come home. When Sister McGurrin arrived, she saw the fire and led Kaesi to safety. I am grateful for the promptings of The Spirit. It can help us all in many ways.

My new companion, Elder Hancock, called today and said, "Elder Todd, how are you doing?" It was very refreshing to have a companion utter those words. Elder Hancock will be the first full-blooded, permanent "California" missionary companion to me since Elder Hedelius last summer. I know that the Lord will bless us both in this magnificent work. I am totally excited.

Gratefully, Elder Hancey and I are getting along much better. He gave me some lame excuse about how leaving his beloved Rialto area and hanging with me in Fontana for a week was hard on him. (Pooooor baby!) I am trying to stay positive, and it's neat how the Lord works when I'm down in the depths of humility. God really comes through, and he does answer prayers. Elder Hancey decided to leave again, so Elder Rogers, Jr. will be my companion for another day. The revolving door of companionships continues, and it is crazy, but I'm getting tons of work done. Despite certain people wearing on me, I am still excited about my mission life, and I love it.

It was another windy day today. My body is getting used to the punishment of biking uphill against 85–90 mph gusts, dust flying down my throat and lungs, and my eyes drying out so badly that I cannot see where I'm going.

We have an appointment this evening to teach the 2nd Discussion with the Tomlinson family. Brother Adams and I teamed-up for the appointment. We had a good question-and-answer session. Sister Tomlinson said, "I've been struggling with my desire to read and understand the contents of the *Book of Mormon* due to my doubts concerning its validity." She continued, "I prayed for two-hours, asking Heavenly Father to help me receive an answer."

The next day, Sister Tomlinson said that she entered the family room to watch television and picked up the TV Guide. She said, "The very first page I turned to was a large advertisement for the *Book of Mormon*. There was a toll-free phone number to order a free copy. I could not believe my eyes, and I started to cry." Brother Tomlinson, who is a member, walked into the family room and said, "Dear, it looks like you're crying." She denied it, of course, but then admitted that Brother Tomlinson's heartfelt concern made her feel good.

Elder Hancock will be arriving tomorrow at 10:45 a.m. in San Bernardino. I think it will be neat to have a regular, full-time "California" Missionary in my midst again. The Lord fully knows what I have been through over the past couple of months. I pray that the work will continue.

The Lord has blessed me so much by helping me realize not to take my companions for granted—especially California missionaries. Oh, how I long for the days of serving with my trainer and mission "dad," Elder Hedelius. My most recent companions, Elder Clark, and Elder Evans were solid missionaries, but their burning desire to go to Brazil affected their work here in California. However, I look on the positive side. Clark and Evans taught me a lot about being humble and patient. In a spiritual sense, I really did enjoy working with them, but the extra stress I put on my own shoulders as their trainer added to the complexity. It is not an easy job being a trainer, but through these trials I have learned to be more patient.

Moving forward, Elder Hancock, a "California" missionary, is my companion and the new district leader for Fontana. This is what is important. He is a stud from Tooele, Utah, and we are getting along just fine.

Elder Murdoch and I visited Robyn, a man who I have been trying to teach for the past couple of months. The discussion went very well, and we scheduled the next couple of appointments. Robyn is progressing well through the Discussions.

Tonight, 'the three amigos' (Hancock, Murdoch, and I) teamed up and followed through with several people in our "finding pool." It was dark and it was starting to get late, so Elder Murdoch suggested we bike home. In following The Spirit, I felt impressed to continue our journey despite Elder Murdoch's apprehension. I assured him that we had one more family to meet. I am thankful we followed the prompting because we met with the Causey Family, who we learned has an 11-year-old son who hasn't been baptized, yet. I was excited because the experience supported my resolve that when we are in tune with the spirit, the Lord provides.

I was depressed because we failed to achieve our goal in delivering fourteen copies of the *Book of Mormon* this week. Sadly, we only delivered ten copies. I suppose I cannot complain though, because Elder Hedelius and I made up for lost ground by delivering fifty-six copies of the *Book of Mormon* in the past two weeks!

My life has been a little hectic this month to say the least. To add to my woes, I have not had a steady companion for some time. However, I must focus on the positive, which gives me the incentive to work harder. My new goals for this month:

1. Seven hours of companion study
2. Seven hours of personal study and
3. Give fourteen copies of the *Book of Mormons* away.

I don't think anything picks me up more than a wholesome and uplifting letter from my family. Mom really knows how to say just the right words. She touched a chord inside of me that made me realize that I did not necessarily show the utmost respect all the time at home—especially towards her. The older I get, the more I realize how conflict caused damage to my relationship with my parents. I want to forget the issues and pain I may have caused them.

Elder Hancock and I get a long great. He is a solid missionary. The work is going to carry forth. The Lord is continuing to bless us. I just pray that I am worthy enough to receive His outpouring of blessings.

This evening at one of our teaching appointments, I realized that I have a lot to learn. I know I do not know everything, but it's amazing how much there is to know and learn on a mission. I want to do my best and learn as much as I can to be an effective missionary. My faith in Jesus Christ makes my testimony stronger in the gospel.

One of the most important things that I have learned from my church service is that this mission is not for me; it is for my Heavenly Father. It is for His mission and His glory. I am simply a servant helping to build His kingdom here on earth.

The change which has taken place within me is incredible! I do not think I will realize the mighty change until I return from my mission and look back on my spiritual progress. There is nothing easy about my mission. It is a tremendous sacrifice that brings forth marvelous blessings. The ideas and concepts I learn in the field will last a lifetime.

I am so grateful for my family, wonderful friends, this opportunity to serve, and my mission. Most importantly, I am grateful for Jesus Christ because He is my Savior, and my best friend. Imagine the blessings that can be ours if we obey Him and keep the commandments! I believe firmly in prayer. I know the gospel is true because God answers prayers.

Our District Meeting was short-and-sweet because Elder Hancock and I traveled to his old area in Lake Elsinore, California to attend a baptism. Elder Hancock taught Gary, an eighteen-year-old investigator, who is now ready to be baptized.

It is a solid forty-five-minute drive south of Fontana. It was interesting traveling to a new area. Geographically, the Lake Elsinore area is a lot different than Fontana. Elder Hancock and I rode in the back of the minivan with the cutest girls (primary age), and we were the main attraction.

The baptismal service went well. The power of the priesthood is so neat because it bonds us together spiritually. The Brother who drove us to church baptized and confirmed Gary. I felt The Spirit so strong as this good Brother confirmed Gary into The Church of Jesus Christ of Latter-day Saints and gave him a blessing. He said, "Gary, you will go on a mission and serve others." Elder Hancock was thrilled to be a part in

Gary's decision to be baptized. Now, he can serve, teach, and baptize other people.

After the confirmation, we had a testimony meeting. A sister stood up and shared her testimony about her son serving a church mission. She said, "Every time I see a missionary it reminds me of my son." This good sister shared her thoughts on missionary work, and it was very spiritual. She was obviously very proud of her son.

After the baptismal service, we climbed back into the minivan. When we sat down, the little girls climbed onto our laps and asked what we would like with our order— "French fries, hamburgers, or chicken?" We were so tired that we dosed off and slept the rest of the way home. We awoke from our nap just as the minivan pulled into the parking lot of our apartment complex. It's nice to be back to my "home sweet home."

When we exited the vehicle, we noticed Elder Murdoch and Elder Rawson working on Steve Holstrom's car. Later, Ms. Holstrom (Steve's mom) stopped by to see how Steve's car repairs were coming along. Then she told us that she was ready to get baptized. She is having a lot of family issues, but with the Lord's help, Ms. Holstrom will find peace and happiness.

After speaking with Ms. Holstrom, Elder Hancock and I met with Sister Tomlinson and her sister, Rhonda Youngbloom, to teach the 2nd Discussion, "The Gospel of Jesus Christ." We had a three-hour discussion about the Savior and His purpose and asked the sisters, "Will you be baptized on February 4th?" Elder Hancock and I could tell by the hesitant look on their faces that we needed to pray. So, we invited them to kneel with us and ask the Lord about baptism in prayer. The Spirit was strong, and it bore witness to them that the things that we were teaching them were true.

Later that evening we attended a "Know Your Religion" Series at the Randell building. The main speaker was Captain Larry J. Chesley from Burley, Idaho. Captain Chesley was a prisoner of war (POW) for almost seven years in Vietnam. He served in the U.S. Airforce for thirteen years and had been in

Vietnam for only four months when his fighter airplane was shot down. Tragically, he was captured. Captain Chesley said, "The thing that really kept me going was my family, knowing that they loved me and that they cared for me."

My goodness did he share an unbelievable story about living as a POW. The North Vietnamese kept the POWs in 3 ft. x 6 ft. shacks, and they lived in filthy and deplorable conditions. The guards fed them all kinds of various parts from pigs and chickens. Captain Chesley was beat up constantly. He reiterated again that the one thing that kept him going was family and prayer. In fact, he said, "I prayed night and morning." He stressed the most about how powerful prayer is in our lives.

The other important advice that he gave was about marriage and quoted something that President Spencer W. Kimball said to his wife while serving in the Quorum of the Twelve Apostles. He said, "There are two things to a glorious marriage. The first is to be selfless in your love to your spouse and second is to be dedicated in the gospel of Jesus Christ." I thought that was neat because being selfless is the key to a successful marriage. I think I will use that quote on my first date when I get home to Georgia. Just kidding!

Missionary work is moving along. It is so amazing to see the growth that has taken place in my spiritual life. The Lord has blessed me beyond measure. I am so blessed and fortunate to serve and grow in the gospel. I absolutely love my mission here in California San Bernardino.

★★★

After eight hours of church service, duties, and responsibilities, missionary work drains me physically, mentally, and spiritually. Elder Hancock and I sat with Rick in Sacrament Meeting in Fontana Fifth Ward, our last church service of the day. Afterwards, we walked with him to his car. We talked for a few minutes and then I asked Rick, "Have you prayed about being baptized January 28th or 29th?" He replied, "Yes, and I and feel good about January 28th." I was so excited because it was not me who told him to be baptized; our Heavenly Father did. And I am so thankful for the answer he received. It is an answer to all our prayers.

Elder Hancock and I waited patiently for Brother Hadden to arrive for Ward Correlation Meeting. I had a few minutes so I opened my scriptures to Alma 7:23. "And now I would that ye should be humble and be submissive and gentle; easy to be entreated; full of patience and long-suffering; being temperate in all things…" I stopped reading and gazed at the last phrase "being temperate in all things." I said a little prayer when Brother Hadden walked through the door.

At this point there was a definite feeling of contention in the room. However, I mustered up my courage to be tactful, mature, and to use temperance. I gave the missionary report, and I assured Brother Hadden that we would schedule Rick's baptismal interview date at least a few days before January 28th. This way we would be able to carefully plan and prepare the program. I specifically followed Brother Hadden's request. I utilized The Spirit, as I am expected to do. I am immensely proud of myself for inviting the spirit of cooperation during the meeting.

We continued and discussed Ms. Holstrom's desire to be baptized. She seems sincere and she gets my approval. Ms. Holstrom is a good lady.

The last individual we talked about in Ward Correlation Meeting was Sister Tomlinson. She wants to get baptized on February 4th. To prepare for her big day, she committed to quit smoking for two-weeks. Elder Hancock and I will contact her every day to help encourage her progress along the way. The Lord has truly poured out His spirit among us and I am greatly thankful for that. The opportunity to serve is truly a gift and blessing from our Heavenly Father.

It has been an incredible day. I do not think I can really pen or express in words the tremendous blessing The Spirit has poured into my soul. Where should I start? Well… how about the beginning?

This morning I received a phone call from Karyn Tillett, Rick's old girlfriend. She is a neat gal; I really like her a lot. She said some complimentary things to me as a person and as a missionary. Karyn said, "I'm happy that you endured to the end with Rick." He had told her, 'Elder Todd really just wants to be friends and he cares about me as a person.' Karyn emphasized that he likes me a lot, and that made me feel good inside. After I hung up the telephone, I could not help but ponder on Karyn's kind words. I realized that the key to conversion is love. I must love my investigators unconditionally and sincerely with all my heart. I firmly believe that. It is a Christlike attribute because the Savior loves everyone no matter what.

During companion study this morning, we planned our day for tomorrow. We have a packed day, so we are planning to teach Rick two full Missionary Discussions (Fourth and Fifth) between 9:30 a.m. – 10:15 a.m. Then Elder Lloyd, district leader from south Fontana, is going to interview him for baptism. During Rick's interview, Elder Hancock and I are going to administer to Sister Tomlinson and give her a special blessing to help her quit smoking for good. After the blessing, we will head to Multi- Zone Conference at 12:00 noon.

After companion study, we attended Zone Conference and one of the speakers was Brother Christianson from the Fontana First Ward. He gave an incredible talk on using The Spirit as a special witness and as a friend. Brother Christianson also shared about a marvelous spiritual experience he had while administering a priesthood blessing on his church mission.

He began telling a story about Sister Griffin, a very spiritual lady in their ward. Sister Griffin had a major health condition known as heart-valve disease. In other words, she had a broken heart-valve. Brother Christianson and his companion gave her a blessing. While the missionaries administered, Sister Griffin saw a vision of the Salt Lake temple and Jesus Christ counseling with the prophet. In her vision, the Savior stopped what he was doing, rose, and stepped out of the meeting for a few moments, and listened to the blessing she was being given. She could see that the Savior took time out of his busy schedule to care for her needs. After the blessing, through Sister Griffin's faith, her heart valve was healed.

But that is not all. I do not think Brother Christianson came out and said it, but what The Spirit impressed upon me the most was that the prophet calls each individual on a church mission and signs his name on a piece of paper. In other words, each mission call is truly inspired. After hearing Brother Christianson speak, I believe that Jesus Christ himself is present with the prophet and assigns where each child of God should go on their mission. The Spirit bore witness to me of that truth.

My day was packed with spiritual experiences. Our companionship taught three discussions and the Lord has blessed us so much! Elder Hancock said something cool. He said, "Elder Todd, I do not care what anyone else says; you are a great missionary, and don't let anyone tell you different." I need positive reinforcement to build me up, and it's great.

I love the church, my family, and my Savior most of all. My mission is so sacred. I feel very fortunate to serve my Almighty Master. What an eternal blessing.

Again, my heart is full of gratitude for the many blessings that the Lord has given me. During companion study this morning, Elder Hancock and I prayed and asked Heavenly Father for His spirit to help us with Rick in about an hour. We did not have a lot of time scheduled for him due to Multi-zone Conference.

To prepare Rick for baptism we needed to teach him two discussions, so we left our apartment at 9:30 a.m. and headed to his house. Elder Hancock and I, with the aid of The Spirit, were able to teach him the 4th and 5th Discussions and then committed him to three major principles of the gospel: The Word of Wisdom, the Law of Chastity, and the Law of Tithing. Elder Lloyd was waiting in the wings to interview him for baptism.

In our hurry to complete the Discussions, we barely had time to catch our breath and nearly forgot to give Sister Tomlinson her special 'quit smoking' blessing! Thank goodness she lives right down the street from Rick's house.

When we arrived, Sister Tomlinson was lying on the couch with a blanket. She said, "I'm feeling sick to my stomach." Elder Hancock anointed her head, and then I had the opportunity of sealing the anointing and giving her a blessing. In the blessing, The Spirit whispered to me the following. I said, "Sister Tomlinson, you will be made whole again and recover soon from your illness. You will be given the strength to overcome smoking and Heavenly Father will help you quit smoking." After the blessing, we wished Sister Tomlinson well and biked back to Rick's place.

We arrived 15-minutes later but Elder Lloyd and Rick were still in their interview, so we waited in the family room. When Rick finally entered the room, he looked happy. He is going to be baptized this Saturday, January 28th. I am so excited for him!

The Lord has blessed me immensely, and I have gained so much. I have gained a strong testimony that Jesus Christ lives, and that Heavenly Father has a glorified resurrected body of flesh and bones. I know these things because the Holy Ghost has witnessed it unto me. Elder Hancock and I were able to teach two discussions, make three commitments, conduct a baptismal interview, and give a special priesthood blessing all within an hour and 15 minutes. There is only one explanation—The Spirit. The Spirit made it possible. Incredible!

We could not have done it without the Lord's help. That is one reason how I know Heavenly Father and Jesus Christ live. They have bodies that are immortal and perfect. Heavenly Father is true, kind, and just.

We arrived at Multi-Zone Conference and took a seat in the chapel. President Gourdin gave us instruction on the Beatitudes of Jesus Christ. He said that Christ wants us all to achieve spiritual perfection one day. The three covenants Jesus wants each child of our Heavenly Father to obtain are.

1. Be obedient and keep the commandments.
2. Make and keep covenants.
3. Receive all the saving ordinances.

He continued and taught us what the word Beatitude means. It means "the attitude of becoming like Christ." To become something, we must change. To become like Jesus Christ, we must change our attitude and thoughts. President Gourdin names several characteristics in Matthew Chapter 5 and 3 Nephi 12. These are the eight characteristics or elements of Godliness that Jesus taught.

1. Broken Heart
2. The poor in spirit.
3. Those who mourn.
4. Contrite Spirit—Mosiah 3:19—the meek.
5. Sanctification
6. Those that hunger and thirst after righteousness.
7. The merciful—be compassionate and selfishness.
8. The pure in heart.
9. The peacemakers.
10. Endure to the End—Persecution inside and outside of the church.

And all these points or characteristics revolve around our Lord and Savior Jesus Christ—come unto me. Sister Gourdin said a couple of things that are very worthwhile. She said, "We are what we have willed to be by our own free agency. And our actions have put us where we are today. Let us hope that they are righteous ones." She talked about habits found in the *Book of Mormon* in 3 Nephi 12:48 and 3 Nephi 27:27. There are two questions you should always ask yourself about a decision. What would Christ have me do? How can I become like him?

I love my mission and I love serving my Lord and Savior Jesus Christ to build forth His Kingdom for His mission and His glory. I would not trade this mission opportunity for anything in the world.

The next day, Elder Hancock and I met with Rick to teach the 6th Discussion, "Membership in the Kingdom" and talk about the gospel in general. After teaching the 6th Discussion,

Rick decided to flip through the Gospel Principles manual to the chapter on the Second Coming of Jesus Christ. We had a spiritual meeting, and we believe Rick is ready for baptism. It is the Lords' will.

After our meeting with Rick, Elder Hancock and I met with Mrs. Janet Wade. Initially we received a referral from one of Janet's sisters to visit with her. It was a humbling experience as we talked about her husband, Mr. Wade's battle with cancer and recent passing. Mrs. Wade is going through a tough time.

I was amazed at how receptable she was to The Spirit during her time of grieving. I began to reminisce about my own life and reflect on the times in my life when I needed Heavenly Father's love and support the most. When I was in pain. And that is when he helped me the most.

We had small talk, but I felt uncomfortable, and I did not know how to approach the subject of Mr. Wade's passing. Then we began to talk about her husband's death. I realized that it was comfortable, and it came easy to all of us. Mrs. Wade revealed a very spiritual experience that she had with Mr. Wade.

Mrs. Wade said, "Immediately after his death, I was comforted by peaceful thoughts that came to my mind. My husband was letting me know that everything was all right. It felt like someone was rubbing my forehead with their forehead. This was a loving gesture that we did with one another while he was still alive."

Mrs. Wade continued and said, "My sister saw a vision of Mr. Wade in the spirit world. He was walking with other people in a group setting. Mr. Wade was being taught the gospel of Jesus Christ." In addition to her sister, Mrs. Wade also had manifestation by her husband that she should be baptized and attend the temple to be sealed. I felt Elder Hancock and I were there for a purpose.

After tracting the rest of the day, we decided to go home for dinner. When we arrived, the telephone was ringing. We received a phone call from Sister Rogers asking us if we would not mind giving the McCook family a priesthood blessing. About 10–15 minutes later, Brother Rogers picked us up and we traveled to the McCooks'.

When we arrived, the McCooks' were all lying around deathly ill. Brother and Sister McCook and the son all had sore throats, fevers, and pneumonia. One of the boys could not even walk. Every time he would try to get up from the couch, he would fall. Brother Rogers proceeded to bless Brother McCook and Elder Hancock performed the blessing for the son. I had the privilege to bless the mother, Sister McCook. It is so neat to do this marvelous work for my fellow man.

At the end of the day, Elder Hancock and I delivered eight copies of the *Book of Mormon*. I feel the Lord blessed us because we are trying to play catch up.

I spoke with Sister Tomlinson. She is a good lady. I do my best to show my love and care for my investigators. The Savior taught that we must love another. This is a Christlike attribute He taught his whole life. I am so blessed because Sister Tomlinson said that she wanted me to baptize her. She also offered to prepare a meal of delicious tacos, just like home. I'm dependent on the Lord and the gospel is so true.

Today is my "hump day" for being in the mission field for six-months. Elder Hancock and I had a breakfast meeting with Rick to outline his baptismal program. We are all excited about His "BIG" day and we are looking forward to it. He is a neat guy and I feel that my life has been blessed for being able to teach him.

After visiting with Rick, we met Brother Tomlinson at his home. We had the sacred privilege giving him a priesthood blessing to help him stop smoking. Elder Hancock gave the blessing directed by The Spirit. He said, "Brother Tomlinson the Lord is pleased with your desire to keep the commandments. Our Savior is the one who we lean towards for guidance and protection." Sister Tomlinson is doing well, and she will be baptized on February 4th. She told me that she is calling President Gourdin to request that I complete the rest of my mission in Fontana. She is a neat lady and I really appreciate the compliment.

Jeremy Causey is another person who the Lord has prepared to be baptized. Jeremy is eleven years old, and he is excited about taking the Discussions. He is a sharp kid, a choice spirit.

Well, Elder Hancock and I have been extremely busy with two major conferences and a lot of proselyting activity. We completed our weekly mission reports and here is what we accomplished. We taught twelve standard Discussions, delivered fourteen copies of the *Book of Mormon*, taught eighteen investigators, and had sixty-six hours of proselyting. In summary, if we follow thy commandments, Jesus will greatly bless us. Although, I am incredibly happy with my progress as a servant of the Lord, I can do better.

The next day, Ricardo Perales (Rick) was baptized, confirmed, and entered the kingdom of our Heavenly Father's gospel and Jesus Christ church. Rick's baptism went extremely well. In fact, it was the most fulfilling baptism that I have attended, yet. He has been converted and the Holy Ghost is now in his life one hundred percent of the time.

Even though the water was cold, the feeling within our souls was warm and peaceful. I felt so good, and the baptismal prayer was stated with authority and conviction. It felt good. It impressed upon me this is truly the Lord's baptism, not mine. Moving forward, I need to continue praying to Heavenly Father asking for His help to find those individuals who are ready for baptism. I must first submit specific names to the Lord in prayer and ask Heavenly Father who he would like to baptize.

Elder Hancock along with the companionship of the Holy Ghost, gave a wonderful and spiritual confirmation. In the blessing Rick is going to be a great missionary in bringing other souls into the gospel of Jesus Christ. It is important to inquire of the Lord, first, before performing a sacred ordinance in His name.

Elder Hancock and I had nine and half hours of church and missionary meetings today. It is very fulfilling but very exhausting at the same time. I enjoy shaking hands and fellowshipping with the members because it makes me feel important.

Brother Broderick, Ward Mission Leader, set a lofty goal to deliver six hundred and one copies of the *Book of Mormon* by the end of February. He asked the ward members for their assistance in this massive effort to "flood the earth" with the *Book of Mormon* as directed by the Prophet Ezra Taft Benson. We are going to need our Heavenly Father's help and guidance in this huge effort. I'm all for it and it can be done, but each one of us must do our part.

***

It was neat to see Rick at church this morning. He was dressed in his suit, white shirt, and tie. He looked sharp. Brother Woods invited Elder Hancock and I to share our testimonies to the congregation. I focused my remarks on the importance of baptism and the gift of the Holy Ghost (Doctrine & Covenants 76: 51-52). It was a wonderful opportunity to tell Rick publicly how much we care about him.

Tonight, Elder Hancock and I are visiting with Tomlinson Family. Before leaving the apartment, Elder Hancock and I prayed that our companionship will be unified in feeling The Spirit as we are only tools in the Lord's hands.

During our bicycle ride, I began to reflect on priesthood blessings. Am I speaking or is The Spirit? I know I am just the mouthpiece for the Lord. Will The Spirit manifest itself in a vision? What is it really like?

When we arrived, Sister Tomlinson told us that she completely stopped smoking. What a marvelous manifestation to our prayers. God answers when we ask. He really knows what is best for His children. We must do our part and listen.

On the other hand, Rhonda was having a tough time and she asked me to give her a special priesthood blessing. During the opening prayer, I said a prayer in my heart and asked my Heavenly Father to help me feel The Spirit and be guided on what to say in the blessing.

Elder Hancock and I placed our hands on Rhonda's head. I said, "Rhonda Youngbloom, by the authority of the holy Melchizedek Priesthood which we hold...." I paused for a few seconds. I really listened to the promptings of The Spirit. It came quietly and without any noise or confusion. The Spirit was gentle. I continued, "Rhonda, Heavenly Father gives you comfort during this time of your hardship to quit smoking." In the past, Rhonda had difficulty feeling the Spirit. This time when said "Amen" and rose my hands from her head there was no doubt. The Spirit was extraordinarily strong.

Rhonda immediately said, "Elder Todd, your hands must be on fire. Boy, it's hot in here!" Then she waved her hands to cool herself. She knew it was The Spirit of our Heavenly Father. I said the things my Heavenly Father wanted me to say. I praise Him because He's a kind, just, and loving father that speaks boldly, but in a loving way. It was marvelous to behold.

I love The Spirit; it is wonderful to have in my life. Above all, I am most grateful to my Heavenly Father for giving me the Melchizedek Priesthood. When we returned home, Elder Hancock told me that I gave a beautiful blessing, but honestly, I cannot take the credit. All power and glory go to God!

Today things are moving at lightning speed. In fact, every day lately seems cruising with work, work, and more work. However, we were able to rest briefly during "Personal Interviews" with President Gourdin at the Rialto Stake Center.

The interviews occupied almost the entire day. President Gourdin met with all the missionaries in alphabetical order. Since my last name is Todd, I waited quite a while. In fact, I was the last Elder in the Zone to be interviewed.

President Gourdin sat down in his chair and said, "I can tell there is a difference in you. I can see it in your countenance. You have been temperate, haven't you?" I replied with an astounding, "Yes, sir and boy have I ever been temperate and long- suffering." He continued, "I'm very proud of you and all the great work you're doing." I thought to myself, "Cool!"

I appreciate the counsel President Gourdin has given me to be temperate. Additionally, I've done my part by praying and exercising temperance with Brother Hadden. Although he is a good guy, Brother Hadden is a <u>difficult</u> man to live with.

The reason why I'm bringing up the subject of Brother Hadden is because he wants to take control of the conversion process with the Tomlinson's and Rhonda. He expressed concern that we're moving too quickly through the Discussions, and that our investigators need more time to quit smoking. I feel very close to this family, and I know Heavenly Father knows the intentions of their hearts. The Tomlinson's and Rhonda are good people who have a sincere desire to follow Jesus.

It is really interesting how the adversary tries to tempt those who are very close to repent and change their lives around. Satan knows what is going to happen to those souls who get baptized. The new members will help our Father in Heaven build forth His kingdom.

Before leaving the Stake Center tonight, I telephoned Sister Tomlinson tonight. She said, "Elder Todd while I was praying, I felt scared." She told me that she felt tremendous pressure to smoke a cigarette. Her favorite brand was left by one of her friends. To make matters worse, Rhonda lost her job today without warning. She felt so depressed that she lit up a cigarette and started smoking. I encouraged Sister Tomlinson to stay strong and be positive. I tried to inspire her by staying the course. Then, I asked, "Please call Rhonda to let her know there's still hope for repentance, and she can still get baptized."

After my phone conversation with Sister Tomlinson, Elder Hancock, and I had an appointment with Sister Curtis, a young adult in the Fontana First Ward. It was neat to visit with Sister Curtis and Brenda and talk about the *Book of Mormon*. We walked through the process on how they can share it with their friends.

During the closing prayer, Elder Hancock paused allowing them to feel The Spirit. The sisters felt the calming influence of the Holy Ghost. Sister Curtis and Brenda received their own witness about sharing the *Book of Mormon* with their friends. Before leaving Sister Curtis' house, Brenda used The Spirit in talking with a nonmember friend tonight and told us that we have an appointment at 2:00 p.m. tomorrow. The spirit of missionary work is great and exciting.

After meeting with the sisters, we had a teaching appointment with Brother Krueger. Elder Hancock was leading the discussion about baptism and Brother Krueger politely said, "I've already been baptized." There was a little tension between us, and I prayed in my heart for The Spirit, and it came into the room. Elder Hancock gave me permission to speak next. I spoke with Brother Krueger about the importance of being baptized by a person who has the proper authority. We all felt The Spirit and were edified together.

Today it was so wonderful to give Sister Tomlinson and Rhonda Youngbloom another blessing today. Rhonda is making another honest attempt to stop smoking. This time, Elder Hancock offered a blessing. The Spirit was present, and I pray that Rhonda will continue to read the scriptures and pray. I had the sacred opportunity seal the anointing and bless Sister Tomlinson. It is so neat to be a worthy mouthpiece for my Heavenly Father. I simply say the things that The Spirit wants me to say. It is so wonderful. I know the Lord is going to bless Sister Tomlinson and Rhonda to lighten their load and the pressures of life.

After visiting with the Tomlinson's, we followed through with a member, Brenda to meet her friend, Debbie. She attends a non-denominational church. It was really a neat experience to see the difference between how a member of the church approaches a missionary opportunity versus the elders.

After explaining a little bit about the church, we introduced the *Book of Mormon* to Debbie. She was hesitant at first, but I said a prayer in my heart and asked for The Spirit. The Spirit was present and softened her heart. When I opened the *Book of Mormon*, I gave Debbie a passage to read. We read a few verses together from 3 Nephi Chapter 11. Her entire mood changed for the better and The Spirit was strong. We left Debbie with a copy of the *Book of Mormon* and gave her a challenge to read and pray about its contents. We left with a positive experience and that's why missionary work is so spiritual.

It is so neat how the Lord works. Elder Hancock and I knew that there was bad blood and contention between the Tomlinson family and Brother Hadden. We talked about practical solutions, and nothing seemed to gel or feel right. We decided to kneel as a companionship and pray. We asked, "Heavenly Father, please help us know what to do. How do we help alleviate the contention between the Tomlinson's and Brother Hadden?" Afterwards, we felt The Spirit and it whispered to do nothing. We need to leave it up to the Lord because it is in His hands. We did not understand the answer, but that is exactly what The Spirit told us.

I decided to telephone Brother Tomlinson and speak with him. He told me that he is feeling well even without smoking. Most importantly, he is excited about the baptism. Brother Tomlinson said, "I prayed before calling Brother Hadden. My answer was to share our baptismal schedule with him. When I called and talked to Brother Hadden giving him our thoughts on the program, he did not give me any hassle." I was astonished and happy at the same time. The Lord answered our prayers and softened Brother Hadden's heart. Brother Tomlinson continued, "You guys are special missionaries who bring The Spirit into my home." I cried with joy! I am so grateful that I have chosen to come on this mission to learn and grow stronger.

It rained the rest of the day. It is neat to see how the Lord blesses me even during inclement weather. Despite the rain, we managed to pick up another investigator. It was a great blessing. We biked in the cold and wet weather; however, it is awesome to serve the Lord. I just look at how much I have grown on my mission, and it is incredible. For example, I feel that I've grown spiritually and I'm more mature than I was before. I also take life more seriously, and I'm focused on my goals. Jesus Christ and my Heavenly Father love and appreciate every one of His children. It is a wonderful feeling.

It continued to rain through the next day. It is miserable because it is cold, rainy, and windy. The Lord blesses you when you work hard and obey his commandments. The members in the Fontana First Ward are giving us referrals like crazy. I think several factors have contributed to our success. (1) A diligent and spiritual ward mission leader. (2) The members are excited and have the spirit of missionary work. (3) Hard working and obedient missionaries. (4) The Lord's spirit and His blessings are poured upon us. Currently, I am so grateful for the wonderful success. I love Jesus Christ for allowing us to receive such great blessings.

Sister Tomlinson was interviewed by Elder Norton, one of the "Traveling Assistants to the President." The Lord has worked mighty miracles upon the hearts of this family. I pray for the continuing blessings and the spirit for each of them. Elder Norton is companions with Elder Rawson (Rawhide) temporarily.

***

It snowed in Fontana, California! It really snowed. It happened on the Fifth of February in the year of 1989 at 1:30 p.m. and it was cool. It was coming down hard, but it is not sticking to the ground in the valley. However, the mountains are covered in white snow, and it looks beautiful.

It is interesting, just when things are going my way and I'm doing what the Lord asks me to do, God changes things. We received a phone call from the 'zone heads' that from now on Elder Hancock and I are only responsible for the Fontana First Ward. Elder Berry from South Carolina and his companion will cover the Fontana Fifth and Sixth Wards. Essentially taking over our responsibilities of the Fifth Ward. I thought to myself, "Ummm. Interesting. I wonder if Brother Hadden had anything to do with it?" Despite my reservations, I feel good because I know that through my hard work and by the grace of the Lord and His spirit, the Fontana Fifth Ward is exploding with red, hot investigators. It makes me feel good knowing that I helped the Lord in a small way to build forth his kingdom in the south Fontana area.

Elder Hancock and I had an appointment with Janet Wade. We showed her the video "Together Forever" and The Spirit was there. Janet's oldest daughter, Cherise Chism, asked us for a priesthood blessing to help her re-activate to church. Elder Hancock gave the blessing. I feel good inside when I follow the spirit and say what the Lord wants me to say. By the look on his face, I know Elder Hancock was feeling the same thing.

Our zone is "Zone of the Month" again. President Gourdin said that our success is owed to the Lord. The credit goes to God and His kingdom. My thoughts turned to a recent letter I received from Elder Humphrey. He suggested that I read Mosiah 4:11 because it is a good scripture on how we should be humble because we are nothing without God.

And again I say unto you as I have said before, that as ye have come to the knowledge of the glory of God, or if ye have known of his goodness and have tasted of his love, and have received a remission of your sins, which causeth such exceedingly great joy in your souls, even so I would that ye should remember, and always retain in remembrance, the greatness of God, and your own nothingness, and his goodness and long-suffering towards you, unworthy creatures, and humble ourselves even in the depths of humility, calling on the name of the Lord daily, and standing steadfastly in the faith of that which is to come, which was spoken by the mouth of the angel.

I am glad Elder Humphrey suggested I read this scripture. It seems like when "we" as a people have success that we tend to forget the Lord. When this happens like the people of Nephi in the *Book of Mormon*, the Lord smites us with trials and tribulations until we humble ourselves before Him.

I know that there are great many obstacles that I must overcome to be with my Heavenly Father someday. This earth life is full of tribulations, and I know it is not over. It is one of the reasons why we are here on earth. I pray that I can continue to stay worthy to receive the many blessing that my Heavenly Father pours out.

Last night the temperature dipped to negative 5 degrees below zero. Holy smokes it was cold today! The wind was blowing between 60–70 mph. Elder Hancock is not feeling well so he is staying at Brother Broderick's house to recuperate. Elder Rawson and I ventured out into the frigid wind. Wow! I have never seen anything like this my entire life. This Georgia boy with his thin blood is cold. The dog gone wind has been blowing for two and a half days straight. It is incredible. I hear the wind hissing as it travels from the roof through the HVAC supply vents. The wind even rattles and hisses through our bedroom window seals.

An investigator in the Fontana Second Ward gave me a huge compliment. He asked, "How long have you been out on your mission?" I replied, "Over six months." He began to smile and nodded his head he said, "It seems like it." It is nice to know that other people appreciate what I am doing. I am not looking for recognition for what I do, however, I am glad others benefit from the gospel as much as I do.

Elder Rawson and I worked hard today. It rained last night and then cleared up this morning just in time for proselyting. After our regular morning routine, off we went to follow through with a few call-backs and visit several members so they could give copies of the *Book of Mormon* to their friends.

About three miles from our apartment, Elder Rawson's 10-speed bicycle fell apart all over the wet pavement just in time for a complete downpour. So, I grabbed the only thing that I had, one of my bungy cords from my rear bike rack and handed it to Elder Rawson. I said, "You need to hang on to the chord tight while I pull us, o.k.?" Elder Rawson replied by nodding his head and said, "O.k." Now I understand what Noah and his family felt like during the great flood. It was pouring down rain as the tires of our bicycles splashed through the puddles. It felt good even though it was cold, dark, and rainy. I know what we are doing is what the Lord wants us to do. It was great bicycling in the rain. I loved it because I am serving my Lord and Savior.

We bicycled all day traveling from one appointment to the next. We did not even have time to eat lunch because we were so busy. Rhonda Youngbloom and Jeremy Causey both had their baptismal interviews this afternoon. The Lord has truly blessed us. It is the Lord's kingdom, and it is His work and His glory.

Elder Rawson and I gave a special priesthood blessing to Sister Curtis, one of the stake missionaries in the Fontana First Ward. It is important to be in tune with The Spirit. The priesthood power and authority really does work because I see people getting healed right before my eyes.

The Lord has blessed me so much in just the short six-months that I have been on my mission. I have learned so many wonderful things with the aid of the Lord and his spirit. I think the greatest lesson of all can be found in Alma 7:23. I have mentioned this scripture several times in my memoir, so I'll just reiterate the most important words. "...be humble, submissive and gentle, full of patience and long-suffering; being temperate in all things..."

It is important to be patient and temperate in all things. These are two traits that I have developed since becoming a missionary. My secret formula for success is Work Hard + Faith in Jesus Christ = Holy Spirit and Conversion to the Gospel.

I am just starting to understand the true and sacred ordinances I can perform to build up the kingdom of our Heavenly Father. I know for a surety that God has much in store for me as a representative of Jesus Christ. If I continue to keep the commandments and improve myself, I will be given more sacred responsibilities to continue the work.

I pray for the continued guidance and companionship of the Holy Ghost. I know that I must continue being submissive, humble, and temperate in all things to be an effective missionary. I shared Alma 7:23 with Sister Tomlinson today, which was the scripture President Gourdin read to me when I was going through a challenging time. After reading the scripture together, she agreed that it is an excellent passage to follow. She then highlighted the verse in her *Book of Mormon* and wrote, 'When people give you a tough time,' in the margin.

I was speaking with Sister McCook the other day at Church Activity Night. I wanted to know how the family was doing after we gave them priesthood blessings. Sister McCook said, "Jason walked over to me and said, "Mommy, look! The elders helped me walk again!" I replied, "It's a miracle that he recovered so quickly, because he was so ill and couldn't even walk or move his legs." I know for a surety the true and sacred power where special blessings come from. All true healing comes from Jesus Christ.

I am so thankful for my mission call, and I would not change it for the world. I love my mission to death. Let us go forth and baptize.

I cannot believe how much the Lord has blessed my life. I have been given so much, and no matter what I do, I cannot return the Lords gestures with thanks enough. Currently, my heart is very full. It is such a blessing to work on the right-hand side of Jesus Christ. My Heavenly Father has enriched my life for the better. I am incredibly grateful for my companion, Elder Hancock. I have learned two valuable principles from him: (1) The power of prayer and (2) Receiving answers from The Spirit. Prayer is real, and it works. I have realized the true importance of missionary work since fully dedicating my service to God as a missionary. We are servants of our Heavenly Father, and we are helping prepare the world for the Second Coming of Jesus Christ.

It was neat to witness the baptisms of Robyn Tomlinson, Rhonda Youngbloom, and Jeremy Causey. Brother Tomlinson was able to quit smoking and became worthy to receive the Aaronic Priesthood in the office of a Priest. The hand of the Lord has been present every step of the way for the conversion process of the Tomlinson Family.

Elder Hancock and I had the unique opportunity and privilege of giving them all special priesthood blessings more than once. I am so grateful to be able to exercise the priesthood. I am happier now because I am close to the Lord, and I rejoice in following the Savior. I also had the wonderful opportunity of baptizing Rhonda Youngbloom this week, and it was a highly spiritual experience. It reminded me of a scripture found in The

Pearl of Great Price, which says, "For behold, this is my work and my glory—to bring to pass the immorality and eternal life of man." (Moses 1:39)

This month was also a choice time to witness Jeremy Causey's baptism, administered by his uncle James Causey. He received the Aaronic Priesthood in the office of a Priest last Sunday as well. It is neat to see how the Lord works to build families, as this is a family-oriented church. The Causey family are currently less active; however, I believe that Jeremy's baptism will give them strength to return to church.

After Jeremy's baptism, I acted as the mouthpiece of God and confirmed Robyn a member of The Church of Jesus Christ of Latter-day Saints. It was a marvelous experience, and a reminder that I must continue to work and be worthy.

***

The Fontana First Ward is full of young adults, and most of them are single women who are all pumped up about missionary work. As a result, we are getting a lot of solid referrals from them. Lisa, who is one of our investigators, wants to be baptized on February 25th. It is so neat to see the hand of the Lord in all things.

Additionally, the Krueger's—a part-member family in the Fontana Fifth Ward— committed to attend church tomorrow. They even volunteered to pick us up on the way. How can I express in words my deepest gratitude to my Savior? There are no words; however, I can show Jesus the real intent of my heart. I love the gospel with all my heart, might, mind, and soul.

There is a saying in my mission that once an elder begins to memorize street names and phone numbers, it is time for him to transfer to another part of the Lord's vineyard. I just received a phone call from the 'zone heads' that I am getting transferred to Palmdale. I feel good about it and know it is where the Lord wants me to serve next. It is certainly going to be tough leaving this area. I have met so many good people, made so many friends, and yet I am excited to continue the Lord's work. I feel like this is just another one of my duties as a missionary. The Lord knows where He needs me the most. I will continue to work to combine Hard Work and Faith to acquire The Holy Spirit and Conversion.

I didn't realize how many friends I've made on my mission until now. I have grown close to Rick Perales, Louis Martorella, and the Tomlinson Family. I truly consider them my good friends. Of course, I will remember all the people who I had an opportunity of teaching and baptizing.

I feel that my newly assigned area is inspired of God. I have heard a lot of good things about Palmdale, and I am extremely excited to serve there. The bus route to Palmdale travels through Los Angeles, which means the bus travels outside my mission boundaries. However, I have special permission to travel through Los Angeles because it's the only way to Palmdale. I will have a brief layover in LA, and then I will board the northbound bus to Palmdale. When I arrive in LA, I am going to telephone my mom and dad. I cannot wait to hear their response when I tell them where I am calling from. They are going to freak out! I can already hear them saying, "What!? You are in Los Angeles! What are you doing there??"

The Lord has blessed me so much. Even though I am not a "Greenie" anymore, I know my mission will not get any easier. My experiences have taught me how to be more productive and use my time more wisely. I will continue to rely on The Spirit always.

I am so grateful for the things that I have been given personally from my Heavenly Father, which have helped me grow closer to Him. The Spirit is so sweet and peaceful. I love to feel its presence at all times. I have a couple of things to take care of before I leave, like returning a couple of church books and a coat to members I borrowed from. I love Fontana and I have really grown spiritually, mentally, and physically.

Before leaving town, Elder Hancock and I visited a few members and investigators. We had the privilege of giving two priesthood blessings—one to Sister Tomlinson and the second blessing to Christine Hilt.

When we visited the Tomlinson house, Robyn told us that she was having a tough time feeling the Holy Ghost and was getting discouraged. She also admitted that she was holding a grudge against her mother, and that this could be one of the reasons why she was struggling spiritually. I had the opportunity to give Robyn a special priesthood blessing of comfort. I believe it is important to exercise faith in Jesus Christ to receive the fullness of His blessings. I think once Robyn forgives her mother with sincerity of heart, she will begin to feel the comfort of the Holy Ghost in her life again.

Elder Hancock and I were disappointed in Rhonda's decision to not completely quit smoking. I know that the Lord will help her in making the right decision. She needs the continued love and support of the ward. Even after baptism we make mistakes, and we still have our free agency. I believe Rhonda will quit soon.

Our last visit was with Christine Hilt. During the meeting I felt impressed to offer her a priesthood blessing, to which she nodded her head and said, "Yes." Then I turned to Elder Hancock and asked him if he would offer the blessing. He got a surprised look on his face and then responded, "Yes, I'd love to." It was a beautiful blessing. The Lord inspired Elder Hancock as he said, "The missionaries are teaching you correct principles of the gospel. The Church of Jesus Christ of Latter-day Saints is the church that you have been searching and praying about." The Spirit was there; it was great.

It sure is tough leaving Fontana. It is amazing to feel so much joy and peace in my heart knowing that I did my best. I did all that I could to help share the gospel with the wonderful people in Fontana. I have a lot of friends here, and I have become remarkably close with several people. The common theme I kept hearing this week during our visits was, "Boy, Elder Todd, we're going to miss you!" I know that I have grown so much in this area. When I think back on my days in the MTC, I can see now how reading the scriptures and sharing my testimony daily has helped me to grow spiritually. I wrote a letter to my ward in Georgia for their newsletter, which sums up my experience over the past six months:

To My Family and Friends of the Roswell Third Ward:

The mission life is fantastic! The Lord has blessed me beyond compare, and no matter what I do on my mission, I can never repay Him because Jesus keeps blessing me. Even though I love my mission, I have gone through many trials and tribulations that have helped me grow stronger. The Lord tests me because he knows what He wants me to become. He has placed obstacles in my way to humble me and help me grow closer to Him. Beth Moore who wrote "To Live is Christ," said, "A man is tallest when he is down on his knees in prayer." This is so true!

In John 14:6 (KJV), the Apostle John said, "Jesus saith unto him, I am the way, the truth, and the life; no man cometh unto the Father, but by me."

What keeps me going strong every day? It is your continued love and support. Thanks Roswell Third Ward. See you soon!

Sincerely Yours,

Elder Stephen M. Todd

It is a sad feeling to leave so many friends and loved ones behind, but the Lord needs me in another part of His vineyard. I will continue to work hard and strive to please my Heavenly Father.

Companions
James Evans October 1988–January 1989
Mark Hancey January 1989
Elder Rogers, Jr January 1989
Kelly Hancock January–February 1989

Acknowledgements

I would like to acknowledge and thank two gentlemen that made this memoir possible: Pastor Jay Rice and Scott Haslam. Pastor Jay and Scott lent me their woodworking tools and paint equipment so I could complete my custom home office bookshelf. Before the bookshelf, my office was very disorganized, and I couldn't begin my memoir until I organized my thoughts. Many thanks to Jay and Scott for your kindness.

In addition, I would like to thank the East Cobb Creative Writer's Workshop, part of the Cobb County Library System in Marietta, Georgia for giving many useful editing tools to complete my memoir. Also, I would like to give thanks to my cousin, Jennifer Stirling- Campbell and my mom for doing the line and copy editing.

I would also like to acknowledge and thank the many people on my mission for making it one of the best experiences of my life, including my parents, immediate family, friends, local church leaders, members, mission presidents and their wives and my missionary companions. I would especially like to thank all the church members in the San Bernardino, California area who fed my companion and I (we had a dinner appointment almost every night), joined us on team ups, and who gave us emotional and spiritual support. Without your love my mission wouldn't have been possible.

As I stated earlier in the Preface, the purpose of this book was to share with my family, friends, and you (the reader) what I experienced on my mission. In addition, I wanted to emphasize the importance of personal revelation from Heavenly Father and your relationship with Jesus Christ in your life.

In conclusion, there will hardly be another time in my life where I'll be able to focus 100% all of my time and energy for one purpose—to teach, exhort, and baptize souls unto Jesus Christ. It is to this end that I conclude this wonderful chapter in my life that I gained a powerful and heart felt personal testimony that Jesus Christ is my Lord and Savior.

I firmly believe in the scripture found in the New Testament, John 14:6, "I am the way the truth of the life, no man cometh unto the Father, but by me." I pray that we may all be able to spread love, joy, and peace by being gentler and kinder to our fellow man. I say these things in the name of Jesus Christ. Amen.

Book Steve Todd to increase sales

If you organization is looking to improve its sales process and increase sales, please contact Steve Todd at steve@stevetoddauthor.com for a FREE consultation. He specializes in helping organizations in the trades (HVAC, plumbing, electrical, etc...).

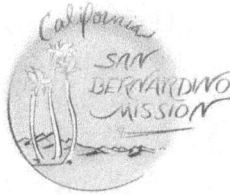

Glossary of Terms

1 Sacrament Meeting—is very similar to communion in the Catholic church or regular church service in Christian denominations.

2 Stake President—is a church leader that is responsible for 6–8 wards within a geographical area.

3 "Setting apart"—is performed by a priesthood leader by laying on of hands and gives you a charge to act in your calling.

4 Priesthood line-of-authority—is a pattern in sequential order of specific ordinations that can be followed back to the original origins of Jesus Christ's church in biblical times.

5 President Thomas S. Monson—was the 16th President and Prophet of the church. The President is also referred to as the prophet, seer, and revelator for the entire world.

6 Elder Hartman Rector, Jr.—he was a general authority of the church from 1968 until his death. The term "Elder" refers to a full-time position within the church and its an office within the Melchizedek Priesthood.

7 Book of Mormon—is a record of ancient scripture written by proph-

ets living on the American continent from 600 B.C. to 421 A.D. It is considered one of the four canons of scripture used by the church.

8 Mission President—is usually a retired couple who accepts a priesthood leadership position to preside over a mission in a geographical area in a specific region of the world.

9 Mormon Pioneers—were LDS church members who migrated from the NY area to the Midwest and finally settled in the Salt Lake Valley from the mid-1840's until the late 1860's.

10 Atlanta Temple—temples are considered by LDS members to be the most sacred structures on earth. Any member and non-member may attend church service on Sunday at a church building. However, you must have a temple recommend entering the House of the Lord.

11 District Leader—is a position and calling within the mission. It's usually an LDS missionary who has trained and served for a minimum of 6-months in the field.

12 1st Discussion, "The Plan of Our Heavenly Father"—this is the first out of six Discussions in the lesson manual.

13 Investigator—The word "investigator" is a missionary term used to describe an individual investigating the church.

14 Personal Priesthood Interview or PPI—A typical PPI usually lasts about five to ten minutes and reviews the spiritual life of a missionary or priesthood holder.

15 Branch President or Bishop—A priesthood leader who is responsible for a specific geographical area within a Stake.

16 Quorum of the Twelve Apostles—A priesthood position or calling within the Melchizedek priesthood. The Quorum of the Twelve Apostles is similar to the Apostles in biblical times.

17 The Discussions—The Missionary Discussions are a set of planned lessons that review the most important points of the restored gospel. The following Discussions or lessons are as follows. (A.) The Plan of our Heavenly Father, (B.) The Gospel of Jesus Christ, (C.) The Restoration, (D.) Eternal Progression, (E.) Living a Christlike Life, (F.) Membership in the Kingdom.

18 Testimony—is a church members personal belief and testimony in the gospel of Jesus Christ.

19 Tracting—The word "tracting" is a missionary term used for proselyting in a large neighborhood.

20 Seventy—is an office in the Melchizedek Priesthood who assist in the administration of the church across the world. Until recently, stakes had their own quorums of the seventy.

21 Area Proselyting Guide (APG)— The APG is a small three-ring binder that stores all the information from missionary proselyting efforts. It includes the information about local church leaders, investigators, and Book of Mormon placements.

22 Stake Missionaries—a church calling to a local member to assist in the missionary efforts within the stake boundaries.

23 Less-active—refers to a church member who does not attend at least one Sacrament meeting or church service a month.

24 Video entitled "Together Forever, The Plan of our Heavenly Father, The First Vision, How Rare of a Possession, and What is Real," are all church sponsored productions for missionary work.

25 Fontana First Ward—a ward is a small geographical area within a Stake. A Stake compromises of at least 6–8 wards in a region.

26 Bishopric—refers to the bishop and his two counselors that assist in the administrative and spiritual affairs within a ward.

27 Relief Society—This is one of the oldest women's organizations in the world. It began in 1842 in Nauvoo, Illinois under the direction of the prophet Joseph Smith. He referred to the Relief Society as "...a select Society separate from all the evils of the world; choice, virtuous, and holy." (Minutes of the Female Relief Society of Nauvoo, 30 March 1842.

28 Zone Conference—The San Bernardino Mission is divided into twelve geographical areas called "zones." For example, the Fontana and Rialto area is one zone. Palmdale and Lancaster area are another zone.

29 Family Presentations— A "Family Presentation" is defined as a spiritual lesson presented to a church- member family. The purpose of the visit is to invite The Spirit and obtain referrals.

30 3 Nephi Chapter 11 and Moroni's Promise—This chapter in the book of Nephi describes Christ visit to the American continent after his resurrection in Israel in 33 A.D. Moroni's promise encourages people to read, ponder, and pray about the truthfulness of the Book of Mormon.

31 Priesthood blessing—is performed by laying on of hands and given by the authority of the priesthood for healing, comfort, and encouragement.

32 Splits—The term "splits" refers to splitting up or pairing with another companionship for training or teaching purposes.

33 Stake Missionary Discussions—The term "Stake Missionary Discussions" are a set of lessons taught after a person has been baptized. It's usually taught by a Stake Missionary who is a member of the church that lives in the local ward.

34 Call back— A call-back refers to a person who was left with a copy of the Book of Mormon and agreed to a follow-up meeting.

35 Zone Leaders—a zone leader is a missionary who has been trained, held the position as a District Leader and usually been on his mission for more than a year.

36 A "team-up" happens when two missionaries meet with two church members to do missionary work. It is effective missionary tool, because Elder Hedelius and I can schedule two appointments at the same time.

37 The elder's quorum is a priesthood quorum, or group of worthy male members of The Church of Jesus Christ of Latter-day Saints, who meet together on Sundays. They also meet throughout the week, or whenever service in the community is warranted. The elder's quorum is also known as the first quorum of the Melchizedek Priesthood, and there are five quorums of the Melchizedek Priesthood: elders, high priests, seventies, patriarchs, and apostles.

38 Part-member family—is a family or marraige that consists of one LDS church member and one non-member.

39 Greenie— A "greenie" is a brand-new missionary entering the field from the MTC. It was just a month ago that I was a greenie!

40 Spanish-Americans—The Span-Ams are English-speaking missionaries who learned Spanish in the MTC.

41 Marked up the Book of Mormon— The term "marking-up a Book of Mormon" means highlighting and earmarking three to four passages. For example, we marked the introduction, 3 Nephi Chapter 11, and Moroni 10:3–5 for quick- reference.

42 Roswell Stake Center— A "stake center" is an LDS term to describe a large church building. There is a difference between a regular ward building and a stake center. In The Church of Jesus Christ of Latter-day Saints, the church membership is divided into different geographical regions (stakes) and wards within these stakes, which typically comprise 125 members or more. Usually, a combined six or seven wards make up a stake.

43 Correlation Meeting—refers to the auxiliary leaders or administrative leaders that run the major functions and positions within a ward.

44 Articles of Faith—a list of thirteen key points or beliefs within the church.

45 General Conference— It is the usual custom in The Church of Jesus Christ of Latter-day Saints to attend the semi-annual General Conference held twice a year; once in the spring and once in the fall.

46 Investigator Fireside— The term "fireside" was first used in the 1930's for a supplementary meeting at the church building held in the evening.

47 Master Teacher— The "Master Teacher" means you're well-versed and know all of the basic principles and scriptures to the Missionary Discussions.

48 A "no show" is an appointment that writes you off as a missionary, in which the investigator doesn't even bother to call to cancel. It's the worst kind of cancelation when they don't even have the nerve to tell you, "No," to your face.

49 Thrifting—is a term we use when we shop for clothes at multiple thrift stores.

50 Companion inventory—The term "companion inventory" is used to describe a one-on-one meeting between two missionaries to resolve an issue.

51 Golden investigator—is a term we use to describe an investigator who accepts the gospel from the beginning. The.investigator does his or her homework and commits to attend church and be baptized.

52 Trunky—The slang term "trunky" describes a missionary who is excited about returning home or serving in another country because his or her bags or trunk is packed.